Shakespeare on the American Stage

From the Hallams to Edwin Booth

Shakespeare on the American Stage

From the Hallams to Edwin Booth

Charles H. Shattuck

The Folger Shakespeare Library

Copyright © 1976 by The Folger Shakespeare Library

First Published 1976
Second Printing 1978

The Folger Shakespeare Library is administered
by the Trustees of Amherst College.

Frontispiece: Nancy Hallam in the Cave Scene from *Cymbeline*.
Painted in Annapolis by Charles Willson Peale in the summer
of 1771 during a return engagement of Miss Hallam, it
represents a scene before a cave from Shakespeare's *Cymbeline*, Act III, scene 6. Miss Hallam plays the part of
Imogen, who is here disguised as the boy Fidele. Her use
of oriental costuming was common in eighteenth-century
theatre, although often historically inappropriate to the
role. Courtesy of Colonial Williamsburg Foundation.

Library of Congress Cataloging in Publication Data

Shattuck, Charles Harlen, 1910–
    Shakespeare on the American stage.

    Includes index.
    1. Shakespeare, William, 1546–1616—Stage history—
United States.   2. Actors—United States.
I. Folger Shakespeare Library, Washington, D. C.
II. Title.
PR3105.S5   792'.0973   75–43999
ISBN 0–8139–0651–2

Printed in the United States of America

For Susan

Contents

Illustrations

Preface

THE NOTION that this book should be written grew out of a conversation with Dr. O. B. Hardison, Director of the Folger Shakespeare Library, who thought that during the Bicentennial Year the American history of Shakespeare should be celebrated as part of the nation's history. We first intended that this book, like the Folger's Bicentennial Exhibition of "Shakespeare in America," should cover the full scope of Shakespearean production down to the present. It soon became apparent, however, that the subject was too vast to be covered in a single volume—hence I have attempted to discuss only the first century of it and a little more, from the first *Merchant of Venice* of the Hallam company down to the major Shakespearean realizations of Edwin Booth.

Grateful acknowledgment is hereby made to the Copernicus Society of America, which helped subsidize this work. Particular thanks are due to Mr. Edward J. Piszek, President of the Society, and Mr. Ernest Cuneo, representative of the Society in Washington.

I am indebted to Dr. Hardison not only for his initial suggestion but for his subsequent encouragement. I am grateful to Dr. John F. Andrews, Director of Research Activities at the Folger, for helpful criticism; to Miss Martha Gibbons of the Folger staff for gathering the illustrations; to Professor Richard Benson of Eastern Kentucky University for providing the scene design for Booth's *Julius Caesar* (Illustration 103); to Mrs. Daryle Carras, who has translated my draft into cleanly typed pages. I am particularly grateful to Miss Megan Lloyd, the Folger Editor, for labors with the text far beyond the call of duty. My greatest debt is to the patience and counsel of the person whose name appears on the page following the title page.

CHARLES H. SHATTUCK

Urbana, Illinois
September 1, 1975

Introduction

IN ITS BEGINNING the art of theatre in America, including Shakespearean theatre, was entirely an importation from the mother country. From 1752 when Lewis Hallam led his London Company of Comedians to Virginia until well into the 1820s, very few native-born Americans took to the stage and none rose to eminence. It should be noted that for most Americans who attended the theatre in the eighteenth century Shakespeare in performance was their first experience with Shakespeare's plays in any form. They knew odds and ends of quotations which had drifted into common lore, like the "To be or not to be" soliloquy, but few had read any of the ten or fifteen Shakespeare plays which, over the years, they might see acted in one of the larger cities. Books of the plays were not readily accessible, and only the most highly educated would have developed the play-reading habit. In this respect, as has often been noted, those Americans who did attend the theatre resembled Shakespeare's first audiences: they were seeing the plays without having read them.

Much of what they saw was not true Shakespeare, of course, but "Shakespeare improved." *Hamlet*, *Othello*, *The Merchant of Venice*, and *Cymbeline* came through fairly straight (though much cut); but *Richard III* was Colley Cibber's melodramatic reworking of the original, *Romeo and Juliet* was David Garrick's version with a surprise ending, *The Tempest* was the Dryden-Davenant refashioning of it to bring it in line with Restoration-period notions of comedy, *Macbeth* was tricked out with choruses of dancing and singing witches, *The Taming of the Shrew* had been reduced by Garrick to a three-act farce called *Catharine and Petruchio*, and *King Lear* had been thoroughly rewritten by Nahum Tate, who gave it a happy ending. All the same it was "Shakespeare" that the American audiences saw—Shakespeare adorned in the current London fashion. Such of Shakespeare's proper qualities as filtered through made their impact; and if audiences credited Shakespeare with the tears they shed over Colley Cibber's lurid additions to the murder of the little princes, with their delight in the comicalities of Dryden's Hippolito and Dorinda in *The Tempest*, and with their excitement during Tate's last-minute rescue of Cordelia from rape during the Storm Scene on the heath, these effects served to keep Shakespeare on the boards until later generations with purer taste would gradually welcome restoration of the "true texts."

The principal actors who arrived from England during the generation after the Peace of 1783 seem mostly to have been either gifted eccentrics like John Hodgkinson and James Fennell or uninspired practitioners of the neo-classic school of acting, given to bold posing and ponderous declamation. Few of them, with the exception of Ann Brunton Merry, could likely have stood up to the competition of the great John Philip Kemble or his sister Sarah Siddons in London; and on the whole, the best level of Shakespearean acting in America down to 1810 seems to have been competent but unremarkable.

But then, between 1810 and 1821, thrown off as it were by the volcanic eruption in England which is palely described as the Romantic Movement, there came to America three actors—George Frederick Cooke, Edmund Kean, and Junius Brutus Booth—whose astonishing personalities and revolutionary methods; whose rigorous attack upon roles; whose vivid pantomime, impetuosity, and bold contrasts of speed, volume, and intensity in their speaking startled American spectators, as they had startled the English, into a new awareness of the living reality of Shakespeare's characters. For the time being, America was too preoccupied with practical affairs—settling its government, expanding into the wilderness, waging its last armed conflict with England—to create a romantic theatre of its own, or even, indeed, to know quite what to make of these romantically rebellious visitors. When the wildest of them, Edmund Kean, had the bad manners once to refuse to perform for too small an audience, America responded in a paroxysm of hurt pride, declared that he had insulted the nation, and sent him packing home.

At last, in the middle 1820s, America produced a great actor of its own. This was Edwin Forrest, a brawny, massive, passionate man, endowed with every strength of body, voice, and mind which he would need to achieve the highest level of histrionic excellence. In the long run, however, he narrowed himself into a symbol of American nationalism—self-consciously parochial, belligerent, and at worst downright bullying. Forrest took his inspiration in part from the blazing emotionalism of Edmund Kean, with whom in his early years he once acted, in part from the Noble Red Man, whose physical culture he emulated. In the Red Man's cause, that of an oppressed race defying the oppressor, he found a symbol of his own favorite cause: the democrats in American society defying the aristocrats, or the New World defying the Old. His patriotism, fervid from the beginning, soured with the turn of events in his life into a relentless hatred of all things English—hatred of the Englishwoman whom he had married and of one particular English rival in the profession. His antipathy to William Charles Macready climaxed in 1849 in the horrible Astor Place Riot, when more than thirty persons were shot dead in the streets. In Forrest, the romantic spirit spent itself not so much in realizing the characters of Shakespeare as in using Shakespeare to fight causes and to do down supposed enemies of himself and the state.

The comedian James Hackett, who was of Forrest's generation, was also deeply rooted in the American (especially the Yankee American) scene; but having nothing of the jingo in his makeup, he actually allied himself with American "aristocrats" and with Englishmen in high intellectual and social circles. The great Charlotte Cushman, approximately contemporary with Forrest, resembled him in physical strength, emotional power, and strong-mindedness, but not in political attitudes or personal vindictiveness. Those early-middle decades of the nineteenth century were frontier days, Paul Bunyan days, and inevitably a shoal of imitators of Forrest—outsized, loud, and muscular—followed in his wake, but they need not individually concern us here.

Yet even as these native-born Shakespeareans were rising in their primitive vigor, they were rivaled on their own stages by an unceasing procession of visiting stars from England, who made the crossing for no grander purpose than to glean fortunes from American box offices. During the 1820s and 1830s these visitors clung mostly to the eastern seaboard—from New York north to Boston and south through Philadelphia, Baltimore, Washington, and as far as Charleston. By the 1840s they would cut across the southern states for a long stand in New Orleans, then complete the grand circle up the Mississippi to Saint Louis and through the Ohio River towns to Pittsburgh and on to New York again. By their foreignness and their glamorous reputation as well as by their polished style, they continued to anglicize and sophisticate American taste in Shakespearean acting.

Thus when William Charles Macready first came to America in 1826, he found an audience weary of the secondhand classical acting of established Americans like Thomas Cooper, and at the same time distrustful of the spectacular but erratic acting of Edmund Kean. They were ready to take lessons from Macready's more thoughtful approach to his art. It was good to see a Hamlet conceived intellectually and played reliably, consistent from end to end. When he came again in the 1840s he had won (or at least he wore) the label of "The Eminent Tragedian." By then he had passed through his celebrated if futile struggles to rescue the great patent theatres of London from animal shows, melodrama, and opera and rededicate them to Shakespeare and the classics. Glorious in defeat, he was welcomed by leaders of the intellectual and artistic community. In the 1830s, the last representatives of the famous Kemble family—Charles and his daughter Fanny—and after them Ellen Tree, drew the world of fashion to the theatre, as much perhaps because of their social reputation and gentility as for their genuine acting skills. In the 1840s Charles Kean initiated patrons of the Park Theatre to the delights of modern scenography, re-creating for them the recent London stagings of *Richard III* and *King John*. He failed to establish a fashion for historically accurate scenery, for the American audience was not yet sufficiently interested in that sort of "educational theatre," but at least he set a standard for scenic investiture of Shakespeare which would be remembered in years to come.

Just after the mid-century a new generation of American actors and managers began to grow up to their Shakespearean responsibilities. They did not altogether reject the refining influence of English models, and probably, too, both performers and audience were becoming serious *readers* of the plays. By mid-century American editions were plentiful (including family and fireside editions), and the lyceum lectures on Shakespeare, such as H. N. Hudson's and Ralph Waldo Emerson's (his enthronization of Shakespeare as "The Poet"), were becoming almost as popular as Shakespeare in performance. The new generation of actors certainly turned their backs on the screaming-eagleism which had inflamed the mobs in Astor Place, and with a new thoughtfulness and sensitivity they fashioned a Shakespeare for the coming age.

William Burton must surely be counted as a catalyst in this process. Born in England and trained as a comic actor there, he spent the second and more important half of his life as an actor-manager in Philadelphia and New York. He not only played a superb Toby Belch, Bottom the Weaver, and Autolycus but mounted several Shakespeare comedies in stagings which would yield nothing to the best theatres of London. Moreover, as an expert bookman he accumulated a vast library of Shakespeareana and other literary rarities. Several leading Shakespeare scholars of the day found source and stimulus for their work in Burton's library. In Edward Loomis Davenport we come at last upon an American-born actor who, though somehow lacking in ambition or sense of career, was so well molded a man, a voice, and an intelligence that even among the hypercritical English he passed as a fine Shakespearean. One of the most gratifying accomplishments during the 1870s and early 1880s was that of John McCullough, a handsome, tall, and stalwart man, who succeeded in bringing the gigantic Lear and Othello of his master Edwin Forrest down to the level of human beings, investing them with something of his own geniality, warmth, and kindliness.

American Shakespeare of the nineteenth century climaxed in the long career of Edwin Booth. Although as an actor Booth lacked humor, sentiment, and physical grandeur, he united beauty of face and voice, brisk wit, gentleness, companionability, an impression of intellectuality, a mysterious power of compelling all eyes and ears and wishes to attend upon him, and a total dedication to theatrical art. For about a decade he strove to emulate the English in the arts of *mise-en-scène*, and he achieved some triumphs in this kind. Fortunately, however, financial disaster put a stop to his indulgence in what was after all a diversion from the true Shakespearean essence. His strength lay in acting. As an actor he won and held the admiration of a nation, revealing to his nineteenth-century audiences such truths about Shakespeare's characters as he and his age could comprehend.

We have no history of Shakespeare in the American theatre. I offer this set of essays as the beginning of one.

At the time of the Shakespeare quatercentenary, there appeared two fine articles which touch upon American performances of Shakespeare, but only cursorily, along with other matters. James G. McManaway's "Shakespeare in the United States" (*PMLA*, 79 [1964], pp. 513–18) discusses most interestingly those American editors and critics whose work has been made possible by the establishment in this country of great libraries of Shakespeareana and Renaissance books. Robert Falk's "Shakespeare in America: A Survey to 1900" (*Shakespeare Survey*, 18 [1965], pp. 102–18) takes note, in turn, of "the actors of Shakespeare, his editors, and aesthetic critics, and . . . the imaginative use of his themes and language in new forms of literature." Especially rewarding are the two final sections of Falk's essay, in which he traces the influence of Shakespeare upon American intellectual life in the nineteenth century (Emerson, Lowell, Whitman) and the transmutation of Shakespearean art and idea in the fiction of Herman Melville.

Behind these essays stand two important books, both published in 1939. Alfred Westfall's *American Shakespearean Criticism, 1607–1865* is a systematic analysis of American editions of Shakespeare and American critical utterances down to the Civil War. It climaxes with the work of Richard Grant White and stops just short of H. H. Furness and the beginning of the *New Variorum*. Except for one brief chapter, largely statistical, on staged Shakespeare in the eighteenth century, Westfall did not concern himself with the theatre at all. Esther Cloudman Dunn's ambitious and wide-ranging *Shakespeare in America* devotes half of its chapters to Shakespeare in the theatre during the eighteenth century and the first half of the nineteenth. Of especial value are two chapters in which Miss Dunn brings together curious information about Shakespeare on the frontier—first in the Ohio and Mississippi valleys, then beyond the Rockies in the wake of the Gold Rush. Miss Dunn's basic concern, however, is to observe Shakespeare as a "barometer of social and cultural history" (these are the last six words of her text), and thus she tends to generalize from the theatrical experience rather than to examine in detail the work of actors and managers, their acting styles and modes of stage production. She is indeed more interesting, and perhaps on surer footing, in her discussions of Shakespeare in the magazines, the rise of Shakespeare studies in school curricula, the early editions of Shakespeare, and Shakespearean influence on the thinking of certain founders of the nation (Adams, Jefferson) and on certain nineteenth-century thinkers (Emerson, Thoreau, Whitman, Lincoln).

My objective in the essays that follow is narrower than Miss Dunn's, although I hope also to contribute something to modern awareness of our cultural history. My objective is to bring the glass down quite close upon certain long-past performers and performances of Shakespeare, to brighten our vision of those persons and events, to improve our understanding of their cultural significance, and to restore something of their forgotten luster in the annals of theatrical art.

We must bear in mind Miss Dunn's cautionary observation that "the business of conjuring the past, making it deliver itself up, 'in its habit as it lived,' is as everybody knows, mostly a failing business." Insofar as is possible, I have endeavored to conjure up this theatrical past through the language and opinions of the actors themselves and of the professional critics of their day. This language and these opinions must be taken with grains of salt, of course. We do not know what such words as *beautiful* or *natural* or *gentlemanly* or *indecent* meant a century ago, or two centuries ago, to the writers who used them or to the readers who then read them. We can pretty well rely on two laws of history which, to be sure, almost contradict each other. The first and more important of these is that in a mere two hundred years human nature has not changed much in its intelligence, its passions, and its fundamental values. But the second law, caught up in the phrase *autres temps, autres mœurs*, reminds us that the surface manifestations of human nature—*manners*—fluctuate wildly from one generation to another. And theatre is intimately tied to manners. A hundred years ago an exposed female "limb" gave scandal; and actors in those days dared not utter the name of God upon the stage, but always substituted a mild "Heaven." In the theatre of our own time, total nudity is the vogue, and profane or blasphemous language is almost as common in film and drama as it is in everyday life. Manners, not morals, is the issue. Thus when we find a critic of the past condemning on moral grounds some theatrical effect —an entire play, a costume, a word, a gesture—which was in fact no worse than a violation of some popularly held code of manners, it is usually not difficult to detect the confusion and to allow for it. We must be extremely wary, though, in detecting shifts in *aesthetic* standards, which are subtle and unspectacular. We must scrupulously adjust aesthetic pronouncements of theatrical effects in the light of what we know about shifts of taste in literature, music, painting, and all the other arts. In using past language to re-create past events, I have made every effort to find statements which I take to be not only reliable but relatively factual, forthright, unambiguous— which exchange at face value in the marketplace of ideas.

I have referred to what follows as "essays" rather than as a "history," for it has been my method to select those few figures in each generation whose work seems to me to typify or to set the tone for the Shakespearean theatre of their time, and to treat those figures in sufficient detail that their significance comes clear. The whole history would do justice (as I have not attempted to do) to the Wallacks (Henry and James William and James William the Younger and Lester), whose careers, taken together, spanned seven decades of the nineteenth century; Thomas Hamblin, actor and longtime manager of the Bowery Theatre; James Murdoch, actor and teacher of actors; to such comedians as Henry and Thomas Placide, William Davidge, W. R. Blake, and Charles Bass; to a number of visitors from abroad—James Anderson, George Vandenhoff, G. V. Brooke, and Barry Sullivan; and to such actresses, famous in their day, as Caroline Chapman, Laura Keene, Julia Dean, Anna Cora Mowatt, Josephine Clifton, Emma Waller, and Mrs. D. P. Bowers. These and dozens more served the cause admirably, but to rehearse their careers would, I think, add little more than bulk to the "idea" of Shakespeare in America.

I have refrained, too, from any attempt to report the spread of Shakespeare across the nation. Shakespeare in New Orleans, Boston, San Francisco, Chicago, Philadelphia, Cincinnati, Baltimore, Saint Louis—and in dozens of lesser towns that built theatres and sustained resident companies—is indeed important. But I have limited my scope mainly to cities of the East and, after the turn into the nineteenth century, mainly to what happened in New York City. For ultimately whatever set the style of Shakespearean playing and production in America came into or came out of the theatrical capital of the country and was well reported there.

Shakespeare on the American Stage

From the Hallams to Edwin Booth

Illus. 1. William Dunlap, first historian of the American theatre.

CHAPTER I

The Eighteenth Century

IN THE YEAR 1752 one Lewis Hallam led a company of actors from London to Williamsburg, Virginia, and there on September 15 they staged what is usually taken to be the first professional Shakespeare in America. The play was *The Merchant of Venice*, with Ravenscroft's *The Anatomist* as afterpiece.[1]

It was not, to be sure, the *first* Shakespeare in America. In 1730 a jocular New York physician named Joachimus Bertrand advertised that he was about to play the Apothecary in an amateur performance of *Romeo and Juliet*. In March and April of 1750 New York audiences saw *Richard III* (the Colley Cibber version) done by a company headed by Walter Murray and Thomas Kean, and during the next year or two Murray and Kean would carry this play and the rest of their repertory into Maryland and Virginia. In December of 1751 a man named Robert Upton, who had been sent to New York in advance of the Hallam company to serve as their agent but who had abandoned his commission and set up on his own, performed *Othello*. Very little is known about these persons, however, and by 1752 their companies had broken up and disappeared. Lewis Hallam would refer to Murray and Kean as "that Sett of Pretenders." William Dunlap, the first historian of the American theatre, described them as "idle young men perpetrating the murder of sundry plays," and a modern historian has called them "stage-struck tradesmen and their wives." Probably none of these epithets is quite fair, but there is so little else to say about them that we simply accept the Hallam company's *Merchant of Venice* as the significant beginning of staged Shakespeare in America.[2]

THE HALLAM COMPANY

If we are to believe William Dunlap (who was reporting from hearsay and some eighty years after the event), the Hallam company was truly professional—organized, equipped, and rehearsed. Yet at the time of their crossing, the members of the company, except for Hallam and his wife, seem to have been theatrical nonentities. This was expectable, of course, for no English actor who was thriving in the profession would willingly have taken on the rigors of "exile" in the colonies. The great Garrick never thought of doing so—although when he heard of the Boston Tea Party he offered whimsically to don his stage tyrant's robes and "make yᵉ Bostonians drink their tea as they ought, or send them after yᵉ tea into yᵉ atlantic."[3] It never occurred to the Woodwards and Barrys, the Woffingtons and Pritchards and Clives to carry their talents to the western wilderness. Charles Macklin quarreled with everyone in London, but his rages never catapulted him farther off than Ireland. "America was looked on in England," so the actor John Bernard would remember, "as a land of fever and fanatics, of swamps and scamps, of self-called saints and savages."[4] The northernmost colonies were populated by psalm-singing Puritans and governed by blue laws as repressive as ever were on the books in Cromwell's Commonwealth. If the living was easier in Virginia, yet there, too, one expected to encounter disadvantages: an unhealthy climate; a developing caste system based on extremes of wealth and poverty; the morally offensive institution of slavery, which was growing at an alarming rate; and a supposed abundance of dangerous criminals. For generations England had been deporting to the southern colonies "all the rogues and runagates who had outraged the laws of Europe," and Ben Franklin once sent Walpole a basket of rattlesnakes "in return for the curious venomous reptiles the minister had been pleased to present to Virginia."[5] Tomahawk-swinging redskins were supposed to lurk in the forests outside every hamlet, and even more murderous was the yellow fever, which in every hot season swept up from the West Indies, sometimes decimating whole southern communities and infecting at least as far north as Philadelphia. Thus it was mainly bankrupts, desperate men, younger sons, and other social castoffs who would willingly emigrate—and actors who could never make the grade at home or who were too fretful to wait their turn on the London ladder.

If the members of the Hallam company were nobodies, at least they were courageous, and it is worth looking into the circumstances which brought them to their perilous adventure.[6] The promoter of the affair, as Lewis Hallam once explained in a broadside to the people of New York, was his older brother William, who organized the company in London but did not travel with it. This William Hallam had achieved a certain notoriety in legal as well as theatrical circles by his defiance of the Theatre Licensing Act—that Act of 1737 which decreed that the "regular" drama could be performed in London only at the patent houses of Covent Garden and Drury Lane. As proprietor of a minor theatre called the New Wells, which he built in 1739, Hallam at first exhibited such entertainments as the Act allowed—tumbling, ropedancing, concerts of music, and pantomimes. But in the autumn of 1744 he put together an acting company and began to perform plays.[7] In order to keep upwind of the law he made it appear in his advertisements that what he was selling to the public was only musical entertainment: the play being offered was incidental to the concert, and it was free of charge. By this dodge (which later proprietors of nonpatent houses would often resort to) he managed during three seasons to stage over fifty-five main plays for a total of nearly three hundred nights. It was a first-rate repertory, too, with plenty of Farquhar, Otway, Rowe, Congreve, Vanbrugh, and Shakespeare, together with some of the most admired or most topically interesting pieces of newest vintage.

Then abruptly in the spring of 1747 the regular drama disappeared from the New Wells, the company was dispersed, and the house reverted to acrobatics, music, and pantomime. Probably the law was closing in. Soon thereafter, in fact, the authorities began to enforce the Licensing Act with a vengeance, suppressing theatricals of all sorts at the nonpatent houses. In December of 1751 the New Wells was closed permanently and Hallam was left without occupation or income and, it is said, with debts amounting to £5,000. A year later he managed to open the house again, but only for six performances, every one of them billed as a benefit for himself.[8]

During these seasons of slow defeat Hallam's thoughts had been turning toward the colonies. News was drifting in of lively theatrical doings in Jamaica. The Jamaican manager John Moody was sending home annually for recruits to his company (as the yellow fever cut down his numbers), and many a minor actor began to look to the New World for his future. Thus Hallam got the notion of sending out a company, not to the Indies, which Moody was in control of, but to the American mainland. As early as 1750 he dispatched Robert Upton to New York with funds and authority to build a theatre, obtain a license, and prepare the way for him—that Robert Upton who, as we have seen, absconded and set up his own company.

Hallam owned some equipment. At the settling of his indebtedness, it is said, his creditors let him keep the costumes, properties, and painted scenes that had accumulated at the New Wells. And he had at hand exactly the right persons to lead his company—his brother Lewis and Lewis's wife, who had been his mainstays at the Wells. Lewis, a low comedian specializing in comic servants and eccentrics (of which he played over forty at the Wells), was gifted with executive ability and would manage the company in the field. Mrs. Hallam had achieved the status of leading lady, capable—at least up to the level expected at minor houses—of everything in the romantic, sentimental, tragic, and high-comic lines. At the Wells she had played some forty-six roles—many a Melinda, Dorinda, Lady Betty, and Violante of fashionable light pieces, but often enough a Shakespearean Miranda or Lady Percy or a tragical Jane Shore.

The company was to consist of a dozen adult performers, and it would operate on the sharing system, the income to be divided eighteen ways according to the pattern long operative in the English provinces. Lewis Hallam would in effect control eight of the eighteen shares: one for himself as manager, one for himself as actor, one for his wife, one for his three teen-age children (Helen, Lewis, Jr., and Adam), and four company shares which were to cover operating expenses and earn profit for William. The other ten shares were allotted to the other ten adults whom William had hired: Mr. and Mrs. William Rigby, Patrick Malone, John Singleton, William Adcock, Miss Palmer (she appears to have become Mrs. Adcock very early in the venture), Mr. and Mrs. Thomas Clarkson, Mr. Herbert, and Mr. Wynell.

And who were these ten players? "A good and sufficient company," said Dunlap, taking his opinion from Lewis Hallam, Jr., who as a twelve-year-old in the year of the crossing may have been unduly impressed by his elders. But Dunlap slyly added that they were "willing to leave their country (and perhaps their creditors)." One finds next to nothing about them in the records of *The London Stage* or other histories. Some were probably old stagers of dubious talent; some, probably, young and promising but as yet untried. All of them dwelt on the fringes of "the legitimate"—were of the sort that haunted inns and taverns of the Covent Garden neighborhood to pore over notices posted there of booth theatres operating at London fairs, lucky if some country Crummles would carry them off to a season of wandering in the provinces. Whatever their condition near the end of 1751—sanguine, despairing, or reconciled to their low estate—they were fortunate in the situation Hallam offered them. America might be a wilderness, its towns a rabble of Yankee-Doodles, but there they could at least labor in their vocation.

"The emigrants were next assembled at the house of William Hallam," Dunlap wrote; "a list of *stock plays* [was] produced by him, with attendant farces, and the *cast* of the whole agreed upon in full assembly of the body politic." They were to ready themselves in some two dozen plays and eight or ten farces, which constituted a thoroughly sophisticated repertory. The list—or half of it—stands up pretty well to modern inspection: six or eight Shakespeares, including *Richard III* (the Cibber version), *Romeo and Juliet* (in its fashionable new tailoring by Garrick), *Hamlet*, *Othello*, *The Merchant of Venice*; five comedies by Farquhar, including *The Recruiting Officer* and *The Beaux' Stratagem*; Congreve's *Love for Love*; Gay's *Beggar's Opera*. We should not much relish the other half of the list, although we can sympathize with our ancestors' preferences. They valued Addison's *Cato*—because as cultivated persons they owed it to themselves to do so—for its eloquence, its "classic" form, and its display of Roman fortitude. Nathaniel Lee's *Theodosius* flattered their allegiance to Christian virtue while it tickled their appetite for pleasures of the flesh. George Lillo's *London Merchant* preached social and business morality in language and situations instantly relevant. Tragedy of the most melting sort was provided in Nicholas Rowe's *Fair Penitent* and *Jane Shore*. Although many of the Hallams' items are out of favor now, in those days discriminating observers held them in high regard, and they certainly imposed weighty demands upon their actors.

The "good and sufficient company" had the entire winter to get up their roles, for it was not until April of 1752 that they sailed from England with Mr. William Lee, captain of the *Charming Sally*. "The pieces had been . . .

put in study before embarkation," Dunlap tells us, "and during the passage they were regularly rehearsed. The quarter-deck of the *Charming Sally* was the stage, and whenever the winds and weather permitted, the heroes and heroines of the sock and buskin performed their allotted parts." They rehearsed the entire repertory, concentrating especially on those pieces which they would first use to "enliven the wilds of America." Dunlap speculated on "the fun" of those rehearsals, the delight which the Jack Tars took in having such a company aboard, and the amusement of the actors themselves in the "nautical drollery" of their sailor audience. The voyage took six weeks. The *Charming Sally* docked at Yorktown on June 2. The company proceeded at once to Williamsburg, but there such matters as fitting up a theatre and securing Governor Dinwiddie's permission to play in it delayed their first performance until September 15.[9]

When William Hallam sent his advance agent to New York he must have intended for the company to appear in New York, and one wonders why they went to Virginia instead. They may have heard that New York was occupied by rival companies and, not knowing that the rivals were dwindling out of existence, may have chosen to avoid a confrontation. Or they may have been drawn to Williamsburg by its peculiarly happy reputation: it was a center of political and social life (the capital city and home of the governor of the Old Dominion), an intellectual center (home of the College of William and Mary, which had long since fostered amateur theatricals as a tool for education), and the business center of a wide and prosperous agricultural area. Or perhaps their decision turned on the matter of local moral codes—the likelihood that in the South, where the Established Church prevailed, there would be far less difficulty in obtaining license to play. In Dunlap's opinion the choice almost certainly depended from "the knowledge that Episcopalians were then more liberal in regard to the drama than most other sects."

Historians remind us not to assume an absolute dichotomy between Puritan North and Cavalier South. They tell us that even during Virginia's very early history, when Oliver Cromwell deposed King Charles I, a Cromwellian adherent speedily and easily replaced the colony's royalist governor. And during the 1740s and 1750s when late waves of the Great Awakening drove the general American populace into a frenzy of religiosity, shaming them out of indulgence in public pleasures, Virginians by the thousands succumbed to the hysteria like everybody else.

Indeed, within a year or two of the Hallams' arrival, the Reverend George Whitefield was spouting evangelical salvationism in Williamsburg itself.

Unquestionably, however, Puritan New England was bastioned against the players as the South was not. New York *would* receive them, albeit grudgingly, its hospitality cooled by an inborn Dutch regard for time and money. But in Massachusetts, down through 1792, plays were legislated against absolutely, and the Quakers of Pennsylvania, seconded by other Protestant sects, sought repeatedly (if not successfully) to impose regulations every bit as restrictive as those in Massachusetts.

The New England hostility to theatre was of a piece with the all-consuming Puritan fear of flesh and the devil. The early Church Fathers may be blamed for it in the long run, but it derived more nearly from the frantic excesses of radical English Protestants of the sixteenth and seventeenth centuries. In 1577 (within a year of the building of Burbage's Theatre and when Shakespeare was a boy in school) one John Northbrooke, a preacher at Bristol, gave classic expression to this hostility, a battle cry against the devil's works which echoes at least faintly in antitheatric pronouncements to this day.[10] "Satan hath not a more speedie way," wrote Northbrooke, referring directly to the playhouses then springing up in the northern suburbs of London, "and fitter schoole to work and teach his desire, to bring men and women into his snare of concupiscence and filthie lustes of wicked whoredome, than those places and playes, and theatres are: And therefore [it is] necessarie that those places and Players shoulde be forbidden and dissolued and put downe by authoritie, as the Brothell houses and Stewes are." Someone had been saying (as in what age have they not!) that plays can teach more sound morality than many sermons do—a notion which Northbrooke howled at. Among their other evil effects, he was certain, plays foster sexual misbehavior.

I speake (alas with griefe and sorowe of heart) against those people that are so fleshlye ledde, to see what rewarde there is giuen to suche Crocodiles, whiche deuoure the pure chastitie, bothe of single and maried persons, men and women. . . . No wiues or maydens, that list to content and please sad and honest men, will be founde and seene at common Playes, Dauncings, or other great resorte of people. For these Playes be the instrumentes and armour of Venus and Cupide, and to saye good soothe, what safegarde of chastitie can there be, where the woman is desired with so many eyes, where so many faces looke vpon hir, and againe she vppon so manye?

She must needes fire some, and hir selfe also fired againe, and she be not a stone; for what minde can bee pure and whole among such a rablement, and not spotted with any lust?

Then comes his exercise in rhetorical *copia*, a fireworks of denunciation:

If you will learne howe to bee false, and deceyue your husbandes, or husbandes their wyues, howe to playe the harlottes, to obtayne ones loue, howe to rauishe, howe to beguyle, howe to betraye, to flatter, lye, sweare, forsweare, howe to allure to whoredome, howe to murther, howe to poyson, howe to disobey and rebell agaynst Princes, to consume treasures prodigally, to mooue to lusts, to ransacke and spoyle cities and townes, to bee ydle, to blaspheme, to sing filthie songs of loue, to speake filthily, to be prowde, howe to mocke, scoffe, and deryde any nation . . . shall not you learne then at suche Enterludes howe to practise them?

This was very much the temper, if not quite the style, of New England Puritanism two centuries later, and the Hallams were wise to keep a safe distance from it on their first arrival into the New World.

In the South, the general attitude toward theatre was quite different. Theatre, along with hunting, dancing, riding, drinking, cardplaying, was one of the pleasures traditionally available to the English leisured classes—pleasures that well-to-do southerners, those who set society's tone, remembered and cherished.[11] Whether as colony or state, Episcopalian Virginia never passed laws banning plays, nor did Catholic Maryland. Fine ladies in their best bonnets attended plays without thought of damnation, and the players—as long as they paid their bills and laid no thieving hands on other men's property or wives—were welcomed.

When the Hallam company arrived at Williamsburg they found a playhouse waiting for them. Erected by a local builder a year earlier for the Murray-Kean company, it stood in the outskirts of the community, just to the east of the Capitol, so near the forest, as Lewis Hallam, Jr., would recall, that his father could stand in the doorway and shoot pigeons for his dinner. It was a crude structure, however, which in no way measured up to Hallam's notion of a proper playhouse, and he spent the summer rebuilding it. No trace remains—not even the foundation lines—of the building as he left it, and only by reckoning from what we know of small English theatres of the time (such as, for instance, the now well restored theatre at Richmond in Yorkshire) can we arrive at an image of the house in which the first American *Merchant of Venice*

Illus. 2. An eighteenth-century provincial playhouse. The Richmond, Yorkshire, Theatre Royal as recently reconstructed. Courtesy of the University of Bristol Theatre Collection, Richard Southern Accession.

was performed.[12] The following statements about it, then, are not facts but likelihoods:

1. It was a rectangular wooden building, small as theatres go: perhaps thirty feet wide and seventy feet long. The auditorium occupied slightly over half the length.

2. The central area of the auditorium, called the pit, was some twenty feet wide and twenty-five feet deep, with ten or a dozen backless benches. Shallow boxes with more comfortable seating stood across the rear and down the sides of the pit; in later theatres there were two or more tiers of boxes, but at Williamsburg probably only one. A small gallery supported by posts stood above the boxes at the rear.

3. The stage consisted of forestage and rear stage, separated by the proscenium arch. A green curtain, whose purpose was not to conceal scene changes but to rise after the Prologue and fall at the end of each act, hung behind the proscenium arch. The forestage, where the actors did most of their acting, extended ten or twelve feet forward of the arch; it was flanked by the actors' entrance doors and, above these doors, by small balconies or bay windows. The rear stage, used mainly for the display of scenery and furniture, was about twelve feet deep. Behind the rear stage were small workrooms and retiring rooms.

4. The forestage was lighted by hoops of candles suspended from above and by candle footlights. The scenic area was lighted by candles above and in the wings. The auditorium was lighted by brackets of candles attached to the front of the boxes.

These are the playhouse features which Hallam would have sought to realize not only at Williamsburg but afterward at New York and elsewhere, and which David Douglass and other builders would emulate throughout colonial America.

Hallam's first advertisement in the *Virginia Gazette* declared that the company's "Scenes, Cloaths, and Decorations are all entirely new, extremely rich, and finished in the highest Taste"; and further that "the Scenes, being painted by the best Hands in London, are excell'd by none in Beauty and Elegance, so that the Ladies and Gentlemen may depend on being entertain'd in as polite a Manner as at the Theatres in London."[13] We must beware of puffery: at least some of the wardrobe and scenery was left over from the defunct New Wells and hence was by no means "entirely new." We must bear in mind too that their "Cloaths" would not have been especially designed to express every character in twenty-odd plays and a batch of farces. No matter what vintage the play, the actors for the most part wore contemporary costume and the same costume for role after role. Except when playing ancient Romans, Orientals, or other exotics, they dressed for the stage pretty much as they would dress at home, in society, at their trades, or on the street. Each actor had something to wear which was appropriate to the "line" of characters he was trained for. Thus Hallam's advertisement meant little more than that each principal male actor owned one or two fine velvet suits, a handsome wig, and other fashionable accoutrements in which to present fine gentlemen, and that each leading lady had two or three voluminous dresses of elegant fabrics, so tailored with bustles and trains that they might grace a banquet or court ball in the year 1752. As for the "Scenes," however splendidly the best hands in London may have painted them, they were built for touring and thus were few and unsubstantial, and, like the costumes, did multiple duty. Any given "set" might consist of four to six wings (two or three to a side) and a backdrop on a roller: the wings were perhaps three feet wide and not much more than twelve feet tall. A few stock sets—a throne room, a street or two, a forest, a cottage, a seascape, and two or three domestic interiors—would be used again and again to back up many diverse dramatic situations.

Yet with these provisos, the Hallam company did have a good deal to boast about. They were a professional company, and at least in the geographical sense they were "from London"; they brought dresses in trunks, not merely the clothes on their backs; their scenery was of sufficient quantity and attractiveness to meet standard

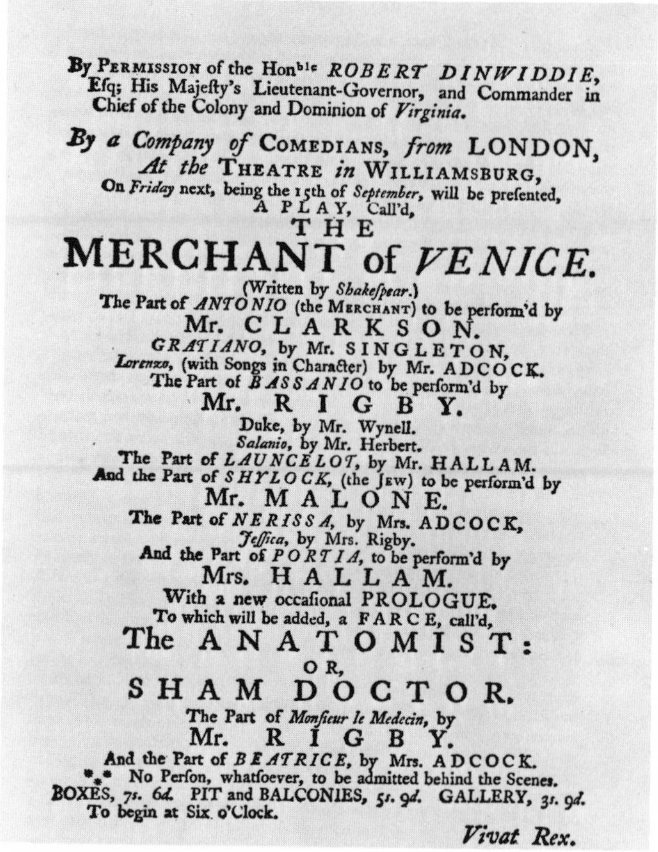

By PERMISSION of the Hon[ble] *ROBERT DINWIDDIE*, Eſq; His Majeſty's Lieutenant-Governor, and Commander in Chief of the Colony and Dominion of *Virginia*.

By a Company of COMEDIANS, *from* LONDON,
At the THEATRE *in* WILLIAMSBURG,
On *Friday* next, being the 15th of *September*, will be preſented,
A PLAY, Call'd,
THE
MERCHANT of *VENICE*.
(Written by *Shakeſpear*.)
The Part of *ANTONIO* (the MERCHANT) to be perform'd by
Mr. CLARKSON.
GRATIANO, by Mr. SINGLETON,
Lorenzo, (with Songs in Character) by Mr. ADCOCK.
The Part of *BASSANIO* to be perform'd by
Mr. RIGBY.
Duke, by Mr. Wynell.
Salanio, by Mr. Herbert.
The Part of *LAUNCELOT*, by Mr. HALLAM.
And the Part of *SHYLOCK*, (the JEW) to be perform'd by
Mr. MALONE.
The Part of *NERISSA*, by Mrs. ADCOCK,
Jeſſica, by Mrs. Rigby.
And the Part of *PORTIA*, to be perform'd by
Mrs. HALLAM.
With a new occaſional PROLOGUE.
To which will be added, a FARCE, call'd,
The ANATOMIST:
OR,
SHAM DOCTOR.
The Part of *Monſieur le Medecin*, by
Mr. RIGBY.
And the Part of *BEATRICE*, by Mrs. ADCOCK.
*** No Perſon, whatſoever, to be admitted behind the Scenes.
BOXES, 7*s*. 6*d*. PIT and BALCONIES, 5*s*. 9*d*. GALLERY, 3*s*. 9*d*.
To begin at Six o'Clock.
Vivat Rex.

Illus. 3. Playbill for the Hallam company's *Merchant of Venice* at Williamsburg, 1752. Courtesy of *Shakespeare Quarterly*.

expectations. As we have seen, they offered a strong and balanced repertory—"all the best Plays, Operas, Farces, and Pantomimes, that have been exhibited in any of the Theatres for these ten years past," as their advertisement put it. And above all, they were rehearsed: their six weeks together on the *Charming Sally* and their three months between arrival and first performance gave them far more opportunity to perfect the teamwork of their playing than touring companies usually enjoyed.

It has been said that the play with which the Hallam company opened its campaign was not Shakespeare's *Merchant of Venice* but Lord Lansdowne's reduced and corrupted version of it called *The Jew of Venice*.[14] This is difficult to believe. The Lansdowne version had held the stage (though not played with great frequency) from 1701 to 1740. But in February of 1741 Charles Macklin not only restored the original but astonished all London by converting Shylock from a funny man, as the Lansdowne character had always been played, to a harsh-tongued, vindictive villain. It was a revolutionary event. The cry went up that "This is the Jew / That Shakespeare drew," and Shakespeare's play (with cuts, of course) suddenly became one of his most popular: it was played at Drury Lane twenty-seven times in the next twelvemonth, and at all the London theatres together over sixty times more during the next decade.[15] It is unthinkable that once Hallam chose *The Merchant* for his opening bill he would revert to the forgotten Lansdowne version, or would offer anything less fashionable than London's best.

Proof lies in the casting. Hallam himself, manager and low comedian of the company, played Launcelot Gobbo, a role that does not appear in the Lansdowne version. And William Adcock sang the "songs in character" of Lorenzo: these songs, addressed to "Jessy" are not in the Lansdowne version but were added to the original play in 1741 or after.

The only review of this famous performance tells us no more than that "a numerous and polite audience" received the play "with great Applause."[16] Thrown upon conjecture we can catch at least faint glimpses of the performance in the light reflected from the several actors' histrionic "lines." Shylock was played by Patrick Malone, whose line in the few later years in which we can trace him was heavy or severe old men, sometimes comic ones like Lockit in *The Beggar's Opera* or Sir Sampson Legend in *Love for Love*, sometimes very serious ones like Thorow-

good in *The London Merchant* and King Lear. If he could play King Lear there is no reason to assume he played Shylock other than in dead earnest, as near as possible to the approved Macklin manner. Mrs. Hallam, being indisputably the leading lady of the company, was of course the Portia of the occasion, bringing to the role something of the dignity and warmth for which she was celebrated in Juliet and Cordelia, Andromache in *The Distrest Mother*, and Calista in *The Fair Penitent*. The title role of Antonio, which from the greenroom point of view was traditionally held to be of secondary importance, fell to Thomas Clarkson, a serviceable actor of indefinite quality, who was sometimes Friar Lawrence, sometimes Edmund the Bastard, sometimes Old Foresight in *Love for Love*; in *The Beggar's Opera* he played the whore named Moll Brazen. The romantic lead, Bassanio, went to the actor who appears beyond all the rest to have been the leading man of the company, William Rigby, who on other occasions was Romeo and Richard III, Beverly in *The Gamester*, Orestes in *The Distrest Mother*, and Valentine in *Love for Love*. John Singleton, the poet of the company, played Gratiano, his line being witty, mercurial parts. Singleton also composed a special prologue for the opening in which he assured his hearers that the Muse herself had inspired this company to come to "Virginia's plains," where they would be "confident to find / An audience sensible, polite, and kind."

During the company's eight months of playing at Williamsburg they seem not to have laid special emphasis on Shakespeare (we do not know that they even repeated *The Merchant of Venice*), but presumably they seeded into their repertory *Richard III*, *King Lear* (the Tate-Garrick version), *Romeo and Juliet*, *Henry IV*, and *Othello*. One well-remembered incident from the season is that when Governor Dinwiddie entertained the Emperor and Empress of the Cherokee Indians at a performance of *Othello*, the Empress became so alarmed at the sword-fight in the second act that she sent "some about her to go and prevent them killing one another."[17]

By July of 1753 the company was in New York, caught up in the expectable battle with conservative authorities over license to perform; and again as at Williamsburg they replaced an inadequate theatre, formerly used by the Murray-Kean company, with a "very fine, large, and commodious" one.[18] From mid-September to March they spun off their repertory, adding at least *King Lear* to the number of Shakespeare plays previously seen in New

Illus. 4. Lewis Hallam, Jr. Courtesy of the Harvard Theatre Collection.

DAVID DOUGLASS AND THE AMERICAN COMPANY

Late in 1758 David Douglass reintroduced the company to the mainland, this time for a stay of five and a half years. The personnel of the company was almost entirely new, and of the Hallam family only two significant figures remained. Lewis Hallam, Jr., though only eighteen, was now ready to play most of the leading roles except the heaviest, like Othello (which Douglass reserved for himself), King Lear, and Richard III: in a few years he would graduate to these roles also. He would continue on the stage for nearly half a century, coming to be regarded for much of that time as America's foremost actor.

Unfortunately the younger Lewis Hallam does not come down to us as a very attractive person.[19] When he became manager and co-manager of the company in the 1780s and 1790s he earned an ugly reputation for stinginess, craftiness, jealousy, quarrelsomeness, and double-dealing. And signs are plentiful too that his histrionic skills were inadequate to the rank in the profession which he assumed and clung to. Contemporary accounts suggest that he was a late hanger-on to acting methods then referred to in England as the Old School, by which was meant rigid posturing and heavily formalized speaking. Given his stubborn temperament and the circumstances of his training, this result was inevitable. During his early teens his mentors had been William Rigby and others whose own methods had developed during the heyday of the Old School of Barton Booth, Lacy Ryan, and James Quin; and rarely if ever in his formative years could he have been exposed to the more natural acting fostered by Garrick and his best followers in London. Thus, although he is said to have fenced vigorously, his general stage movement was stiff and prim. His vocal delivery was excessively declamatory, in moments of high passion lapsing into gabble and rant. An observer in Philadelphia once commented sourly that he ought to "speak plain English whenever he assumes a character that may be supposed to understand the Language."[20] He was the first American Hamlet (the earliest recorded performance was at Philadelphia on July 27, 1759), but when he visited London in the 1770s and attempted Hamlet at Covent Garden, he was allowed to play it only once.

His mother, now Mrs. Douglass, was turning matronly, but her beauty held and her intelligence was unimpaired. At the return from Jamaica she was the principal actress of the company. Mother and son often shared the honors of the evening. On at least one occasion she was the

York. In the spring of 1754 they played a short season in Philadelphia, opposed furiously by the Quakers; in the autumn, another short season in the easier world of Charleston, South Carolina. Early in 1755 they abandoned the Continent for the sweeter climate of the Indies. There Lewis Hallam merged his management with that of the Jamaican director David Douglass, and soon thereafter he died of yellow fever, leaving both company and widow for Douglass to claim as his own.

Illus. 5. Sketch supposedly of Mrs. Lewis Hallam, Sr., later Mrs. David Douglass. Courtesy of the Harvard Theatre Collection.

Juliet to Lewis's Romeo[21]—an odd little Oedipean situation, which may have roused wonder in the more knowing observers but was no cause for the gouging out of eyes.

Douglass began his campaign in New York. Times were very bad financially, and the good magistrates thought people ought not to waste their money on theatricals. It tested to the limits Douglass's not inconsiderable abilities at maneuvering and subterfuge to obtain a license. Finally, beginning January 1, 1759, he was allowed to run off a limited program of thirteen or fourteen plays, in which Shakespeare was represented by *Othello* and *Richard III*.

Philadelphia was even more difficult to break into, for by now not only the Quakers but the Presbyterians, the Lutherans, and the Baptists mounted attacks upon the playhouse as the "House of the Devil": "Consider, therefore, the Play-House, and the Master of Entertainment there, as it consists of Love Intrigues, blasphemous Passions, profane Discourses, lewd Descriptions, filthy Jests, and all the most extravagant Rant of wanton, vile profligate Persons, of both Sexes, heating and inflaming one another with all the Wantoness of Address, the Immodesty of Motions, and Lewdness of Thought that Wit can invent."[22] By June of 1759 the organized religionists put a bill through the Assembly prohibiting plays absolutely. Governor Denny, however, being on the side of the players and knowing full well that the government in London would repeal the bill, postponed its enforcement until the following January, so that the players had a clear half year in which to work. Douglass trimmed his sails to the prevailing winds, making his program as respectable as possible. Of the twenty-eight bills of which we have record, eight were Shakespearean: *Richard III*, *Hamlet* (thrice), *King Lear*, *Macbeth* (twice), and *Romeo and Juliet*. None of these had ever been performed in Philadelphia, and Douglass won support from the intelligentsia for introducing them. At least five evenings were devoted to Colley Cibber's highly moral *Provoked Husband*.[23]

Twice during these early years Douglass actually dared to lead his troops into the heart of New England. Newport, Rhode Island, was even in those early days a vacation town, where in the summer months rich southerners and their families took refuge from the heat and fevers that made their homes unlivable. Some sixty Jewish families lived there too, a result of Rhode Island's original practice of religious toleration, and, as the historian of the Providence theatre put it, "Jews from time immemorial have been conspicuous in their support of the drama."[24] For such an audience Douglass moved his company into the King's Arms Tavern in the summer of 1761 and offered plays in the guise of "Moral Dialogues." His playbill for *Othello* is a famous curiosity:

King's Arms Tavern, Newport, Rhode Island
On Monday, June 10, at the Public Room
of the Above Inn, will be delivered a Series of
MORAL DIALOGUES
in five parts
Depicting the evil effects of Jealousy and
other Bad Passions and Proving that
Happiness can only Spring from
the Pursuit of Virtue.

MR. DOUGLASS will represent a noble and magnanimous Moor named Othello, who loves a young lady named Desdemona, and after he has married her, harbors (as in too many cases) the dreadful passion of jealousy.

> *Of jealousy, our being's bane,*
> *Mark the small cause, and the most dreadful pain.*

MR. ALLYN will depict the character of a specious villain, in the regiment of Othello, who is so base as to hate his commander on mere suspicion, and to impose on his best friend. Of such characters, it is to be feared, there are thousands in the world, and the one in question may present to us a salutary warning.

> *The man that wrongs his master and his friend,*
> *What can he come to but a shameful end?*

MR. HALLAM will delineate a young and thoughtless officer, who is traduced by Mr. Allyn, and getting drunk loses his situation and his general's esteem. All young men, whatsoever, take example from Cassio.

> *The ill effects of drinking would you see?*
> *Be warned and keep from evil company.*

MR. MORRIS will represent an old gentleman, the father of Desdemona, who is not cruel or covetous, but is foolish enough to dislike the noble Moor, his son-in-law, because his face is not white, forgetting that we all spring from one root. Such prejudices are very numerous and very wrong.

> *Fathers beware what sense and love ye lack,*
> *'Tis crime not color, makes the being black.*

MR. QUELCH will depict a fool, who wishes to become a knave, and trusting one gets killed by him. Such is the friendship of rogues—take heed.

> *When fools would knaves become, how often you'll*
> *Perceive the knave not wiser than the fool.*

MRS. MORRIS will represent a young and virtuous wife, who being wrongfully suspected gets smothered (in an adjoining room) by her husband.

> *Reader, attend; and ere thou goest hence*
> *Let fall a tear to hapless innocence.*

MRS. DOUGLASS will be her faithful attendant, who will hold out a good example to all servants, male and female and to all people in subjection.

> *Obedience and gratitude*
> *Are things as rare as they are good.*

Various other dialogues, too numerous to mention here, will be delivered at night, all adapted to the improvement of the mind and manners. The whole will be repeated on Wednesday and Saturday. Tickets, six shillings each, to be had within. Commencement at 7, conclusion at half-past 10, in order that every spectator may go home at a sober hour and reflect upon what he has seen before he retires to rest.

> *God save the king*
> *And long may he sway*
> *East, North, and South,*
> *And fair America.*[25]

This first Rhode Island season did such fine business that in the summer of 1762 the company came again. By this time, though, bigotry was roused and ready for them. When they moved into Providence, after playing a few nights in Newport, a mob marched on their "Histrionic Academy," determined to pull it down. The mob was dissuaded by one John Brown, a heroic friend of the drama, who confronted them with hard words and a loaded cannon. The rescue was but temporary, however. The General Assembly of the colony, whose rulings could *not* be reversed in London, banned theatricals altogether, ordering too that an appropriate officer proclaim their Act through the streets of central Providence "by beat of drum."[26]

Routed from New England they tried New York again, but with unhappy results. The authorities there reduced their customary three nights a week to two, they were pestered in the press (one hostile letter writer accusing them of carrying £6,000 profit out of the community),[27] and at least one performance was interrupted by a "Person who was so very rude as to throw Eggs from the Gallery."[28] They turned southward then, for in the South they were always more comfortable. Throughout Maryland they were welcomed enthusiastically. Then on to Williamsburg, where they settled down for two entire seasons. In Williamsburg a wealthy young gentleman farmer named George Washington was frequently a member of the audience.[29] Finally in November of 1763, having recently assumed the title "The American Company of Comedians," they moved into Charleston, South Carolina, for a pleasant winter.

By happy chance there arrived in Charleston about the same time a young Englishwoman of surpassing loveliness named Margaret Cheer, who agreed to join the profession.[30] Her background appears to have been social rather than theatrical, but her natural talent—"her fine person, her youth, her Voice, & Appearance &c," as one happy Charlestonian listed her attributes—equipped her perfectly for the stage, and by her "Ease of Behaviour . . . she well fits the highest Character she ever assumes." Douglass at once put her into Juliet and other of the more youthful roles of Mrs. Douglass's repertory. Perhaps it was the emergence of Miss Cheer which suggested to Douglass that the American Company needed a general overhauling and refurbishment. At any rate, in the spring of 1764 he dispatched the company to Barbados while he and Mrs. Douglass went on a recruiting expedition to London.

When he returned and reassembled his troops in Philadelphia in the autumn of 1766, Margaret Cheer was at the top of her form. In the next two years she would command at least eight Shakespearean roles—Catharine in *The Shrew*, Lady Anne, Portia, Ophelia, Cordelia, Juliet, Lady Macbeth, and Imogen—and nearly thirty-five other roles, both serious and comic, in modern plays. A Philadelphia critic, contrasting her to the ranting Lewis Hallam, awarded her one of the finest compliments that a classic actor can deserve: "There is no necessity of destroying the least articulate Beauty of Language, thro' Fury, Eagerness, or Passion; Miss Cheer never loses the sweetest Accent, or faulters in the Clearness of Expression, from any or all those Causes, though I believe she is equally delicate, and capable of feeling the Force of Passion."[31] Her years of glory were few, however. In August of 1768 the newspapers reported her marriage to a young Scotch nobleman, Lord Rosehill; about the same time, it appears, Rosehill married someone else. Miss Cheer continued briefly with the American Company, acting under her maiden name, and then dropped out of sight. A quarter of a century later in New York she was identified with a Mrs. Long, who played a season of diminishing roles, took a last benefit, and disappeared.

In 1767 the company was powerfully augmented by the arrival from Jamaica of a huge, handsome young

Illus. 6. John Henry as Ephraim in John O'Keeffe's *Wild Oats*, the only known likeness.

Irishman named John Henry, together with the Storer sisters.[32] Henry specialized in Irish parts, excelled in Shylock, and was said by Dunlap to have played Othello better than anyone before him in America. Indeed, his Othello was sufficiently impressive that when he sojourned in London during the war years it won him a season's contract at Drury Lane. After the Revolutionary War he shared with Lewis Hallam in management of the company until he was driven out by the aggressive rivalry of a younger (and better) actor, John Hodgkinson, and by Hallam's own treacherous dealings. More than for his acting, Henry is remembered for his strange connubial arrangements with the Storer sisters. While in Jamaica he had married Helen, the eldest of them, and had two children by her. But she and they were destroyed in a fire on shipboard during the voyage to the mainland. At once he embraced the second sister, Nancy, who passed for Mrs. Henry (without legal ceremony), bore him a son, and acted with him for many years. Eventually she broke away. Since the third sister, Fanny, had eluded him by marrying outside the family, so to speak, about 1787 he married the fourth, Maria—a tiny and brilliant executant of Ariel in *The Tempest*—who had been a mere child during Henry's early days of keeping house with her sisters.

While Douglass's American Company was at work in the North, a minor competition erupted in Williamsburg and the South—an organization called at first the Virginia Company and then, more boldly, the New American Company.[33] The founder was an ambitious but not otherwise distinguished actor named William Verling, his leading lady one Henrietta Osborne. Both had been brought from London by Douglass during his recruiting expedition, but they could not work in harness with the other actors and so had deserted him. Except for one event their Shakespearean work was not particularly memorable: at Annapolis in 1769, Mrs. Osborne, who looked good in breeches, played Prince Hal in *Henry IV* —apparently the first transvestite Hal in history.

Among the lesser members of the New American Company was our old friend Patrick Malone, who had played the first Shylock in America seventeen years earlier— now no longer esteemed as an actor but by no means diminished in vigor. When Malone chose *The Merchant of Venice* for his benefit this year, Verling took Shylock, but between play and afterpiece Malone performed on the slack wire: he lay on it at full length, he beat a drum, he balanced a pyramid of thirty glasses of jelly in each hand, he stood on his head with a pistol in each hand "which he will Fire, if agreeable to the Ladies." By the middle of 1769 the New American Company disbanded.

Another recruit that Douglass brought over in 1765 was genuinely worth her passage—a young singing actress of the Hallam family, a niece of Mrs. Douglass, whose first name is not certainly known but is generally thought to be Nancy.[34] For her first couple of years she

Illus. 7. John Hodgkinson. Courtesy of the Library of Congress.

was second to another bright vocalist whom Douglass had also recruited, a Miss Wainwright, receiving perhaps two interesting acting assignments to the Wainwright's three. But with Margaret Cheer's withdrawal in 1769, Nancy Hallam began to play more and more leading roles. When she appeared as Imogen at Annapolis in September of 1770, there broke out around her a perfect frenzy of woman-worship. A correspondent to the *Maryland Gazette* who signed himself "Y.Z." told of the "sanguine hope" with which he approached her performance: "But how was I ravished on experiment! She exceeded my utmost idea! Such delicacy of manner! Such classical strictness of expression! The music of her tongue—the *vox liquida*, how melting!" Speaking as if he were a habitué of the London scene, he professed to hear once more in Miss Hallam's voice the "warbling" of the late Susanna Cibber. "How true and thorough her knowledge of the part she personated! Her whole form and dimensions how happily convertible and universally adapted to the variety of her part."

A friend of Y.Z.'s, the Reverend Jonathan Boucher, was so excited by her Imogen that he composed, almost extempore, a dozen quatrains of rhymed adulation. The following selection from them catches something of the Annapolitan fever:

> Hail, wondrous maid! I grateful hail
> Thy strange dramatic power;
> To thee I owe that Shakespere's tale
> Has charmed my ears once more.

It was the poet's ability to *paint* human passions, Boucher declared; it is Miss Hallam's power to enact them. Our eyes flow with tears of pity when she pleads a tale of woe; the pit resounds with shouts when she charms us with strokes of wit.

> She speaks!—What elocution flows!
> Ah! softer far her strains
> Than fleeces of descending snows,
> Or gentlest vernal rains.
>
> Do solemn measures slowly move?
> Her looks inform the strings;
> Do Lydian airs invite to love?
> We feel it as she sings.
>
> Around her, see the Graces play,
> See Venus' wanton doves;
> And in her eye's pellucid ray,
> See little laughing loves.
>
> Ye Gods! 'Tis Cytherea's face;
> 'Tis Dian's faultless form;
> But hers alone the nameless grace
> That every heart can charm.

When as the dead Fidele she is laid on her grassy tomb, Boucher demanded to know, what artist could paint so fair a sleeping saint? No one less than Charles Willson Peale could do so.

This rhetorical call upon the famous artist was successful, and a year later Peale's charming painting of her was on show (see the frontispiece).

> How pleased we view the visionary scene,
> The friendly cave and rock and mountain green—

so hymned Boucher or some other ecstatic rhymster in the *Maryland Gazette* of November 7, 1771. In the painting, Imogen as the boy Fidele, prettily clad in pink trousers and an overdress and a cloak and hat of brilliant blue, stands wonderingly, her sword drawn, about to enter the cave. Far down the sunlit hill (barely discernible near the right-hand edge of the picture) Belarius and the boys are approaching to discover this "fairy," this "angel," this "earthly paragon." The painting, one of the most delightful relics we have of our eighteenth-century theatre, gathered dust in someone's attic for many decades, but it is now one of the treasures of Colonial Williamsburg.

Through the next three seasons, as the company wandered between New York and Charleston, Nancy Hallam continued to charm beholders as Juliet, Ophelia, Imogen, and Cordelia until all theatrical activity in the colonies was put down by law. In October of 1774 the Continental Congress, girding for the Revolution, in an effort to "encourage frugality, economy, and industry," resolved to "discountenance and discourage every species of extravagance and dissipation." These included not only horse racing, gaming, and cockfighting, but "shews, plays, and other expensive diversions and entertainments."[35] The players were defeated. But already the American Company, having ended their season in Charleston, had broken up and taken ship for many destinations. For the next eleven years the only playmaking in America would be the diversions of the British and the American soldiers, who occasionally took a fling at *Othello* or *Richard III*, but whose amateur efforts need not detain us here.

Between 1750 and 1776, according to Hugh Rankin's count, fourteen of Shakespeare's plays were done professionally 180 times, and Rankin would estimate that, considering the loss of records, the total number of performances must have been at least 500.[36] We cannot date the American premieres of these plays with absolute certainty, but the following are the earliest professional performances that have been recorded.

Richard III	New York, March 5, 1750
Othello	New York, December 26, 1751
The Merchant of Venice	Williamsburg, September 15, 1752
King Lear	New York, January 14, 1754
Romeo and Juliet	New York, January 28, 1754
Hamlet	Philadelphia, July 27, 1759
Macbeth	Philadelphia, October 26, 1759

Henry IV, Part 1	New York, December 18, 1761
Catharine and	
Petruchio	Philadelphia, November 21, 1766
(*The Taming*	
of the Shrew)	
Cymbeline	Philadelphia, May 25, 1767
King John	Philadelphia, December 12, 1768
The Tempest	Philadelphia, January 19, 1770
The Merry Wives	
of Windsor	Philadelphia, March 2, 1770
Julius Caesar	Philadelphia, June 1, 1770

SHAKESPEARE BETWEEN THE WARS

With the signing of the peace treaty in 1783, the British military withdrew from New York, and the cheerful rush of social life which they had sponsored during their occupation came to an end—the concerts, banquets, assemblies, bathing parties, balls, and plays. For many of the loyal sons and daughters of the Revolution the cease of theatre was good riddance. Some of them were moral reactionaries for whom the playhouse was still the devil's house; some were the mindless rabble to whom theatre was merely an appendage of monarchy. In easygoing Maryland, to be sure, the actors resumed their work before the war was officially over: a Mr. Wall built a theatre in Baltimore in 1781 and led a company through two happy seasons of standard repertory, including seven or eight Shakespeares.[37] But in 1783 and 1784 when Lewis Hallam and John Henry attempted the northern cities with a reorganized American Company, they met fierce resistance. Philadelphia would not revoke its wartime ban against plays until 1789, so that there the actors had to resort to the old dodge of billing plays as "Moral Lectures." *Hamlet* became a lesson in "Filial Piety," *Richard III* "The Fate of Tyranny," *King Lear* "The Crime of Filial Ingratitude."[38] In New York, too, though there were no legal bans, swarms of correspondents to the newspapers denounced theatre as a thing of evil. The actors' friends rallied to the defense, countering that manly and useful entertainment was being prevented while houses for "carousing, wenching, gaming, drinking" flourished without hindrance. By the end of 1785, happily, the opposition in New York was beaten down, and the American Company was licensed for the rest of the season.

It should have been time for a Shakespearean revival. Throughout the decade of 1774–84 audiences in London were seeing more than two dozen Shakespeare plays; but in America, apart from the amateur theatricals of the military, there were neither plays to be seen nor audiences to see them. Throughout this decade in London, to speak only of major Shakespearean performers and pacesetters, Garrick's reign was climaxing and closing, that of Kemble and Siddons was coming on, and John Henderson's brief but brilliant career spanned the gap between them. The mighty establishments of Drury Lane and Covent Garden had never flourished more vigorously, and the little theatre in the Haymarket began to foster a summer program worthy of its winter rivals. But all this while theatre in America was outlawed, suppressed, and nearly forgotten. The question then was not merely a Shakespearean revival but a revival of the whole theatrical enterprise.

During the quarter of a century between the Revolution and the War of 1812, the established Shakespearean pieces (mostly tragical) would be played and replayed—*Hamlet, Macbeth, Richard III, Othello, Romeo and Juliet, The Merchant of Venice,* and *King Lear*—but there would be very few additions from the canon. *As You Like It* and *Much Ado About Nothing,* popular in England since the 1740s, crept into the American repertory in the 1780s. A few others—*The Comedy of Errors, Henry V, Coriolanus,* and *Twelfth Night*—were seen in isolated performances. To a noticeable extent Shakespeare was crowded out by the new drama. It cost a great many evenings of every season to catch up with the swelling output of contemporary playwrights—not only the masterworks of a Sheridan but the timely if now forgotten plays of Cumberland, the two Colmans, Inchbald, Holcroft, Reynolds, Morton, and America's own William Dunlap. From about 1798 American stages, like stages everywhere, were inundated by the lurid melodramas of August von Kotzebue—*The Stranger, Pizarro,* and *Lover's Vows*—or other offshoots of the exploding romantic imagination.

Yet if the quality of dramatic offerings was being diluted or vulgarized in these years, theatrical organizations on the other hand were being stabilized. Men with a talent for business and public relations, as well as a concern for art, took up management. In the larger cities they built fine theatres (handsome to look at and conducive to audience comfort), assembled large companies of actors with wide-ranging skills, improved production methods, and prepared year-round programs attractive to regular audiences. Actors of quality came off the road, settled down in communities, and developed personal followings. By the middle 1790s five major centers were served by permanent companies: New York by the Old American Company, or what was left of it, managed by Lewis Hallam, Jr., and John Henry, then by Hallam and John Hodgkinson, then by Hodgkinson and William Dunlap; Philadelphia by the company of Thomas Wignell and Alexander Reinagle, at that time the strongest company of all, with outposts in Baltimore, Annapolis, and Washington; Charleston by the company of John Solee; Providence by the company of John Harper; and Boston, whose antitheatre legislation was finally repealed in 1793, by the company of Charles Stuart Powell. Up to this time none of the front-line actors was native born: the managers continued to sustain the numbers and quality of their companies by recruitment in England. In 1792 John Henry brought the Hodgkinsons and Mrs. Pownall to New York. Wignell made two grand sweeps to create and augment his Philadelphia company: in 1793 he secured, among dozens of others, James Fennell and Mr. and Mrs. Charles Whitlock; in 1796 he got Ann Merry, Thomas Cooper, John Bernard, and William Warren. Powell of Boston brought over two lots in 1793 and 1794, though he found none so talented as those discovered by Wignell and Henry.

It is difficult to assess the worth of these early actors. The American theatre was too young to have worked out traditions and values of its own, and its audiences, unsophisticated in the arts of the stage, lacked standards by which to judge what passed before them. There were not enough expert witnesses. Theatrical journalism was at least a generation behind that of England: thus, the *Morning Chronicle* of London, where William Woodfall published his sage counsel to the players almost daily, was founded in 1769; but the *Morning Chronicle* of New York, where the occasional Addisonian ramblings on theatrical subjects by "Jonathan Oldstyle" appeared, was not founded until 1802. America had no Francis Gentleman, Charles Este, or Henry Bate in the eighteenth century, and although a critical club in New York, which Dunlap called the "sharpshooters"—including William Cutting, Peter Irving, and Charles Adams—began in the last years of the century to express its opinions on the literary qualities of the new drama, yet no one with critical acumen comparable to that of Leigh Hunt or William Hazlitt appeared there to monitor the arts of acting and stage production in the early years of the nineteenth century. The most vivid impressions of the actors come to us from the reminiscences of theatrical professionals like William Dunlap and John Bernard, who set down their opinions long years after the events. Their facts and judgments may be flawed by faulty memory, colored by affections and hostilities bred out of relationships in the greenroom, toned up or down for patriotic reasons, distorted through a natural tendency of theatre folk never to spoil a story by the telling of it. Yet even with such uncertain evidence, amended by occasional testimony made on the spot, it is worthwhile to remember some half-dozen leading Shakespeareans of the time and take soundings of them. The characters and careers of all but one or two of them, we shall find, were off center, and, except for Ann Merry, probably none could have measured up to their counterparts in the theatres of London.

John Hodgkinson (1767–1805), sometimes called "the provincial Garrick," sometimes "the American Kemble," was an astonishing creature.[39] If we take Bernard's word for it, he was the most gifted actor who ever lived. He was tall and well built, though inclining to the corpulent. (Dunlap less charitably called him "too fleshy" and emphasized his clumsy legs, thick ankles, and bowed-in knees.) His face was so mobile that it could express every change of feeling, however minute, and his voice was "a many-stringed instrument which his passion played upon at pleasure." His memory was amazing: he could learn a part hundreds of lines long in a single night's study and be ready at the next day's rehearsal to prompt the others. He could dance, he could sing, he was equally expert in comedy and tragedy: "In the whole range of the living drama there was no variety of character he could not perceive and embody. . . . To the abundant mind of Shakespeare, his own turned as a moon, that could catch and reflect a large amount of its radiance." By the age of twenty-five he had run the gamut at the Bath Theatre from Richard III to Romeo, from Hamlet to Petruchio to Othello.

Yet he must have been a singularly unpleasant man to deal with—vain, jealous, greedy, pushful, vindictive— and the truth was not in him. He wrote Hallam and Henry applying for a "first line" in their company, claiming that his Bath salary amounted to £400 a year (an improbably high figure); but later he pretended that Henry lured him to America by misrepresenting the advantages he would find here. His immediate reason for wanting to get out of England was to rid himself of a wife (or connubial partner), whom he had stolen from a fellow actor, because he had come to prefer another woman, an actress

Illus. 8. James Fennell as Macbeth.

named Brett, whom he brought over as Mrs. Hodgkinson. He boasted that he was a protégé of Sarah Siddons and claimed that she had offered to support him in various roles if only he would act in London. His patron, he boasted, was the Prince of Wales, who granted him patronage because with extraordinary courage and in a public place he had rebuked and put down the arrogance of one of the royal brothers.

Once he arrived in New York he persuaded Hallam and Henry to yield to him many of their best parts, for he was greedier than Bottom the Weaver to play everything himself; he attempted, too, to take some of Mrs. Henry's roles from her and assign them to his wife. Then he set about a campaign to drive Henry out of the management, fomenting quarrels with him and conniving with Hallam, whose own mean spirit could be counted on to side with the faithless against the faithful partner. He succeeded in this: Henry sold his shares, withdrew, and went off to die, and his brokenhearted wife, the former Maria Storer, went mad and died soon after him. As soon as he could, Hodgkinson usurped most of Hallam's authority, too, quarreled with him publicly, and squeezed him also out of the management. In 1797 he published an incredibly self-serving *Narrative* of his relations with Hallam, claiming that he alone performed the labors of management whilst Hallam merely collected his share of the profits.[40] Whatever Hodgkinson's values as a performer may have been, it was probably better for the profession that so disruptive a figure died young. The yellow fever took him off in 1805, in his thirty-ninth year.

James Fennell (1766–1816), who came to Philadelphia in 1794, was a strange one—a "whirligig, weathercock fellow" Bernard called him.[41] A tall, handsome man with a rich voice and a knack for platform oratory, he was at best a superb Othello. He came of good family, was educated at Eton and Cambridge, and was training for the bar when he got into trouble over gambling debts. He removed himself to Edinburgh, turned actor under the name of Cambray, and succeeded so well as Othello that in the autumn of 1787 he was engaged for that and other leading roles at Covent Garden. Reengaged in 1789, he made no progress in the profession, and when in 1790 his assignments slipped to mere supporting roles it was plain that acting alone was not enough for him. He wrote two plays, edited a theatrical magazine, was arrested for debt. He fled to France. There, according to some, he lived like a man of fashion until his debts caught up with him; others say that he posed as a friend of the Revolution but was accused of being a spy and had to flee for his life.

Brought over by Thomas Wignell as a leading tragedian at the new Chestnut Street Theatre, he was instantly successful, and his elegance and conversational brilliance won him a devoted personal following among the young fashionables of Philadelphia. But "education" was his undoing. He founded a boys' school, which failed. He attempted to run an institution to improve agricultural methods and another to improve the taste of the lower classes: these failed. He lectured on the natural sciences. He claimed to have discovered a method for extracting salt from sea water, and at least four times he persuaded investors to finance a saltworks for him: it always failed. Whenever he went bankrupt or got out of jail he returned to the stage as Othello to recoup his losses, but art could never keep him long from his projects. Frustration brought on dissipation, which wrecked his talents, mind, and body, and he was dead at fifty.

A pair of tragic actresses whose names are always mentioned in the history books, but whose reputations could have been won only far, far away from Sarah Siddons's London, were Charlotte Melmoth (1749–1823) and Elizabeth (Mrs. Charles) Whitlock (1761–1836). The Melmoth was not drafted to America, as most early actors were, but came to New York on her own initiative, having in mind in the spring of 1793 only to do some public readings.[42] Perhaps she had decided that her acting days were over. She had been on the stage a good twenty years by that time—inconspicuously at Covent Garden in the 1770s, then briefly as Lady Macbeth at Drury Lane, then famously in the provinces (especially in Edinburgh and Dublin) ever after. But she had grown fat. In the well-known portrait of her as Queen Elizabeth in *The Earl of Essex* she appears tall, slender, and graceful, but it was her misfortune by the 1790s "to expand to a size that no tragedy and black velvet had power to subdue." Yet the program of readings she gave in New York—from Shakespeare, Milton, Collins, Sterne, etc.—"afforded infinite delight to every rational mind." She repeated the program at popular demand, and the managers of the American Company requisitioned her services for the following season. According to Dunlap, John Hodgkinson promoted Mrs. Melmoth in order to undermine the position of Mrs. John Henry as leading actress of the company, thus advancing his scheme to get rid of the Henrys. Yet Dunlap did not tell this in order to belittle Mrs. Melmoth: he declared without hesitation that she

Mrs. MELMOTH *in the Character of* Q:ELIZABETE

Essex a Traitor! it can never be ___ Act I. Sc:2.

Illus. 9. Charlotte Melmoth as Queen Elizabeth in Henry Brooke's *The Earl of Essex.*

ACT V.   EARL OF WARWICK.   Scene

M.ʳˢ WHITELOCK as MARGARET.
———— *From my breast I drew*
A poignard forth, and plung'd it in his heart.
London. Printed for J. Bell British Library, Strand, Oct.ʳ 8.1792.

Illus. 10. Elizabeth Whitlock as Margaret in Thomas Franck-lin's *The Earl of Warwick.*

was "the best actress the inhabitants of New York . . . had ever seen." In spite of her bulk, which, to be sure, did sometimes provoke a rude guffaw, she continued to delight New York and Philadelphia audiences as a trage-dienne and much admired Lady Macbeth for nearly two decades longer.

Elizabeth Whitlock, who also specialized in Lady Macbeth, had the misfortune to be born a Kemble without quite the attributes needed to live up to that great name.[43] She was a younger sister of Sarah Kemble Siddons. In 1783, when Mrs. Siddons was midway in her first triumphant season at Drury Lane, she persuaded the management to let Elizabeth try Portia. They allowed her two nights of it, and during the next two seasons she played Rosalind a couple of times, Portia thrice, Imogen once, and eight or nine roles in non-Shakespearean plays. In 1785 she married Charles Whitlock, a country manager, and thereafter she worked the provinces, especially the Newcastle circuit. Thomas Wignell, doubtless eager to catch a Kemble, brought the couple to the Chestnut Street Theatre in 1794.

She was a huge and rather coarse-featured woman, resembling her brother Stephen (the fat Kemble) in face, and, in the words of her niece Fanny, was "like a living parody or caricature of all the Kembles." Mrs. Siddons called her "a noble, glorious creature, very wild and eccentric," but Fanny was more graphic and less kind:

She had the deep, sonorous voice and extremely distinct utterance of her family, and an extraordinary vehemence of gesture and expression quite unlike their quiet dignity and reserve of manner, and which made her conversation like that of people in old plays and novels; for she would slap her thigh in emphatic enforcement of her statements (which were apt to be upon an incredibly large scale), not unfrequently prefacing them with the exclamation, "I declare to God!" or "I wish I may die!" all which seemed to us very extraordinary, and combined with her large size and loud voice used occasionally to cause us some dismay.

When she played Lady Macbeth in Philadelphia, the critics would grant that her big-boned figure and her vocal power equipped her to bring off the "very torrent, tempest, and whirlwind of passion" in the part. In New York, however, where she ran into competition with Mrs. Melmoth, the critics would stumble and temporize:

We trust we shall be acquitted of all malice if we venture an opinion that Mrs. W. falls far short of what might be ex-

Illus. 11. Ann Brunton Merry and Joseph George Holman in *Romeo and Juliet.* Courtesy of the Harvard Theatre Collection.

pected in the performer. In those scenes in which the finer passions are to be exhibited, there is an evident lack of sensibility and feeling; indeed, the attempt to express them is attended with such distortions of countenance as rather to move us to laughter than win us to sympathy. It is in exhibiting the stronger passions that the excellence of this lady consists, and from this walk she should never depart.

Given the choice between a gigantic actress and a merely fat one, the critics obviously preferred the more sensitive Charlotte Melmoth.

In 1796 the same ship brought to America (and to the Chestnut Street Theatre) two genuinely valuable Shakespeareans, Ann Brunton (Mrs. Robert) Merry (1769–1808) and Thomas A. Cooper (1776–1849). Ann Brunton had gone on the stage at Bath in 1785, when she was a girl of fifteen, and had leaped to instant fame as a tragic actress.[44] That autumn she became a principal at Covent Garden, playing forty-six performances of nine different roles (mostly in tragedies of eighteenth-century vintage) throughout the season. For six years the Covent Garden management matched her appeal against that of Mrs. Siddons over the way at Drury Lane. The two were very unlike: Sarah Siddons queenly, thoughtful, and passionate; Ann Brunton loving and tender. In their Shakespearean appearances, the one was grand as Queen Katherine, Constance, and Lady Macbeth, the other appealing to hearts as Juliet, Cordelia, and Perdita. "With a voice that was all music," John Bernard wrote of Mrs. Merry in after years, "and a face all emotion, her pathos and tenderness were never exceeded."

In 1792 she married the fashionable Della-Cruscan poet Robert Merry, who for reasons of family pride persuaded her to withdraw from the stage. Merry's poetry did not pay, however, and his devotion to the French Revolution and other revolutionary causes soon cut off his sources of income and reduced his means to nothing. Therefore in 1796 when Thomas Wignell made an attractive offer, Merry not only permitted his wife to resume her profession but was glad to accompany her to republican America. For a dozen years Mrs. Merry was America's leading actress, so excellent in her art as frequently to rob the critics of all but superlatives. "In the praises of Mrs. Merry we do but echo the public voice," said one. "It is almost needless to mention, [she] was perfect," said another. In 1805, the *Evening Post* critic described her Ophelia as "the most chaste, highly finished, and exquisite piece of scenic representation we ever witnessed. The

young lady of high birth and refined manners, was visible in all her deportment. In the distressing mad scene she almost surpassed expectation, and though no professed singer, yet the soft and plaintive melody of her simple tones was in the highest degree impressive and affecting." Her best Shakespearean role was always Juliet, and she was most effective in those roles which she could infuse with sentiment. Yet she was a remarkably intelligent actress, too, and now and then a critic would wake from his dream to acknowledge her impeccable technique: her unfailingly right accentuation of the syllables that carried meaning, her breath control, her cunning use of pauses, her ability to match vocal tone to author's meaning. She could compel an audience into "expressive silence" by sweetness of voice and the right placing of a word. Writing a quarter of a century after her death, William Dunlap called her "the most perfect actor America has seen."

Apart from professional triumphs Mrs. Merry's life in America was checkered with personal disasters. In the second winter after their arrival Robert Merry died in a fit of apoplexy. Her second husband, the manager Thomas Wignell, died in 1803 only a few weeks after they were married. In 1806 she took a third husband, the actor William Warren, but by then her own health was failing, and in 1808, in her fortieth year, she died after a difficult pregnancy. Against her doctor's advice, she traveled to Alexandria, Virginia, where Warren had planned a summer season. She and her stillborn son are buried in Christ Church churchyard in Alexandria.

Thomas Cooper did not achieve instant success in 1796, as Ann Merry did, for he was then a twenty-year-old beginner, a youth of high promise but without a ready-made reputation.[45] Furthermore, at the Chestnut Street Theatre he had to compete with James Fennell, who was ten years older, established in his art, and then at the height of his popularity. Two years later, however, Cooper broke his agreements at the Chestnut Street and moved to the Park Theatre in New York, where, notwithstanding the competition of John Hodgkinson, he leaped at once into a series of leading roles, including five Shakespeares. Dunlap, then manager of the Park, declared of Cooper's Hamlet that the role had never before been played so well in America, and thought it at the time "the best acting I ever saw." In rapid order he ran through King John, Romeo, and Iachimo, and before the season ended he added Macbeth, which eventually came to be regarded as his very best role. According to Dunlap's record of box-office returns Cooper was not yet a great draw, but in 1798 he laid the foundations for a career of nearly four decades, during most of which he would be regarded as America's leading classic actor. Visiting English actors greater than he would come and go, but not until the emergence of Edwin Forrest would any native-born actor challenge his eminence in the profession.

Illus. 12. Thomas Abthorpe Cooper.

His boyhood in London had been spent in the household and under the tutelage of the philosopher and novelist William Godwin, who grounded him well in Shakespeare, modern literature, modern and classical languages —and enough radical political attitudes so that at the age of sixteen he declared that he had had enough education and was going to Paris to join the Revolution. Godwin persuaded him to give up sansculottism in favor of the stage and called in his friend, the playwright Thomas Holcroft, to coach him in some roles. Holcroft got him an engagement under Stephen Kemble at Edinburgh, but he failed so badly there (as Malcolm in *Macbeth* he forgot the concluding lines of the play and was hissed off) that Kemble dismissed him. Three years later, after further coaching by Holcroft, he succeeded brilliantly (but briefly) as Hamlet at Covent Garden. When his Lothario in *The Fair Penitent*, which followed next, was not satisfactory, the management offered him a regular engagement to play secondary roles, but he declined that and, hurt and indignant, withdrew to the provinces. There Wignell found him in 1796 and offered him handsome terms for America. Holcroft, who was still ambitious for Cooper to rise to the top in London, strenuously advised him against emigrating: "As an actor you would be extinct," Holcroft declared, "and the very season of energy and improvement would be for ever passed." But Cooper accepted.

Holcroft probably distrusted a certain light-mindedness or instability of purpose in Cooper, and rightly so. In the years to come Cooper often seemed to take the easy way, relying on his natural gifts rather than on hard thinking about his art, and whenever he did return to England audiences there rejected him as not up to London standards. He settled too easily for mere popularity. Women adored him for his personal beauty—his handsome face, sweet voice, and graceful movement—and men admired him for such offstage skills as riding and shooting. Countless anecdotes were told about his good companionship, his love of sport, his addiction to gambling, his astounding physical courage. His marriage in 1812 to Mary Fairlie, a leader of New York society, floated him

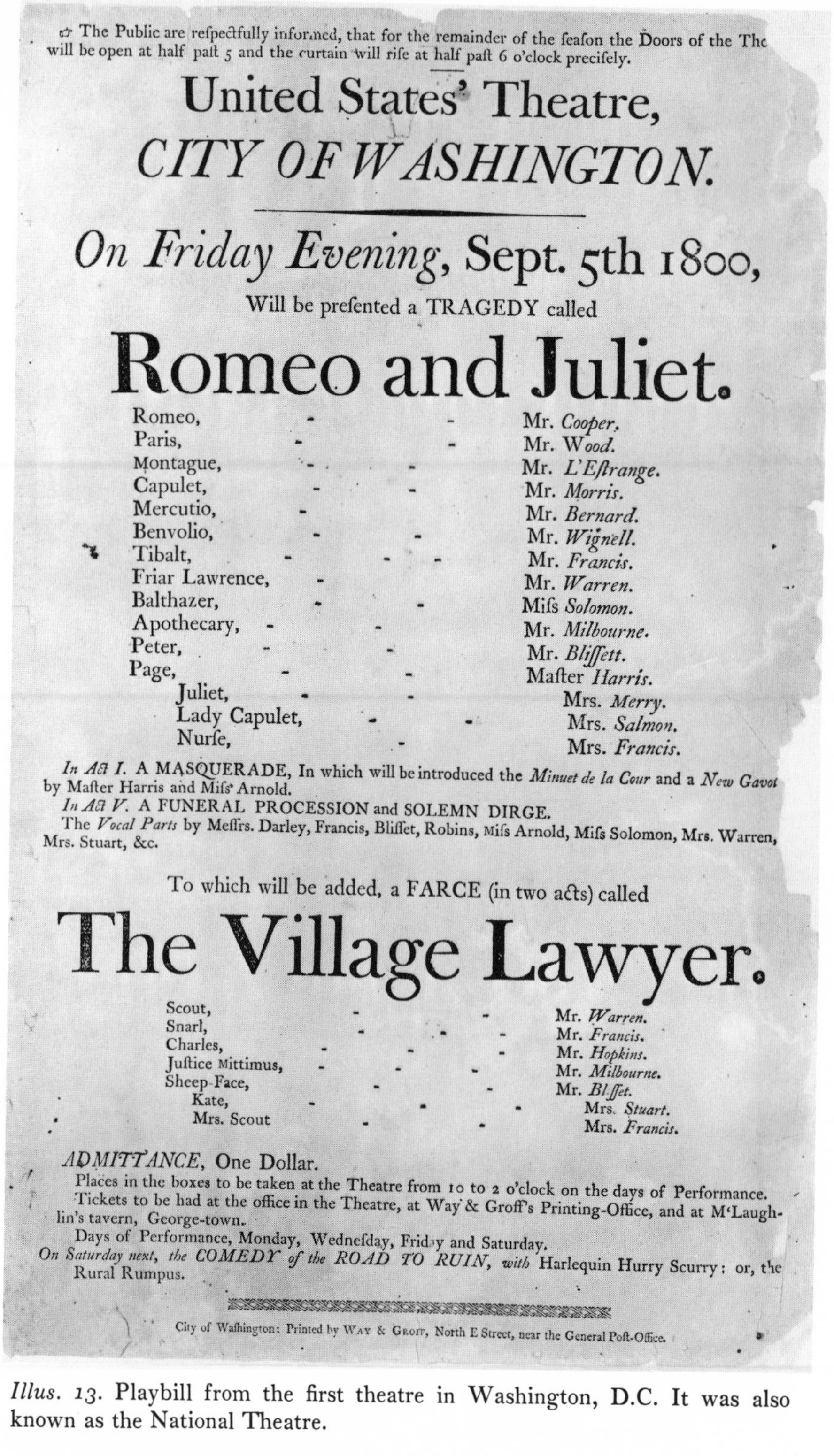

☞ The Public are respectfully informed, that for the remainder of the season the Doors of the The will be open at half past 5 and the curtain will rise at half past 6 o'clock precisely.

United States' Theatre,
CITY OF WASHINGTON.

On Friday Evening, Sept. 5th 1800,

Will be presented a TRAGEDY called

Romeo and Juliet.

Romeo, - -	Mr. *Cooper.*
Paris, - -	Mr. *Wood.*
Montague, - -	Mr. *L'Estrange.*
Capulet, - -	Mr. *Morris.*
Mercutio, -	Mr. *Bernard.*
Benvolio, - -	Mr. *Wignell.*
Tibalt, - - -	Mr. *Francis.*
Friar Lawrence, -	Mr. *Warren.*
Balthazer, - -	Miss *Solomon.*
Apothecary, - -	Mr. *Milbourne.*
Peter, - -	Mr. *Bliffett.*
Page, - -	Master *Harris.*
Juliet, - -	Mrs. *Merry.*
Lady Capulet, - -	Mrs. *Salmon.*
Nurse, -	Mrs. *Francis.*

In Act I. A MASQUERADE, In which will be introduced the *Minuet de la Cour* and a *New Gavot* by Master Harris and Miss Arnold.

In Act V. A FUNERAL PROCESSION and SOLEMN DIRGE.

The *Vocal Parts* by Messrs. Darley, Francis, Bliffet, Robins, Miss Arnold, Miss Solomon, Mrs. Warren, Mrs. Stuart, &c.

To which will be added, a FARCE (in two acts) called

The Village Lawyer.

Scout, - -	Mr. *Warren.*
Snarl, - - -	Mr. *Francis.*
Charles, - -	Mr. *Hopkins.*
Justice Mittimus, - - -	Mr. *Milbourne.*
Sheep-Face, - -	Mr. *Bliffet.*
Kate, - - -	Mrs. *Stuart.*
Mrs. Scout - -	Mrs. *Francis.*

ADMITTANCE, One Dollar.

Places in the boxes to be taken at the Theatre from 10 to 2 o'clock on the days of Performance.

Tickets to be had at the office in the Theatre, at Way & Groff's Printing-Office, and at M'Laughlin's tavern, George-town.

Days of Performance, Monday, Wednesday, Friday and Saturday.

On Saturday next, the COMEDY of the ROAD TO RUIN, with Harlequin Hurry Scurry; or, the Rural Rumpus.

City of Washington: Printed by WAY & GROFF, North E Street, near the General Post-Office.

Illus. 13. Playbill from the first theatre in Washington, D.C. It was also known as the National Theatre.

into a social eminence quite independent of his career in the theatre. By the end of his life he hobnobbed with presidents: his daughter was married to the son of President Tyler, and he was himself made inspector of the New York Customs House by President Polk.

Almost at the beginning of Cooper's New York career we find a critic complaining that during the burial of Ophelia he was "carelessly surveying the boxes and recognizing his acquaintance, we will not say gazing at particular ladies." He lapsed into rant, too, during that same performance, and he read the line about the Everlasting fixing his canon against self-slaughter with such misplaced emphasis that the word "canon" appeared to mean "cannon." In *Hamlet* again, later in the same season, he was found "extremely and shamefully defective in his study": he failed in "To be or not to be," introduced lines from another play, and again stared about the boxes during the Funeral Scene. A decade later a Philadelphia critic complained that despite "the amazing beauties which he frequently displays," one cannot praise the whole of any of his performances when "our patience is put to trial by some defect, or our feelings left to grow cold and languid for want of an appropriate continuous excitement." And he stayed on the stage too long: by 1831 he would be scorned for stalking about the stage "in all the by-gone glory of ten years since, when his misconceptions were esteemed originality," and was dismissed as "an old fallen oak, putting out a few green branches," "a broken column," a "once idolized veteran," "old Cassius still."

Cooper's acting style, expectable in a child of the nineties, was a variety of the classic, adopting, as it were, from Sir Joshua Reynolds's Thirteenth Discourse the "deliberate and stately step, the studied grace of action, which seems to enlarge the dimensions of the actor, and alone to fill the stage." His enunciation was clear and precise, his gestures formal, his poses elegantly statuelike. Noah Ludlow identified the style as that of the John Kemble school, "a little modified, perhaps; rather more impulsive in passionate scenes, but possessing all the towering grandeur of that great English tragedian. You beheld the silent and gradual approaches of the storm of passion, and you stood transfixed with the grandeur of the scene." His affinity to Kemble is caught in one belittling account of that moment when Macbeth emerges from the murder chamber. As Garrick did it, said the critic, the door burst open and Macbeth appeared, "a frightful figure of horror, rushing out sideways with one

dagger and his face in consternation presented to the door, as if he were pursued, and the other dagger lifted up as if prepared for action. . . . In this breathless state, he hastily said in a whisper, as if to himself, 'I have done the deed.' " But as Kemble did it, and after him Cooper, "Macbeth closes the door with the cold unfeeling caution of a practised house-breaker, then listens, as if to be secure, and addresses Lady Macbeth as if, in such a conflict, Macbeth could be awake to the suggestions of the lowest kind of cunning."

Nonetheless this same critic regarded Cooper's Macbeth as a superb performance, "in which he unquestionably takes the lead of all the actors that have appeared in this country; and is in our judgment preferable in many parts to either Kemble or Cooke." Another called it "one of the sublimest efforts of histrionic genius" and observed that in the latter part of the play "the moral reflections are given with such exquisite beauty and feeling that we almost forget the crimes of the murderer, and pity the wretched victim writhing with the tortures of his own conscience."

Cooper's Shakespearean repertory was far more inclusive than that of any other American actor of his generation, embracing thirty roles in seventeen plays—from Romeo to Falstaff, Benedick to Coriolanus, Cassius to King Lear. John Bernard, who had acted with him before they came to America, thought his Macbeth second only to Garrick's, his Hamlet second only to Kemble's, and his Othello equal to that of Spranger Barry. Bernard had seen them all.

NEW THEATRES IN THE 1790S

Besides the great influx of actors in the 1790s, it was also the time for the construction of well-designed theatre buildings, modeled after the best (not the biggest) theatres of Great Britain. The two principal houses still in use had both been built by David Douglass in the 1760s: the Southwark Theatre in Philadelphia, described as "an ugly, ill-contrived affair," and the John Street in New York, "an unsightly object, painted red." Three of the new ones were the Chestnut Street Theatre in Philadelphia (1794); the Federal Street Theatre in Boston, designed by Charles Bulfinch (1794); and the Park in New York, designed by Marc Isambard Brunel (1798).

The Chestnut Street, for which we have excellent pictorial records, well illustrates the best conditions under

Illus. 14. The Park Theatre and the City Hall, New York. The theatre is the building at the right.

which Shakespeare was staged in America in the early nineteenth century.[46] The design for it came from London. John Inigo Richards, then chief scenic artist at Covent Garden, sent over not merely drawings but a three-dimensional model for it and painted for it a handsome drop curtain and several sets of scenery. In principles of arrangement it did not differ essentially, of course, from the barn theatre rebuilt by the elder Lewis Hallam at Williamsburg in 1752, for throughout the eighteenth century all theatres followed the model set when the idea of an indoor theatre was perfected at Drury Lane in 1674. Only in size, materials, finish, and details do we perceive a growth. The Chestnut Street was a shapely building of brick and stone, 134 feet long and 60 feet wide (or 90 feet wide counting the 15-foot auxiliary structures at-

tached to the sides). When it opened in 1794 its façade was disappointingly plain, but before 1804 it acquired a handsome porch to shelter the entrance, fronted by ten Corinthian columns and flanked by projecting wings, as shown in Illustration 15. It seated about 1,200. The semicircular pit, with thirteen curved benches, held some 400. Three levels of boxes held about 240 along the sides of the house and 525 in the deeper boxes facing the stage.[47] The box fronts, painted gray and gold, supported brackets of wax candles which illuminated the auditorium. (Gas lighting was installed sometime before 1820.)

The forestage of the Chestnut Street, some fifteen feet deep and thirty-six feet wide, was flanked by the actors' entrance doors with the usual balconies directly above them. The footlights were oil lamps, which were con-

Illus. 15. Exterior of the Chestnut Street Theatre, Philadelphia, as it appeared in 1804 after completion of the portico. Courtesy of the Free Library of Philadelphia.

cealed behind a low masking board and which could be lowered beneath the stage level when dark scenes were called for. The distance from the footlight row to the back wall of the stage was seventy-one feet. The inner stage (behind the proscenium opening) was trapped, and at every six or seven feet of stage depth there lay crossways of the stage a set of grooves (six or seven sets in all) to accommodate sliding wings and shutters in the old approved style. The scenery was illuminated by oil lamps from above and from the wings.

So little testimony exists concerning scenery in the eighteenth-century American theatre that it is customary to assume that it was both minimal and crude, but by the 1790s it was surely not far inferior to what was then used in London. As early as 1765, in fact, David Douglass brought to Charleston "scenes and decorations . . . designed by the most eminent maker in London."[48] This was Nicholas Thomas Dall of Covent Garden. In 1771 Douglass brought another lot of Dall's work to Annapolis. Illustration 17 shows on the Chestnut Street stage a

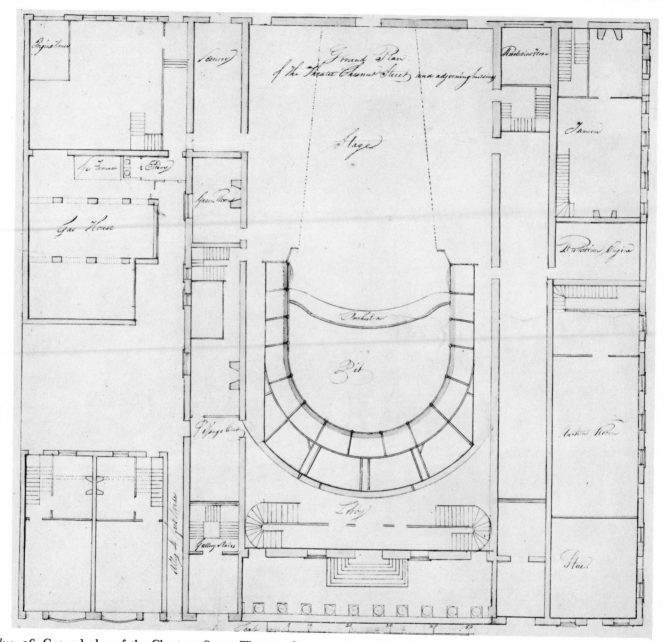

Illus. 16. Ground plan of the Chestnut Street Theatre. Courtesy of the Historical Society of Pennsylvania.

Illus. 17. Interior of the Chestnut Street Theatre. Courtesy of the Free Library of Philadelphia.

conventional but well-wrought Wood Scene leading to what appears to be a river or seascape. It was six grooves deep—that is to say, about forty feet deep—and matched in dimension any usual "deep scene" that one would have found at Covent Garden or Drury Lane.

In accounts of various plays and pantomimes we discover street scenes, domestic interiors, forests, temples, palaces, seascapes, armed camps, caverns, and all other expectable backgrounds to action. Buildings burned, gods flew down to the stage on the wing or chariot-borne, ships sank during storms at sea. One scenic artist who was brought from London to the Chestnut Street but soon joined Dunlap in New York was often given credit in the playbills of the time. This was Charles Ciceri,[49] who seems to have been an artist of great skill. In January of 1795 he created entirely new settings for a spectacular *Macbeth*—this less than a year after (and perhaps in imitation of) the famous London *Macbeth* with which John Kemble opened the newly rebuilt Drury Lane. In 1798 he painted *As You Like It* for the first production at

the Park; his scenery for Cooper's Hamlet debut was "uncommonly elegant and gratifying"; and as for *King John*, "a more splendid exhibition of scenery was never witnessed in this city, and probably never in this country." When the Kotzebuvian fantasies came on—especially *The Virgin of the Sun* and *Pizarro*—Ciceri's talents, not only as painter but as machinist, were given full play. There was a "Temple of the Sun, displaying all the Magnificence of Peruvian superstition"; a "Landscape, with a Rock and Tree upon which a Boy climbs to see the Battle"; a "Forest . . . the background Wild and Rocky, with a torrent falling down a Precipice, over which a bridge is formed by a fell'd Tree." That bridge, we remember, is a practical and trick one: not only must Rolla run across it bearing Cora's child, but he must then collapse it so that the Spanish soldiers cannot pursue him. By the turn of the century, it appears, scenic effects in the American theatre were in all essentials as sophisticated, elaborate, and skillfully executed as in the best theatres of England.

Illus. 18. Portrait of Stephen Price by John Simpson. Courtesy of the Walter Hampden–Edwin Booth Theatre Collection and Library at The Players, New York.

CHAPTER II

The Wild Ones

THE AMERICAN COLONIES claimed independence from England in 1776, won it at the Treaty of Paris in 1783, and confirmed it in the War of 1812, but well past all those times the American theatre operated as if America were still an outpost of the mother country. As for Shakespeare, for a long time books of his plays had to be imported, for none was printed in America until the mid-1790s and not many until after the turn of the century. The westward flow of Shakespearean actors continued without abatement.

Most of the actors who came during the first quarter of the new century were a respectably talented lot—good citizens, too—who had not yet risen to distinctive place in the profession or who in a few cases were on the decline. They chose to gamble on speedier advancement or greater profit where the competition was less keen than in London. At least one of these, Mary Ann Duff, chose wisely, for she enjoyed steadily rising success in America through nearly three decades—but in the long run suffered a conversion to piety and turned her back on the profession altogether.

Three who came, though, outweighed all the rest —George Frederick Cooke, Edmund Kean, and Junius Brutus Booth—actors endowed with such magnetic personalities and transcendent skills (not to mention ready-made reputations) that everyone who cared for theatre had to see them. Of Cooke and Kean it may be said that their triumphs in America were assured before they landed. Unfortunately, though, their triumphs collapsed almost as predictably. For they, and Booth too in his turn, behaved as their passions drove them. Whether acting out lofty scenes upon stages or drinking to the bottom of the bottle, they plunged into temptations of the flesh and riotous living without concern for the devil, themselves, or their neighbors. All three were quite mad at times, or were so keyed up emotionally and behaved so irrationally, or were so fantastically drunk, that they could be taken for madmen. If their best stage performances provided the greatest thrills and deepest revelations that American audiences had ever known, their worst performances and extratheatrical carryings-on stirred up excitements of another kind. Their brawling or boozing or whoring amused some observers, disgusted others, but could not go unnoticed. Their insults to audiences, real or fancied, incited outrage, even riot. They were the Wild Ones.

STEPHEN PRICE, IMPRESARIO

Apart from his acting, Thomas Cooper's most significant theatrical contributions were to bring Stephen Price into the management of New York's Park Theatre and to lure to America the actor George Frederick Cooke. Price (1782–1840) was a businessman, the first of his kind in the American entertainment world.[1] In 1808 he bought shares in the Park from Cooper, who had been sole manager since 1806; he shared control with Cooper until 1815, and until his death twenty-five years later either managed it himself or deputized Edmund Simpson to do so. Price never acted, never stage-managed, never wrote plays, but simply endeavored to feed the box office by giving the public what it wanted. The public wanted *stars*—actors of full-blown reputation whom everybody craved to see because everybody else had seen them. Since America was not yet ready to produce her own stars, Price developed a regular trade of importing them, profiting not only from the business they brought to the Park but also from commissions he exacted in farming them out to theatres of other cities. Eventually he even took up residence in London in order to push the trade at its source.

It is customary to blame Price for the decline of the resident companies in American cities. For as the starring system grew, audiences of local theatres would withhold their patronage between starring visits; and once the stars had carried off their immense fees, there was not much left at the box office to pay the resident company. Talented actors turned stars themselves rather than remain in residence at diminished wages. Nonetheless, Price's system quickened the life and raised the sights of the American theatre. By exposing American audiences to the most brilliant imported talents, Price challenged American provincialism and set standards for emulation.

George Frederick Cooke

Price and Cooper made their first great catch in 1810. This was George Frederick Cooke (1756–1812), who next after John Philip Kemble and Sarah Siddons was the most famous actor in England.[2] Cooke was no beauty. He was physically powerful, something above middle height, turning fleshy, not particularly well proportioned: James Boaden, who disliked him, spoke of "his fin-like arms moving like a tortoise."[3] Yet he overwhelmed audiences with his vigor, his intelligence, his rapidly expressive countenance and fierce eyes. Saturnine in temperament, often rude or even violent in personal manners, he invested stage villains with an energy worthy of Hogarth, or of Gillray at his roughest—a welcome antidote to the classical dignity of the Kemble school or to the idealizing and sentimentalizing tendencies of the day.

For twenty-five years of his professional life Cooke had trudged about the English provinces unknown to theatregoers of the metropolis, hardening his manner and drowning in brandy his envy of luckier men. His drinking bouts became legendary. In 1801, when he was in his middle forties, he was brought to London by the managers of Covent Garden and thrust into competition with Drury Lane's John Kemble, whom he had long ago vowed he would one day make shake in his shoes. In the ensuing contest Kemble retained command of those roles in which dignity was indispensable: Hamlet, Othello, Macbeth, and the noble Romans. Cooke bested him in Richard III, Iago, Shylock, and Sir Giles Overreach and took instant possession of the late Charles Macklin's old creations of Sir Archy MacSarcasm and Sir Pertinax MacSycophant. They split honors (or failures) in King Lear. When Kemble moved to Covent Garden in 1803 and took over the artistic direction of that theatre, he kept Cooke in the company and allowed him to retain all the leading roles in which he excelled.

For too many years tragic acting in London had been forced into what Charles Lamb called the "frozen declamatory style"[4] as Kemble practiced it, or what Thomas

Illus. 19. Portrait of George Frederick Cooke by Thomas Sully.

Holcroft scorned as the "sing-song defect, the puerile schoolboy habit of whining out a lesson."[5] It was Kemble's style in tragedy to apply a sustained "tone" to the verse line, to suppress specific emphases or to cultivate only that sort of emphasis that "swells the passion of the scene, and ennobles the sentiment."[6] Cooke deliberately broke that style. He attacked speeches vigorously and varied the speed of his attack. He resisted the roll and swell of iambic pentameter or any other compulsive rhythm. In studying his parts, we are told, he transcribed verse to look like prose and "scored the emphatic words, with one and sometimes two or three lines, according to their respective value and importance."[7] Having established the emphases which best conveyed meaning, he delivered those emphases with planned exactitude.

Cooke often sharpened meaning through bold vocal transitions, and he cultivated different "voices" with which to do so. The sarcastic Boaden claimed that Cooke had only two voices, "one of which was harsh and acrimonious, the other mild and caressing," and likened him to Stephano's Caliban, whose "forward voice is now to speak well of his friend; his backward voice is to utter foul speeches and detract."[8] But William Dunlap, who knew how valuable it would be if actors "could have handed down to them clear and minute descriptions of the manner in which the great masters of the art delineated their most effective characters," preserved for us a few instances in which Cooke used his changes of voice to convey "such unutterable things as defy language." When, for instance, Cooke's Macbeth heard that the Queen was dead he exclaimed in an agitated manner, "She should have died—" and then, after a pause, he whispered, "hereafter." And again after "It is a tale / Told by an idiot, full of sound and fury, / Signifying —" he would drop his voice to a tone expressive of heartbreaking disappointment and add the word "nothing." Anyone can roar and then whisper, of course, but evidently when Cooke made these transitions the effect went far beyond mechanical trick.

His stage business, too, was wonderfully expressive —"anticipating, extending, and improving the conception of the author," as Dunlap put it. At times he elaborated stage business almost into independent pantomime. When Othello urges Iago to kill Cassio, Cooke's Iago's response was reported by Charles Durang of Philadelphia as follows:

Cooke used to start as if he appeared horrified at the deed, appeared to hesitate, and then, with sudden impulse, drew his hand across his face, looked at the Moor, which told plainly, "I do this for love of thee," and then, in a voice almost choked—"My friend is dead!" The effect was irresistible. We distinctly remember the effect of this beautiful point . . . and the electrical excitement it produced upon the audience and the critics in the pit. It was responded to by three immense bursts of applause, succeeded by a dread pause, as if the audience was lost in contemplation of its sudden sublimity.[9]

Cooke's acting did not gratify every palate, of course, and one did not have to belong to the Kemble coterie to find him crude, unfeeling, coarse grained. Charles Lamb thought that his hypocrisy in the role of Richard III was "too glaring and visible. It resembles more the shallow cunning of a mind which is its own dupe than the profound and practised art of so powerful an intellect as Richard's." Lamb objected that Cooke missed entirely the "habitual jocularity," the "unstrained mirth" of Richard, and expressed only "the coarse taunting humour, and clumsy merriment of a low-minded assassin."[10] Boaden declared that Cooke had no capacity for pathos and suggested that if he had appeared with a white handkerchief in hand (that is to say, in a tearful scene) the audience would have been thrown into a fit of laughter.[11]

When Cooper went to England in 1810 on a recruiting expedition and landed at Liverpool, he found Cooke, whom he had known in earlier days, filling a summer engagement in Liverpool and the environs. Cooke was in the doldrums about his position at Covent Garden, and with the coming on of autumn he was not eager to return there. At the age of fifty-five he was little better off than when he went to London a decade earlier. He had won all the battles with Kemble that he could ever win, and yet he stood in Kemble's shadow, subordinate to him in the profession and in public favor. Time and again he had lost his private battle with the bottle, had been unable to perform, and had been compelled to apologize for public drunkenness. Cooper made him an offer for America. To Cooper's astonishment he accepted it, and after numerous brandy-soaked arguments and indecisions, he was at last got aboard a sailing vessel bound for New York.[12]

Americans generally could not believe the news that Cooke was coming. "It appeared as impossible to many, that the great London actor should be removed to America," said Dunlap, "as that St. Paul's Cathedral should be transported across the Atlantic."[13] Price, who did believe it, "was extravagant in his demonstration of Joy, triumphantly repeating, 'Now is the winter of our discontent made glorious summer by this son of York.'"[14]

The excitement attending Cooke's opening at the Park on November 21 was like nothing ever seen before in an American theatre. The play was *Richard III*. The rush at the doors was so great that many got in without paying; hundreds were turned away. The box-office receipts came to $1,820 (somewhat under capacity), but an estimated 2,200 persons (well over capacity) crowded into the house. When Cooke strode to the center of the stage for his opening soliloquy—"his head elevated, his step firm, his eye beaming fire," said Dunlap—the crowd roared its welcome, and Cooke responded not like a humble player but proudly, "as a victorious prince, acknowledging the acclamations of the populace on his return from a successful campaign—as Richard Duke of Gloster." As a matter of fact, he was suffering an acute attack of stage fright because of the importance of the occasion, and he pitched his voice too high at first, producing sharp, grating tones; but he soon settled into the role, and point after point brought down thunders of applause. The critic of the *Columbian*, called Thespis, declared him "unquestionably the best representative of the part that has ever appeared on the American boards."[15]

In his Shylock, a week later, "the alternate passions of avarice and revenge were exquisitely pourtrayed," and Thespis provided a rather feverish account of "the shocking depravity and fiend-like revenge of this subtle and malignant Israelite": "From the moment Shylock whets his knife . . . to the favorable decision of the judge, his rising expressions of demoniac joy and exultation at the prospect of obtaining unqualified revenge, were strikingly expressive, and executed with masterly skill." When Antonio bares his bosom to the knife, but Portia halts Shylock's blow by insisting on the legal condition of the forfeit,

no language can do justice to the excellence of Cooke. His countenance in an instant lost its wonted glow of malicious satisfaction, and became horribly convulsed with disappointed rage. His manner of dropping the scales at the annihilation of his hopes, was strongly indicative of the writhing tortures of a despairing soul. When Antonio offers to remit half his estate, on condition of leaving the other half to the use of Lorenzo, and of his immediately embracing the christian religion . . . the groan of convulsive agony that seemed to burst from the very innermost recesses of his soul, was electric in its effects.

From these notes one can understand why Charles Lamb disapproved of Cooke, and perhaps a modern audience

Illus. 20. George Frederick Cooke as Richard III, from the painting by Thomas Sully.

would find his acting of Shylock misconceived, excessive, and far more appropriate to Sturm und Drang melodrama than to Shakespeare; but it exactly suited the taste of American audiences in 1810.

During his two seasons in America—mainly in New York, Boston, and Philadelphia—he played about twenty roles for a total of 160 nights.[16] Ten of the roles were Shakespearean, the favorites being his three famous villains, Richard III, Iago, and Shylock. He also played the Falstaffs of *Henry IV* and *The Merry Wives*, and King Lear, Macbeth, King John, Othello, and Henry VIII. At the beginning he brought in enormous profits for the managements and a healthy fortune for himself, but as popular curiosity became sated and audiences were too often disappointed by imperfect performance or even non-appearance on account of drunkenness, his appeal diminished.

Through Cooke's first performances in New York, the audiences were not aware that anything was seriously wrong with him: when he was too hoarse to play well, they ascribed his trouble to a head cold and cheered him on. For eleven nights his box-office average was $1,350. On the twelfth night, which was his benefit, the receipts went up to $1,878—"an audience so numerous, or more genteel, had never graced the walls of the New York theatre." The play was Addison's *Cato*. He drank heavily that day ("I always have a frolic on my benefit day"), declined to rehearse, failed even to read over the part. At performance time he could remember little of it: he stumbled through lines, substituted speeches from other plays, improvised. The audience was disgusted. Two nights later his Shylock, which had drawn over $1,800 earlier, dropped to well under $500.

During his Boston engagement, which followed in January, Cooke's box-office returns were middling, and according to Dunlap he was ill or drunk nearly the whole time. When he returned to New York for fourteen nights in February, his average receipts fell to $485. This was the nadir of his first season. He pulled himself together for Philadelphia, where he acted from March 25 to April 30, and his average these rose to more than $1,100. Under the faithful shepherding of William Dunlap he kept reasonably sober in Philadelphia on playing days, and toward the end of his run Thomas Cooper, who had got home from abroad, gave him a boost by costarring with him.

What the general public and probably even those close to him did not recognize was that this lonely old dragon was dying. He suffered pains in the chest and belly almost constantly, his liver hardened and failed its function, his legs swelled with dropsy. He anesthetized his body with alcohol, but the cure often wrecked his voice and brains. Stories about his crazy doings offstage, which only gradually became public, are numberless. After a midnight drinking bout he would outfox whatever watcher had been assigned to see him safely in bed: he would pretend to sleep until the watcher slept, then creep out of the house and make straight to a brothel. Once while a guest in Stephen Price's house, Cooke grossly insulted Price and then seized a decanter to throw at him; Price saved himself by wrestling Cooke to the floor. But all that Cooke could remember of it afterward was that Price had struck him a foul blow, and in drunken stupor he would vow to duel Price with pistols and drop him at the first shot. He nursed an unaccountable grudge against Thomas Cooper and would denounce him as the "wooden god" of the American theatre. Once when he heard that President Madison might come to see him act, he declared that he had played before His Royal Majesty King George III and would not play for this contemptible "King of the Yankee Doodles." And he fantasized. He would weep for grief that he had no sons, then presently drink toasts to *both* his sons, who, he declared, were both named George Frederick. He would boast of his exploits (entirely imaginary) as a British soldier during the American Revolution, recounting with remarkable vividness how during the battle of Brooklyn Heights—if it had not been for the interference of that forever-to-be-damned Lord Howe—he, George Frederick Cooke, would have captured General Washington single-handed.

At the opening of the 1811–12 season he was at the Park again, but, as Odell pointed out, Price hardly mentioned him in the preseason announcements. Although he played there throughout September and October (except on nights when he canceled and during one period of two weeks when he was truly ill), the bloom was gone. Even in Philadelphia, where he never missed a performance, the box office rarely rose above the $1,000 level. In July of 1812 he wound down his career with nine performances at a small theatre in Providence, averaging a pitiful $215 per night. His body was breaking down with a half-dozen disorders. He withdrew to New York, where on September 26 he died.[17]

Cooke's early death saved his reputation in America. His professional irresponsibility, together with his barbarous social behavior—his quarrelsomeness, his contempt for "Yankee rebels," his drinking and whoring

Illus. 21. Mary Ann Duff as Mary in J. N. Barker's *Superstition*. Engraved from a painting by John Neagle. Courtesy of the Library of Congress.

Illus. 22. James William Wallack as Hamlet.

—could never have been mended and would not have been endured much longer. But in the American memory these faults diminished into astonishing eccentricities, something to gossip about, while his powerful acting became a legend of excellence against which to measure actors of the future.

The Good Citizens

The second decade of the century saw the arrival of many more Shakespeareans from England. John Duff (1787–1831) and his wife, Mary Ann (1794–1857), appeared in Boston only a few weeks before Cooke came to New York, and they became permanent residents.[18] Their careers developed mainly in Boston and Philadelphia, and Mrs.

Duff, who gradually emerged as the more attractive talent, was recognized by the middle 1820s as "one of the richest dramatic treasures which our country has ever possessed." Her Juliet was once compared to Milton's Eve: "Grace was in all her steps—heaven in her eye. In every gesture dignity and love." The elder Booth, Cooper, Forrest, and other major tragedians rejoiced in opportunities to perform with her. By 1838 Mrs. Duff had played 221 roles, of which 19 were Shakespearean: but then she abruptly abandoned the stage and the Roman Catholic church, turned Methodist, and devoted the last twenty years of her life to piety and charitable works.

In August of 1812 Cooper and Price announced that they had all but engaged the great John Kemble for America but that circumstances (the outbreak of the War of 1812?) had prevented the final agreement. In his stead, they were happy to announce, they had engaged Joseph George Holman (1764–1817) and his daughter, who were already on the high seas. Holman, gentlemanly and university educated, had been a distinguished Shakespearean at Covent Garden from 1784 to 1800, often rivaling Kemble in popular esteem. He had left London after a dispute with the Covent Garden proprietors, had gone into management in Dublin, then had retired for several years, and was now making a comeback. Although his health was declining, (he died in 1817) he enjoyed mild success for a season, sharing with his daughter in young lover and husband-wife combinations: he was Romeo to her Juliet, Benedick to her Beatrice, Othello to her Desdemona, etc. The daughter married into the profession and as Mrs. Charles Gilfert continued to act down to 1831.

James William Wallack (1795–1864) came of an English acting family and, along with his brother Henry (1792–1870), founded an American one. He arrived at the Park in 1818, and by his brightness and vitality made a great hit in both New York and Boston in a wide range of roles, including the usual Shakespearean leads. During the next twenty years he played both sides of the ocean, crossing it repeatedly. From about 1837 he mainly settled in New York, where he managed several theatres in sequence and where, in the long run, he came to excel in light comedy and melodrama. In the same autumn of 1818 there also came to the Park George Bartley (1782–1858) and his wife, Sarah Smith Bartley (1783–1850) —he a famous Falstaff and later on the stage manager of Covent Garden under many proprietors, she an artist of greater range and stronger personal appeal than he. She supported Wallack as Lady Macbeth, Imogen, and various non-Shakespearean roles. On March 29, 1820, she played what may have been America's first transvestite Hamlet. In May, after two successful seasons, the Bartleys went home.

EDMUND KEAN

In the autumn of 1820 New York welcomed an actor far greater than any of these, greater than George Frederick Cooke. This was Edmund Kean (1787–1833), the diminutive genius, the Byron and Napoleon of the English stage, the foremost English actor of the day.[19] Kean was then at the peak—or not much declined from the peak—of his popular reputation. When he burst upon the London scene in the winter of 1814, the romantic critics, led

Illus. 23. Sketch of Edmund Kean by Samuel Cousins.

by William Hazlitt, hailed him at once as the actor who most nearly realized their ideal of histrionic art. The Tory press and die-hard proponents of the Kemble school at once attacked him as a vulgar upstart without any art at all, but they could not bring him down.

In the long run he brought himself down, for Kean was his own worst enemy, doomed to self-destruction. He lived violently. He took up prizefighting, was arrested once for brawling in the streets. He kept a pair of black horses and went in for demoniac gallops through the streets at midnight. He kept a lion for a pet. Like Cooke, whom he took as a patron saint, he drank too much, and probably too, as with Cooke, his addiction to alcohol was exacerbated by disease. In a kind of reverse snobbism he rejected overtures from fashionable society, even snubbing Lord Byron, who of all the lords in the land was nearest him in taste and temperament and would have been his influential patron. Turning his back on Clubland, he organized a club of his own, the notorious Wolf Club, made up of hard-drinking rowdies who gathered nightly at the Coal Hole Tavern and were thought to make up a theatrical claque sworn to applaud Kean and drive out potential rivals. He was not often caught with common whores, but he lapsed into a stupid, long-drawn-out adultery with a silly woman named Charlotte Cox, the wife of an alderman, and he wrecked his domestic life and his reputation through this folly. Tales drifted out from behind the scenes of his intransigence and arrogance in professional dealings, and at least occasionally he offended audiences by failing to appear or by playing when drunk.

Nonetheless he was a genius, and his reign over the English-speaking stage, though comparatively brief, was as compelling as it was tumultuous: he set rolling, as Cooke could not, waves of romantic naturalism which have swept over English and American stages through all the generations to our own day.

So many eyewitness critics said their say about Kean that it would cost a long chapter to catalogue their opinions. For a shortcut into the matter we may take the experience of a junior member of the tribe of Kemble, who in spite of family allegiance could not resist Kean's magnetism. Fanny Kemble was a susceptible eighteen-year-old when she first saw Kean's Shylock in 1827, and although Kean was past his meridian he converted her at once into "a violent Keanite."[20] His performance was bloodcurdling, she tells us; and, although it violated her artistic principles, yet "under the influence of his amazing power of passion it is impossible to reason, analyze, or do anything but surrender one's self to his forcible appeal to one's emotions."

One evening four years later she had a long conversation about Kean with her father, Charles Kemble, who himself sometimes played Shylock.

I cannot help thinking my father wrong about him. Kean *is* a man of decided genius, no matter how he neglects or abuses nature's good gift. He has it. He has the first element of all greatness—power. No taste, perhaps, and no industry, perhaps; but let his deficiencies be what they may, his faults however obvious, his conceptions however erroneous, and his characters, each considered as a whole, however imperfect, he has the one atoning faculty that compensates for everything else, that seizes, rivets, electrifies all who see and hear him, and stirs down to their very springs the passionate elements of our nature. Genius alone can do this. . . . He may not be an actor, he may not be an artist, but he *is* a man of genius, and instinctively with a word, a look, a gesture, tears away the veil from the heart of our common humanity, and lays it bare as it beats in every human heart, and as it throbs in his own. Kean speaks with his whole living frame to us, and every fiber of ours answers his appeal.

She admitted that not one of his roles was a "*whole work of art.*" He did not become Othello, Shylock, or Sir Giles; he compelled them to become *him*: "It is Kean, and in every one of his characters there is an intense personality of his *own* that, while one is under its influence, defies all criticism—moments of such overpowering passion, accents of such tremendous power, looks and gestures of such thrilling, piercing meaning, that the excellence of those *parts* of his performances more than atones for the want of greater unity in conception and smoothness in the entire execution of them." Her father wanted to make Shylock "poetical" ("in the superficial sense," Fanny said). But that is wrong for Shylock. Shylock's passion is not poetical—it is "close, concise, vigorous, logical, but not imaginative." There is intense passion in his language, but "no elevation." Besides, "there is a vein of humor in Shylock. A grim, bitter, sardonic flavor pervades the part, that . . . infuses a terrible grotesqueness into his rage, and curdles one's blood in the piercing, keen irony of his mocking humility to Antonio, and adds poignancy to the ferocity of his hideous revenge. This Kean rendered admirably, and in this my father entirely fails."[21] Fanny Kemble wrote these words in 1831, but she put them into print over forty-five years later, far into the sentimentalizing age. The sweetened Shylock of Henry Irving had not yet appeared, but one doubts that even it could have

Illus. 24. Edmund Kean as Shylock.

persuaded her to delete a syllable of her admiration of Kean.

Kean was a very small man (five foot four), but what he lacked in size he made up for in the passion which so impressed Fanny Kemble, in facial expression (he could say marvelous things with his great black eyes), in physical grace and agility, and in striking contrasts of speed and tone in his speaking. It was very likely these contrasts that Coleridge had in mind when he declared that to see Kean act was like reading Shakespeare by flashes of lightning. Hazlitt, who was Kean's most eloquent champion, often doubted the depth or correctness of his overall conceptions—doubted, for instance, that he distinguished clearly enough between brutal Richard and thoughtful

Hamlet, or between Richard and sensitive, fearful Mac-beth.[22] He blamed him repeatedly for showing off tricks (his "overdisplay of the resources of the art"), blamed him for overdoing transitions, for stretching out pauses interminably while he ran the gamut of facial expressions which no one could see except the pittites nearest the stage, for drawling some speeches and gabbling others. Yet there was no question for Hazlitt that Kean's acting was "more significant, more pregnant with meaning, more varied and alive in every part, than any we have almost ever witnessed." Kean had all that Kemble lacked, he reminded one of the "far-darting eye" of Garrick. " 'Take him for all in all,' " said Hazlitt, "it will be long, very long, before we 'look upon his like again,' if we are to wait as long as we *have waited.*"

Kean's forte was naturalism—the vivid realization of exactly what emotional state, vocal tone, and bit of behavior was to be called up at every instant in the stage life of a character. "Other actors," John Keats said, "are constantly thinking of their sum-total effect throughout a play. Kean delivers himself up to the instant feeling, without a shadow of a thought about anything else. He feels his being as deeply as Wordsworth."[23] We can best understand what Keats meant by this through the fragmentary records of Kean's byplay, which, Hazlitt said, took the place of the stage directions that Shakespeare neglected to write.

As Richard III, for instance, he would rub his hands together in self-gratulation when he felt things were going his way. Such actions immensely delighted Leigh Hunt. They tend, he said, "in a very happy manner to unite common life with tragedy—which is the great stage-desideratum"; or, to put it the other way, they depart from "the usual solemn pedantry of the stage."[24] A famous bit of business in his *Richard III* occurred at the end of the Night Scene before the tent, as Richard dismissed his followers. For a long moment Kean stood silent, drawing lines on the ground with the point of his sword as if lost in thoughts of tomorrow's battle. Then he recovered himself with an abrupt "Good night, my friends." This, Hazlitt tells us, was greeted with shouts of applause. The scene in which he took the deathblow from Richmond was also much admired: "He fought like one drunk with wounds: and the attitude in which he stands with his hands stretched out, after his sword is taken from him, had a preternatural and terrific grandeur, as if his will could not be disarmed, and the very phantoms of his de-

Illus. 25. Edmund Kean as Richard III, after the painting by John James Halls.

spair had a withering power."[25] Two of his "lucky hits" in *Hamlet* became fixed in stage tradition. In the scene where Hamlet breaks away from his friends to follow the Ghost offstage, Kean pointed his sword behind him to prevent the friends from following, instead of pointing it ahead to protect himself from the Ghost. And at the end of the scene with Ophelia, having gone to the place of exit he turned and hurried back, "from a pang of parting tenderness," to kiss Ophelia's hand. This, Hazlitt said, "had an electrical effect upon the house," and for Hazlitt it was "the finest commentary that was ever made on Shakespeare."[26] One of his most memorable inventions was the behavior of Macbeth when he reenters after the murder of Duncan: "The hesitation, the bewildered look, the coming to himself when he sees his hands bloody; the manner in which his voice clung to his throat, and choked his utterance; his agony and tears, the force of nature overcome by passion—beggared description. It was a scene, which no one who saw it can ever efface from his recollection."[27]

When Kean came to America in 1820 he encountered a strangely suspicious, even hostile press. Two sets of reasons for this have been distilled out of the circumstances by his biographer Harold Hillebrand—the one personal, the other professional and aesthetic.[28] It probably did not matter much to the typical American newspaper writer that Kean had been a boozing rakehell, but he was also reputed to be "a pretentious, arrogant fellow who laid dogmatic claim to being the greatest living actor," and the American newsman, dogmatic and arrogant himself, would have none of that. Also, as far as London was concerned, he was supposed to have blown up the whole classic school (the Kemble school) of acting, and this posed a threat to America's own leading Kembleite, Thomas Cooper. Since Cooper's fashionable marriage and rise in society he had many friends in positions of influence, including the press, who would resist any challenge to his authority. It is plain, too, that whatever advance information about Kean's style the American critics possessed came from hostile sources. On November 30 (the day after the opening), the critic of the *New York Evening Post* actually admitted his prejudgment that Kean's "excellencies consisted in sudden starts, frequent and unexpected pauses, in short, a complete knowledge of what is called stage trick, which we hold in contempt."[29]

It took Kean but a few performances, however, to convince his audiences that they had never seen his like before and that he was a superb artist. As the *Post* critic went on to say, "He had not finished his soliloquy, before our prejudices gave way, and we saw the most complete actor, in our judgment, that ever appeared on our boards." His Richard III, with which he opened, may have put some people off by its excessive flashiness. Edmund Simpson, the stage manager, wrote to a friend that "the people don't know exactly what to make of him—his strange manner surprises them but his style gains converts every night & before he leaves us, I expect they will be unanimous in calling him as they express it the greatest creature they ever saw."[30] His Othello, which had come to be recognized as his masterpiece; his Shylock, with which he had first conquered London and which continued to be a *tour de force* of fiendish energy; his Hamlet and Macbeth, which, to be sure, called for more restraint and dignity than were easily available to him but in which through striking effects he held his own; and finally his awesome King Lear—these roles cemented his hold on the public. Simpson reported "great business"

Illus. 26. Edmund Kean as Othello.

of some $1,000 a night.[31] After King Lear the *Post* declared, "When we lately . . . said upon seeing the second representation of Richard, that 'acting could go no further,' it was because we had not then witnessed his Lear."[32]

In his offstage behavior, too, surprisingly enough, Kean seems to have conducted himself with exemplary good manners. Simpson found him "extremely agreeable" in his dealings behind the scenes, and the editor of the *National Advocate* was pleased to inform his readers that "he is a modest, unassuming gentleman—securing the esteem of all who have become acquainted with him—easy in manners—always accessible, refined, and classic in conversation—and, when animated, the very life of the festive board."[33]

At the end of 1820 he played seventeen nights in New York, then on January 8 opened in Philadelphia for sixteen nights, and on February 12 opened in Boston for sixteen nights. All three of these engagements were critical successes and triumphs at the box office. Kean's profits from each exceeded $5,000 and each month he dispatched £1,000 to his London bankers. A further round of seventeen nights at New York and six at Philadelphia drew smaller but still respectable tribute, and Kean began to firm up plans for a second year in America. A sixteen-night engagement at Baltimore, running deep into May, should have concluded the present season, but unfortunately it did not.

Kean had fallen in love with Boston, which in a curtain speech he had called the "Literary Emporium of the New World," and he was determined to return there for a final stand.[34] Because of the lateness of the season Manager Dickson advised him not to come, but Kean insisted. On May 23, 1821, he opened in Lear to a fair house; on the twenty-fourth he played Jaffier in *Venice Preserved* to a slim house; near to curtain time on the twenty-fifth, when he was to play his favorite Richard III, he counted only twenty persons present and despite the remonstrances of the manager he dressed and left the theatre. By curtain time there was a fair house, but Dickson could only send word out that Kean refused to play.

He had insulted Boston.

The press howled at him, not only in Boston but everywhere. It did not matter that Cooke, safely dead and practically deified, had canceled many a performance and staggered through others that he ought to have canceled; that Hodgkinson and Fennell and even the admired Cooper had sometimes snubbed or disappointed audiences. A

special venom had been storing up for Kean. All of a sudden he was a "mountebank," a "mock Roscius," "scarcely a second-rate actor." His action was "too foul and dishonoring to be overlooked." According to the *Galaxy*, "They ought to have taken this insolent pretender, this inflated, self-conceited, unprincipled vagabond by the nose, and dragged him before the curtain to make his excuses for his conduct."

Kean published a long letter in the *National Advocate*, hardly apologizing at all, but almost smugly *offering* to apologize if he was found to be in error. This brought down on him a further storm of newspaper abuse. There was nothing to do but go home. He stopped in New York long enough to fulfill a vow that he had made long since —to see the remains of George Frederick Cooke removed from the Strangers' Vault at St. Paul's Church and properly buried in the churchyard and to set up a monument over him. On June 7 he took ship for England.

A dismal sequel followed four years later. In 1824 Kean's affair with Charlotte Cox became the scandal of London when her alderman husband sued Kean for alienation of affections. It even became a public joke. All the sordid evidence was recited in the law court and printed in the newspapers. Street musicians celebrated the affair in song. Kean's personal reputation was ruined, and the pharisaical press, bellwethered by the *Times*, undertook to drive him from the stage. Common sense should have taught him to go underground for a season, but he chose to fight back.[35] His doggedness won a partial victory. Beginning at Drury Lane on January 24, 1825, for a few nights he faced divided houses, who roared, hissed, hurled things, clobbered each other, and heard nothing of the play; but in the long run he got the London audiences well in hand. In the provinces, though, he was hooted at from Chichester to Glasgow, so that finally, weary and broken in spirit, he sought refuge in America.

Under the circumstances it was the wisest way. To be sure, his disgrace was as well known in America as at home, and right-thinking Americans were eager to do him down. Right-thinking Bostonians could hardly wait to avenge the insult he had put upon them in 1821.[36] But luckily the moralists were far outnumbered, in New York at least, by ordinary theatregoers who cherished their memories of Kean's past great performances and would rather see him act again than cast stones at a sinner. Luckily, too, most of the newspapers chose to punish Kean by simply ignoring his existence, and thus they lost their opportunity to stir up opposition.

He got through his New York run pretty well. When he opened at the Park (the play was *Richard III*) on November 14, 1825, two thousand persons ("and not a single respectable female") jammed the house, and the evening was a sustained hullabaloo. Not all the shouting was directed at Kean, however. It was quickly realized that the anti-Kean force consisted mainly of a hundred or so Bostonians who had come to town to make what trouble they could, and the New Yorkers vented their wrath on the invaders. By the second and third nights the opposition was quite eliminated, and Kean enjoyed a brief but prosperous run.

He insisted on going to Boston, however. "My misunderstandings took place in Boston; to Boston I shall assuredly go to apologize for my indiscretions." The impulse toward self-destruction was running strong in him. He even announced his coming in a letter to a Boston newspaper, acknowledging past error but attempting clumsily to dignify the wretched business by clothing it in the language of religion: "The first step toward the Throne of Mercy is confession—the hope we are taught, forgiveness. Man must not expect more than those attributes which we offer to God." Boston was not taken in. An editorial in the *Courier* put the case fairly but brutally: "No one can sincerely respect him; no one can love him. But every one can pity while he condemns, and no one can carry his resentment so far as to drive from the face of the earth the wretched fallen creature on whom the Almighty seems to have set the seal of his displeasure."[37]

The outcome was disastrous. Kean was scheduled to open in *Richard III* on December 21. All tickets were sold to an all-male audience a day in advance, and the theatre was packed on the night, the pro-Keanites in the boxes being vastly outnumbered and outyelled by the anti-Keanites in gallery and pit. Outside, a mob milled in the streets. When Kean appeared on the stage in street clothes to make his apology he was not allowed to speak. They pelted him with nuts, cakes, bottles of "offensive drugs," and more insulting missiles. He retired to the greenroom, weeping like a child, and, convinced of the hopelessness of the situation, fled from the building and the town. When the anti-Keanites realized they had lost their prey, they fought the pro-Keanites and smashed chandeliers, windows, benches, and boxes, until the police, aided by friends of the management, drove them out. Kean had precipitated in the "Literary Emporium of the New World" the first really all-out theatre riot in America.

He finished the season with a series of brief engagements in Philadelphia, New York, and Charleston, all reasonably serene; in early June another riot broke out against him in Baltimore and foreclosed his engagement there. In later summer he was hospitably received in Montreal and Quebec, although at least once in Canada he had to stop a performance of *Hamlet* at the end of the first act because of the intolerably bad supporting company. His major gratification during the Canadian visit was to be made an honorary chieftain in the Huron tribe of Indians. His Indian name was Alanienouidet.

Meanwhile in London Stephen Price had taken over the management of Drury Lane Theatre, and he called Kean home. On January 8, 1827, Kean opened in London as Shylock. The evening was a triumph. For a while at least London forgave him his sins.

EDMUND KEAN ESQ.

Illus. 27. Edmund Kean as Alanienouidet.

Illus. 28. Junius Brutus Booth in the title role of John Howard Payne's *Brutus*. Painted by John Neagle. Courtesy of the Museum of the City of New York, Theatre and Music Collection.

JUNIUS BRUTUS BOOTH

Kean was gone, but Kean's manner was not lost to America. Just as Thomas Cooper carried forward in America the classical style of the Kemble school, so Junius Brutus Booth (1796–1852), who in his youth had been taken almost for Kean's double, sustained the romantic mode in America for a quarter of a century after Kean's final departure.[38] Unfortunately, because Booth spent so much of his career as an itinerant, significant criticism of his work is rather sparse, and thus it is customary among theatre historians to bypass or downgrade him. Considering the length of his career in America and what we can glean of his genius, he contributed far more to the development of the romantic style in American acting than did either Cooke or Kean. According to one of Booth's American devotees, he actually excelled Kean: "Booth took up Kean at his best, and carried him further. Booth was Kean, *plus* the higher imagination. . . . To see Booth in his best mood was *not* 'like reading Shakespeare by flashes of lightning,' in which a blinding glare alternates with the fearful suspense of darkness; but rather like reading him by the sunlight of a summer's day, a light which casts deep shadows, gives play to glorious harmonies of color, and shows all objects in vivid life and true relation." Thus rhapsodized Booth's artist-friend Thomas Gould in his memorial volume called *The Tragedian.*[39]

Booth grew up in London and at the age of seventeen joined the provincial company of Jonas and Penley, whose wanderings in 1814 carried him to the Continent. There, in the Low Countries, besides learning his trade and advancing rapidly into leading roles, he acquired a mistress —a Belgian girl named Adelaide Delannoy, whom he brought back to England and married.

One night in the autumn of 1816, while he was acting at Brighton, he had to stand in for Kean, who failed to arrive for a performance of Sir Giles Overreach. This was the role in which Kean had been overwhelming audiences all that year: during his first London performance of it in January, ladies in the boxes collapsed in hysterics at the violence of his finale, Lord Byron suffered a convulsive fit, and even the actors on the stage were frightened out of their senses.[40] We do not know whether Booth attempted a facsimile of Kean's Sir Giles on that night at Brighton, but certainly he held his audience, and during the months following it came to the attention of the Covent Garden managers that he was a near facsimile (and valuable to them as a potential rival) of Kean himself. He was slightly smaller than Kean (five foot three?) and, unfortunately, bandy-legged. His hair was dark brown; his complexion pale; his features clean-cut, handsome, and resembling Kean's; his eyes blue instead of black; his voice of wider range, pleasanter tones, and subtler management than Kean's.

On February 12, 1817, he appeared at Covent Garden as Richard III, playing the role, or much of it, so much like Kean's Richard that William Hazlitt dubbed it a plagiarism and dismissed Booth as only one more of Kean's several imitators.[41] It was a mistake to dismiss him. The audience applauded him to the rafters, and they swarmed to a second performance of the "plagiarism" in such numbers that Kean and the Drury Lane managers took alarm.

Kean's defense was swift and cunning. He visited Booth at his lodgings, offered him better terms at Drury Lane than Covent Garden had allowed him, and proposed to introduce him as Iago and to "support" him by playing Othello himself. Naively Booth accepted the offer, flattered by Kean's friendliness and generosity, delighted to share honors with the greatest actor in England. Kean intended, of course, to sink him by outacting him, and he very nearly succeeded. Booth protected himself as well as could be expected of a novice caught in a surprise attack. He won at least qualified praise from Hazlitt, who observed that "the two rival actors hunt very well in couple."[42] But the audience knew that what they were witnessing was no friendly collaboration but a duel in deadly earnest, and at the end they knew that Kean was still the champion. The next day Booth gave a careful reading to his Drury Lane contract: the roles he would play in the future, he discovered, would amount to nothing better than Richmond to Kean's Richard or Laertes to his Hamlet. Excusing himself from a second night of *Othello*, he scurried back to Covent Garden.

Although defeated, Booth was by no means at the end of his career in England. For a few nights, that part of the public which was insulted by his defection from Drury Lane attempted to howl him off the stage, but he outlasted their displeasure and went on to act with fair success at Covent Garden and in the provinces for over three seasons. In 1820 when the lunatic George III died and the Lord Chamberlain lifted the ban against performances of *King Lear*, Booth was the first actor to reintroduce Lear to the London stage, and Hazlitt praised him for it.[43]

But then he fell in love. A Covent Garden flower girl named Mary Ann Holmes took his fancy, and in 1821 he abandoned his wife, Adelaide, and their two-year-old son and decamped with Mary Ann to America.

Unlike other well-known actors of the time, Booth did not make for New York or Boston. For the time being he had to avoid old friends in the profession lest someone, getting wind of his irregular domestic arrangement, should carry word of it to London and Adelaide. (Adelaide knew only that he had gone to America to make money, and it appears that for nearly two decades she expected him to return to her.) He landed at Norfolk. For several months he acted only in Virginia and neighboring states.[44] With the birth of Mary Ann's first child coming on, he settled her at Charleston. Eventually he would acquire a farm outside of Baltimore where he could keep his family in seclusion. Ten children would be born to this union, of whom six lived to maturity and three— Junius, Edwin, and John Wilkes—went on the stage.

Booth would serve the American theatre for three decades. Partly because of the star system, partly because of the remote location of his family, he was always on the wander, rarely taking an engagement of more than a few weeks duration, never long-identified with any theatre, region, or city. From Boston southward he played every town and city of the seaboard. In most seasons he played at least one stand in New York—at the Park, the Chatham, and after 1830 at the Bowery. He worked inland to Albany, to Pittsburgh, to Cincinnati. He was familiar to audiences of Nashville, Natchez, and New Orleans. In 1852, the last year of his life, he answered the call of his son Junius, then a theatre manager in San Francisco, to visit the Gold Rush country. Over and over throughout the years he repeated his classic repertory, never augmenting it and gradually limiting it to the few roles most often called for. Typically he would open a run with Richard III, and would follow it with such Shakespearean roles as Shylock, Iago, Hamlet, Macbeth, Lear, Othello, or Cassius. Non-Shakespearean roles which he regularly seeded in included Sir Giles Overreach, Mortimer in *The Iron Chest*, Pierre in *Venice Preserved*, and Pescara in *The Apostate*.

Booth's quality as an actor was often put in doubt, especially in his later years, because at intervals he was quite mad. His son Edwin theorized that this mental imbalance was simply the concomitant of genius, likening his odd antics to the behavior of Hamlet: "Great minds to madness closely are allied. Hamlet's mind, at the very edge of frenzy, seeks its relief in ribaldry. For a like reason would my father open, so to speak, the safety-valve of levity in some of his most impassioned moments."[45] But from Hamlet's "country matters" to Booth's wilder outbreaks the distance is too great for Edwin's pious explanation to bridge it. In the swordfight at the end of *Richard III* (Cibber's) he would sometimes refuse to be downed by Richmond and would drive his amazed opponent off the stage, out the stage door, and into the street. On one occasion in *Othello* he would have smothered Desdemona in earnest if the other actors had not rushed in from the wings and pulled him off his victim. He broke down in the middle of a performance in Boston and was led off the stage jabbering, "I can't read—I'm a charity boy—I can't read. Take me to the Lunatic Hospital." And before his friends could do just that he slipped away from them, shed his shoes, and walked barefoot to Providence. His broken nose, visible in photographs taken during the last dozen years of his life, was the result of a crazy misadventure that took place in Charleston one night in 1838: he rushed into a room where his friend and fellow actor Tom Flynn was sleeping and attacked Flynn, possibly under the delusion that he was Othello avenging himself on Iago; in the tussle Flynn struck him across the face with a fire iron, disfiguring him for life. His most famous (and harmless) bit of fantasizing occurred in Louisville in the early 1830s: he summoned a young clergyman to his hotel room and requested him to arrange a burial place and perform the funeral service for his deceased friends—the "friends" being a bushel of dead pigeons.[46]

Occasionally it was brandy that set off Booth's erratic behavior. It is said, though, that awareness of curtain time was often sufficient to clear his brains of alcohol and steady him for the evening's work. Once when drunk and late and on his way to his dressing room, he heard the impatient clamor of the audience out front: he staggered downstage, pulled apart the curtains, and shouted, "Shut up! Keep still, and in ten minutes I'll give you the goddamnedest Lear you ever saw in your lives." His performance that night, so the story goes, was superb.[47]

When in his right wits Booth was admirable in every way—intelligent, upright, sensitive, humorous, lovable. Highly educated, he was skilled in several languages, both ancient and modern, and he read Plutarch, Terence, the Talmud, Dante, Tasso, and Racine in their originals. Once in New Orleans, at the request of the French community, he even performed in French, the role being Oreste in Racine's *Andromaque*. His library contained not only Shakespeare and the standard English dramatists, but Burton's *Anatomy of Melancholy*, Locke's *Essay concerning Human Understanding*, Thomas à Kempis's *Imitation of Christ*, and works of such modern writers as Shelley, Byron, Keats, and Coleridge. He was a mystic of intense conviction, deeply read in several religions, including the Mohammedan. He believed in metempsychosis, and since he knew that animals had souls as immortal as his own, he was a confirmed vegetarian. He loved to read aloud from the Scriptures or recite the Lord's Prayer, and in a company susceptible to religious suggestion he could reduce them to tears by his powerful elocution. He inherited from his father an ardent spirit of republicanism, including admiration for John Wilkes (by naming a son after that fiery champion of human liberty he set in train one of history's most devastating ironies). A loving father to his family, he inspired profound affection in his children. In later years when Edwin Booth played Hamlet, he imagined in his scenes with the Ghost that he was communing with his own father, and he carried his father's picture on a chain about his neck.[48]

It is necessary, though not easy, to free Booth from the imputation that he was merely an imitator of Edmund Kean. Hazlitt at first glance called him that, and Hazlitt's eloquence and authority are so persuasive that his opinion is quoted to this day. But according to James Murdoch, the American actor and teacher of acting, the English romantic critics so overcommitted themselves to the supremacy of Kean that they had no room to withdraw from that position, and they could not find a niche to accommodate another genius like Booth.[49] However that may be, Hazlitt's opinion followed Booth across the Atlantic and served as a handy cliché for unthinking scribblers in the American press.

That Booth looked like Kean is undeniable, and evidently when he first played Richard III in London—a role which Kean had made peculiarly his own—he lapsed into certain attitudes and emphases resembling Kean's. He may even have adopted bits of Kean's stage business at that time. Yet eventually, if not at once, he made his Richard thoroughly distinct from Kean's. Arthur Colby Sprague has called attention to the remarkably different first entrances of the three major Richards of that era: Cooke came out of the wings in a "martial stalk," expressive of command; Kean rushed onto the stage in a burst of energy, provoking nervous excitement; Booth's

Illus. 29. Junius Brutus Booth as Richard III.

entrance was slow and brooding.[50] Walt Whitman's description of it is the best:

The curtain rising for the tragedy, I can, from my good seat in the pit, pretty well front, see again Booth's quiet entrance from the side, as, with head bent, he slowly and in silence, (amid the tempest of boisterous hand-clapping,) walks down the stage to the footlights with that peculiar and abstracted gesture, musingly kicking his sword, which he holds off from him by its sash. Though fifty years have pass'd since then, I can hear the clank, and feel the perfect following hush of perhaps three thousand people waiting. (I never saw an actor who could make more of the said hush or wait, and hold the audience in an indescribable, half-delicious, half-irritating suspense.)[51]

Murdoch tells us that in Booth's early days in America he would on one night act Richard in Kean's style and the next in his own, thus demonstrating his versatility, his perfect control of the medium, and the total independence of his own methods.[52]

It is not surprising, however, considering the resemblances between the two, that Booth's American advocates should resort to comparisons with Kean in order to assert the excellence of their hero. They claimed, for instance, that he differentiated between similar characters as Kean did not. Fanny Kemble was not alone in suggesting that Kean never really impersonated Shylock, Iago, Macbeth, or Othello, but made them over into so many versions of himself. Thomas Gould declared that Kean's method was "limitary" and that he lacked the imaginative power to project any character but his own: "He took just those words, and lines, and points, and passages, in the character he was to represent, which he found suited to his genius, and gave them with electric force."[53] Booth, on the other hand, could project a character so clearly that "no suggestions of the actor's other impersonations mingle with and mar the impression."[54] John Foster Kirk noticed three characters in Booth's repertory which might be said to belong to the same type: Richard, Iago, and Sir Giles. They are all "unscrupulous, malignant, versed in the arts of treachery, profound dissemblers, indefatigable plotters, with the one redeeming virtue, if such it can be called, of indomitable courage." In another actor's hands their differences might fade into a general resemblance, but "in Booth's performance of each of these parts it seemed as if the walk, gestures, attitudes, looks, and tones belonged to that particular char-

acter and to no other." And Kirk declared that "no tragedian whom I have seen displayed this power in the same degree as Booth."

Kean was famous for "making points"—for carrying his hearers by storm, for holding them spellbound by "volcanic eruptions of frenzied passion," for overwhelming them with "floods of pathos and tenderness." But through long stretches of dialogue that lay between these points, these "flashes of lightning," he would rattle his way indifferently.[55] On the other hand, partisans of Booth claim for him that he dealt in whole characters, not in "partial scenes"; that his conceptions were "sustained and all-related"; that a performance was "a consistent and beautifully graduated order of vocal effects."

Hazlitt said that Kean spoke with the voice of a raven (except, of course, in tender passages), and it is well known that he overused breathy, harsh, guttural tones. Booth used these tones only to express malign and ugly sentiments and never let them intrude into passages that were heroic, serene, sentimental, or purely poetic. Indeed, he prided himself on his studies of "vocality" and was endlessly testing the limits of what the voice was capable of expressing. Over and above the obvious techniques of inflection, pause, and emphasis, he thought deeply about the "hardness or softness" of words, their "roundness or sharpness," the values to be got from extending and contracting them, and "all the forces of sound from the hum of a bee to the blow of a sledge-hammer." He related sounds of the voice to the sounds of musical instruments, and he imagined sounds as having colors. Thus he would say that spoken words could exhibit "the sombre note of the bassoon," "the scarlet tone of the trumpet," and "every variety of tint that can be produced by the violin."[56]

We who live in prosier times distrust these miracles of vocality which Booth aspired to, and when Thomas Gould tells us that at Iago's cry of "The Moor! I know his trumpet," Booth "gave the word, with the very sound of the instrument, and tossed it from his lips with the careless grace of an accomplished musician,"[57] we are almost inclined to distrust Booth himself. Perhaps, however, this is but an extreme instance of Gould's faith in metaphor.

Elsewhere we can accept more easily, and even enjoy, Gould's high-colored efforts to describe Booth's vocal effects. Thus, when Booth's Hamlet spoke of "this majestical roof fretted with golden fire," his voice, which had been "sombre and husky in the preceding lines, suddenly darted upward like light; seemed to penetrate the sky; to run all over the firmament; to search out and give back the remotest echoes of heaven."[58] The opening lines of the "To be or not to be" soliloquy were "uttered in a voice like the mystic murmur of a river running under ground"; the words "That undiscovered country" were given "in a manner unimaginably remote"; and the next words, "from whose bourn no traveller returns," issued "with accelerated and vibrating intensity, the stroke of emphasis coming surprisingly on the last word."[59]

When Booth's Macbeth invoked Neptune's ocean to wash the blood clean from his hand, he did so while "looking on his hands with starting eyes, and a knotted horror in his features; and wiping one hand with the other *from* him, with intensest loathing. The words came, like the weary dash on reef rocks, and as over sunken wrecks and drowned men, of the despairing sea." And then on the lines that follow,

> *No: this my hand will rather*
> *The multitudinous seas incarnadine,*
> *Making the green—one red.*

"he launched the mysterious power of his voice, like the sudden rising of a mighty wind from some unknown source, over those 'multitudinous seas,' and they swelled and congregated dim and vast before the eye of the mind. Then came the amazing word, 'incarnadine,' each syllable ringing like the stroke of a sword, and, as it were, '*making* the green—one red.' "[60]

Booth gave Othello's mighty "farewell" speech in a voice not loud but deep, looking out over the heads of his audience.

In the mere word "farewell," his great heart seemed to burst as in one vast continuing sigh. The phrase, "the tranquil mind," immediately succeeding, came in clear brain-tones, with a certain involved suggestiveness of meaning almost impossible to define, but as if the tranquil mind *had* flown. The whole passage, with its successive images of glorious war, filing and disappearing before his mind's eye, employed some of the grandest elements of voice, subdued to retrospective and mournful cadences. "Othello's occupation's gone." And he stood with a look in his large blue eyes—the bronzed face lending them a strange sadness—as if all happiness had gone after.[61]

Booth's voice could express everything, Gould tells us, except mirth: "There were tones of light, but none of levity." It was "deep, massive, resonant, many-stringed,

Illus. 30. Junius Brutus Booth in his later years.

changeful, vast in volume, of marvelous flexibility and range; delivering with ease . . . trumpet-tones, bell-tones, tones like 'the sound of many waters,' like the muffled and confluent 'roar of bleak-grown pines.' "[62]

We need not follow the worshipful Gould to his conclusion that Junius Brutus Booth was "the greatest of all actors."[63] Booth's range, like Kean's, was limited. He was incapable of comedy, as even Gould admitted, and other witnesses testify that he was less able to project heroes than to project villains—Richard, Iago, or Shylock—when he could snarl and bite and play the dog. Yet even John Foster Kirk, who disliked his Hamlet, sneered at his Macbeth, and "took good care not to be present" at his Othello, praised him generously in his "best impersonations": "His features were wonderfully mobile and expressive. The eyes were the most brilliant I have ever seen. The feeling that was about to express itself in words leaped forth and announced itself in their piercing gaze, their fiery gleams, or their concentrated glow. In moments of exultation the sudden lighting up of the countenance could not but suggest the trite comparison of the sun bursting through the clouds and chasing away the shadows."[64] Booth's beautiful elocution, Kirk said, was enhanced by a kind of melodious intonation which in figurative or pictorial passages could "create a scene with the sound." Kirk praised Booth's vivacity of speech, intensity of feeling, absorption of thought, his picturesqueness and his realism—qualities which "gave the effect of constant variety and contrast without infringing on the unity of conception or breaking the continuity of the performance." By such talents as these "the mad tragedian," as Booth came to be called, improved the romantic mode of interpreting Shakespeare: he moved away from Byronic sensationalism and flash effects toward a more sensitive, intelligent, and coherent art—more sustained than that of Kean, more suggestive than that of the first generation of native Shakespeareans who were at last coming into their own.

DEVELOPMENT OF THE PLAYHOUSES

Between 1820 and 1850—in the time of Junius Brutus Booth and the first generation of significant American actors—there was a vast increase in the number of permanent theatres (as distinct from small-town makeshifts) in America.[65] The rising population expanded the market for entertainment, and the rising prosperity after the War of 1812 made the building of theatres in the larger cities an economically attractive enterprise. New York, whose population more than doubled every twenty years (60,000 in 1800; 123,000 in 1820; 312,000 in 1840; 813,000 in 1860) saw well over a dozen important new houses go up during Booth's time. The Park, which burned in 1820, was rebuilt in 1821, and among those that followed were the Chatham Garden in 1824, the Bowery in 1826, Niblo's Garden (Sans Souci) in 1827, the National in 1838, the Broadway in 1847, the Astor Place in 1847, and Burton's in 1848. The Bowery, which was strangely subject to conflagrations, had to be entirely rebuilt five times in the first two decades of its existence. All these houses, it must be remembered, stood far down the Island, well to the south of Greenwich Village.

In Philadelphia (which had gained the Walnut Street Theatre in 1809), the great Chestnut Street went up in flames in 1820, a few weeks before the burning of the Park. It was built again in 1822, and another house in Arch Street was added in 1828. Boston, which retained the old house in Federal Street, gained a "new and splendid Temple of the Muses" in Tremont Street in 1827 and the Boston Museum in 1841. Providence and Charleston each acquired one theatre during these years, and Washington, D.C., two (the United States Theatre in 1800 and the Washington in 1804).

In the West, New Orleans, with its sophisticated multilingual population, had enjoyed French plays since the 1790s. James Caldwell opened the American Theatre there in 1824, the St. Charles in 1835, and the St. Charles again in 1843 after its burning. Sol Smith and Noah Ludlow built the New American in 1840. Both Saint Louis and Chicago had permanent theatres by the late 1830s. With the opening of the goldfields a rash of theatre building spread through central California in 1849 and after.

Except for the widespread introduction of gas lighting and the enlargement of stage areas to accommodate grander spectacle, no striking advance was made in the technology of play production. Gradually, as we shall see, there was a move toward strict historical accuracy in the mounting of period plays; and scene painters may have refined their brushwork as gaslight improved over the more feeble glow of oil. But the age-old system of perspective painting on flat wings and drops and shutters prevailed without essential change. When the Chestnut Street burned in 1820, William Wood reckoned that his most irretrievable loss was that of the "splendid English scenery," which had been in constant use since 1794 when it was imported. As the new Chestnut Street rose from the ashes, Hugh Reinagle, the house artist, presumably undertook to re-create those same lost scenes, in number and theme and style.

The builders seem mainly to have lavished their funds and ingenuity on the front of the house, interested in the size, comfort, and decoration of the auditorium and its adjuncts—concerned often, too, for the building's streetside attractiveness. When William Niblo, who had grown rich in the Boston fish trade, moved to New York and took up the entertainment business, he began by convert-

Illus. 31. (opposite) Interior of the New Park Theatre, New York. Courtesy of the New York Historical Society, New York City.

Illus. 32. Walnut Street Theatre, Philadelphia.

ing a commercial amusement park into a lovely pleasure garden—a gift to the public. He transplanted trees there, cultivated exotic flowers and shrubs, built fountains and a bandstand, and provided nightly fireworks. The first theatre he built was a long, low, airy-looking structure, many windowed on the garden side; his later one responded to the new-found romantic taste for things Moorish, being decorated within by architectural motifs from the Alhambra. Other builders followed the Greek Revival: the facade of the second Bowery (1828) was almost a perfect Parthenon.

Inside the houses, much space was devoted to social uses—coffee rooms, punch rooms, retiring rooms, and richly upholstered lobbies designed for pleasant strolling. The auditorium typically ran to great height, usually boasting three (sometimes four) tiers of boxes. In seating capacity these theatres vied with the more famous theatres of London: the Park held 2,600, the Chestnut Street upwards of 2,000, the first Bowery 3,000, the third Bowery "800 persons more than . . . Drury Lane," the Broadway over 4,000.

Lavish attention, and sometimes good taste, went into the trimmings—the furnishing of the boxes, the decoration of boxfronts, proscenium, and ceiling. At the Chatham Garden, for instance, the boxes were lined with crimson cloth, the seats covered in green, and the posts supporting the tiers of boxes painted to resemble pale green marble. At either end of the forestage stood a tall alabaster vase on a pedestal of green marble; above the stage doors were busts in high relief of Washington and

Illus. 33. Exterior of Niblo's Garden, New York.
Courtesy of the Library of Congress.

Illus. 34. The second Bowery Theatre, New York,
1828. Courtesy of the Library of Congress.

Illus. 35. Interior of Niblo's Garden.

Jefferson, Franklin and Jackson; higher still in niches was a statue of Shakespeare at one side and a statue of Garrick at the other. Elsewhere the artistry was less discreet. The proprietors of the Park were proud of the fact that all concerned in the making of their building were "*Americans who never have been abroad or have seen a foreign Theatre*"; but at least one foreign visitor, the comedian Joe Cowell, found the decorations pretentious, tasteless, and comparable to what one might find in London at a vulgar melodrama house like the Coburg.

The particular glory of many a theatre was its great chandelier, which hung over the center of the pit. The chandelier in the first St. Charles Theatre in New Orleans measured thirty-six feet in circumference, contained 23,300 cut-glass drops, was lighted by 176 gas jets, and weighed over two tons. The decoration of theatre ceilings,

of vaults over the proscenium, and of act drops was often a *tour de force et majesté* of the scene painter's art. Allegorical groups abounded—Shakespeare flanked by Thalia and Melpomene, Apollo in a chariot surrounded by the Muses, the Goddess of Wisdom presenting a picture of George Washington to the Goddess of Liberty while Justice protected American Commerce and Manufacturing. George Washington on horseback was a favorite subject for act drops: he might appear as a live man on a live horse approaching Mount Vernon, or sometimes as an equestrian statue backed by a monumental building or by a pleasant landscape. The American Eagle frequently came to roost on the keystone of the proscenium arch. In the second St. Charles Theatre in New Orleans he flew in on the act drop, carrying Shakespeare, ringed with light, upon his back.

CHAPTER III

Three Natives–and Another Visitor

N o native-born actors of consequence, and certainly no notable Shakespeareans, emerged in America until well into the 1820s. It is true that as early as 1809 young John Howard Payne (1791–1852) went on the New York stage.[1] Payne has even been called "America's First Hamlet," but that designation must be taken as a half-playful one. Billed as Master Payne, he was the first in America of a long line of Young Rosciuses and Infant Wonders spawned on English-speaking stages in the wake of the original Young Roscius, Master William Henry West Betty, who at thirteen had monopolized the theatres of London a few years earlier.[2] Like Betty, Payne did indeed play Hamlet, and Romeo too, along with Young Norval in Home's *Douglas* and other heavy roles of non-Shakespearean vintage. Like Betty, too, he was "a perfect Cupid in his beauty," and "his sweet voice, self-possessed yet modest manners, wit, vivacity, and premature wisdom, made him a most engaging prodigy."[3] From New York to Boston to Charleston he was lionized for a year or two, and William Clapp of Boston tells us that "his action was elegant, his attitudes bold and striking, and his most prominent defects were those of pronunciation."[4] But of his Hamletizing we really know very little. In 1813 he went abroad. He acted in England and Ireland briefly, then devoted himself largely to playwriting and other literary work. In the early 1840s and at the end of his life he was serving as United States Consul in Tunis. He is remembered not for his Shakespearean acting but for having written the words of "Home, Sweet Home" and for his second funeral. Some thirty years after his death W. W. Corcoran, the art collector and philanthropist, caused his remains to be moved from Tunis to Washington, D.C., and reburied in Oak Hill Cemetery in the presence of Chester A. Arthur, the presidential cabinet, a tentful of newspaper correspondents, and two or three thousand of "the select of the capital."[5]

When a generation of native-born Shakespeareans did appear, they were deliberately and strenuously "Ameri-can." James Henry Hackett, who will serve to represent the native-born comedians, was first and always an exponent of that peculiarly American invention, the stage Yankee. "Essentially the Yankee was always the chip-on-the-shoulder American," says Francis Hodge in *Yankee Theatre*," proud, chary of his independence and freedom, and cocky toward the rest of the world about him, particularly toward England and Englishmen."[6] Hackett himself, as we shall see, was not at all cocky toward the English—was, in fact, rather an anglophile; and, having mastered the punkin-and-broomhandle humor of his Yankee characters, he carried them to the London stage and strove valiantly (but usually to shouts of "Off! Off!") to persuade English audiences to enjoy them. His Shakespearean work, confined mainly to Falstaff, was of course colored by his Yankee beginnings. With the tragedian Edwin Forrest, belligerent nativism became almost a living principle. When, for instance, he endowed the Edwin Forrest Home for retired actors, he limited residency there to actors who had substantially served the theatre of the United States. When he once gave $100 to a club library, he specified that the money could be used only to buy "purely American" books. And, of course, his quarrel with the English Macready blossomed into steadfast hatred which mushroomed into the bloody horror of the Astor Place Riot.

To qualify as a tragedian during this first generation, an American was expected to exhibit burly masculinity. Success in the heroic school depended upon strength and agility of body, volume and range of voice. Forrest trained like an athlete with special diet, daily scrubbing, and gymnastics until his body was all hard muscle; in his early studies with teachers of oratory he developed vocal patterns of extraordinary variety, distinctness, and carrying power. Novice actors apparently took Forrest as the model of what a serious actor should look like and sound like. Three Forrestians whose debuts occurred in the mid-1830s (about a decade after Forrest's own emergence as

Illus. 36. Cartoon of John Howard Payne as Hamlet.

be second only to Charlotte Cushman as tragedienne, was of amazonian proportions, as tall and nearly as muscular as Forrest, whose acting partner she was in the early 1840s and whose mistress she was reputed to be. Miss Cushman was so mannish in physique and temperament that she frequently played male roles.

JAMES HENRY HACKETT

When James Henry Hackett (1800–71), who had made a small fortune wholesaling groceries and liquor in up-state New York, went down to the city in 1825 and lost everything in a financial speculation, he turned to the stage for a livelihood.[7] Or, rather, he restored his wife to the stage. Mrs. Hackett, the former Catherine Leesugg, had been a successful singing actress in 1819 when he married her, and Manager Simpson of the Park Theatre was glad to have her back again. Hackett himself, whose acting experience had been strictly amateur, crept onto the stage behind her skirts, so to speak. He first appeared, unremarkably, on March 1, 1826, playing Justice Wood-cock to his wife's Rosetta in *Love in a Village:* Woodcock was not a role in which to make much of an impression.

His real talent was for imitations, a mode of entertainment with which the English comedian Charles Mathews had recently been enthralling American audiences, and Hackett undertook to emulate Mathews. He could ape the manners of well-known actors, and he also had in mind a great store of yarns about Yankees and other country cousins which he would deliver in Yankee dialect. On March 10, when his wife took a benefit, he presented himself in *Sylvester Daggerwood*—a popular afterpiece in which one of the characters, an actor seeking an engagement, demonstrates his ability by spouting familiar passages in the manner of various contemporary stars. Hackett took off Mathews himself, then Thomas Hilson and Jack Barnes (both well-known comedians), and finally told a Yankee story entitled "Uncle Ben and the Squirrel Hunt." The house was crowded, though presumably more on Mrs. Hackett's account than on his, and if his imitations were pleasing there seems to have been no call for him to repeat them. He did not appear again until late June, when for his wife's sister's benefit he imitated Edmund Kean in some scenes from *Richard III.*

At Mrs. Hackett's benefit the following autumn he gave a special turn to the art of mimicry by playing

a star) were Augustus A. Addams (d. 1851), who played the whole range of Shakespearean heavy heroes for a few seasons but declined from public favor and died young; John R. Scott (1809–56), a robustious performer who, in fact, gave Forrest serious competition as a Shakespearean but presently lost his nerve and dwindled into sailors, pirates, and other prime functionaries in melodrama; and J. Hudson Kirby (1819–48), whose violent groans and contortions in Shakespearean death scenes prompted the once-famous saying, "Wake me up when Kirby dies." Even the women of this generation, it seems, were bred in the heroic mold. Josephine Clifton (1813–47), said to

Dromio opposite the Dromio of Jack Barnes, and imitating Barnes with such confounding accuracy that the audience absolutely could not tell which was which. This *Comedy of Errors*, the first in New York in over twenty years, was liked so well that it was kept on for several performances and won a place for that lesser play in the nineteenth-century American repertory. Finally, for his own benefit on December 12, just one week after Edmund Kean's last performance as Richard III in New York, Hackett played that entire role in exact imitation of Kean. Then he sailed for England, where he got himself billed at Covent Garden Theatre as a "leading American comic actor."

Much of Hackett's reputation in his own day depended upon his creation of Yankee characters and other shrewd or loutish American Originals—Jonathan Doubikins, Solomon Swap, Rip Van Winkle, Major Joe Bunker, Nimrod Wildfire, Job Fox, and the rest. But his reputation persists to our time mainly because he hitched his wagon to Shakespeare. He became the regular proprietor

Illus. 37. James Henry Hackett.

of the role of Falstaff. There were other mid-century Falstaffs, to be sure—Charles Bass, Ben de Bar, William Burton, John Gilbert—but in popular estimation "Falstaff" Hackett was the only one. "When he, and you, and I, and sixty years have gone," an enthusiast prophesied, "old gentlemen will say to the play-goer of the day, 'I saw Hackett in *Falstaff*, sir. He was the finest *Sir John* that ever enacted the character' . . . the real *Falstaff* died with Hackett; and one of Shakespeare's masterpieces is, as yet, no more!"[8] He experimented with some of the tragic characters, too, and left commentaries on them, and we also value highly the judgments he has left us of other Shakespearean actors of the day.

When Hackett worked up his imitation of Kean's Richard III, having watched Kean through the part some dozen times, he recorded in an interleaved copy of the play an exact account of what he was imitating.[9] He marked all of Kean's emphases and major pauses, and scattered over the pages countless adverbs of mood and manner: *archly, sneeringly, rapturously, fretfully, piteously, vehemently*. He wrote down all of Kean's principal movements and business. Thus, in notes to the opening soliloquy he preserved for us a full account of Kean's hasty entrance—head down, arms folded; how he unfolded his arms, tugged his gauntlets, writhed his body; how he grinned and fretted at "the lascivious pleasing of a lute," played with his sword belt, struck his breast three times at "this mis-shapen trunk," chuckled at the thought of a "glorious diadem," hesitated after the final line, then made a sudden exit. Next in the book comes, complete, Kean's butchering of King Henry; then the wooing of Lady Anne, marked with at least fifty notations of Kean's business. Dozens of instants in the Prayerbook Scene, the Throne Scene, the Tent Scenes, the duel and death are caught and fixed in precise, vivid detail, like so many dozens of stills from a movie. No other performance of that era can be visualized so completely, thanks to Hackett's care and skill as a reporter. We notice, too, that for all his devotion to the subject he was not entirely taken in by it. His ultimate judgment of Kean's Richard, entered a few years later, discriminates nicely: "Captivated, as I once was, with the giant genius of *Edmund Kean*, in bending this stubborn character to his own personal peculiarities, subsequent study & reflection convinced me that *Cooke*, from the various traditionary & graphic accounts I have had from *eye-witnesses*, must have been much nearer *Shakespeare's* ideal of Richard 3ᵈ."

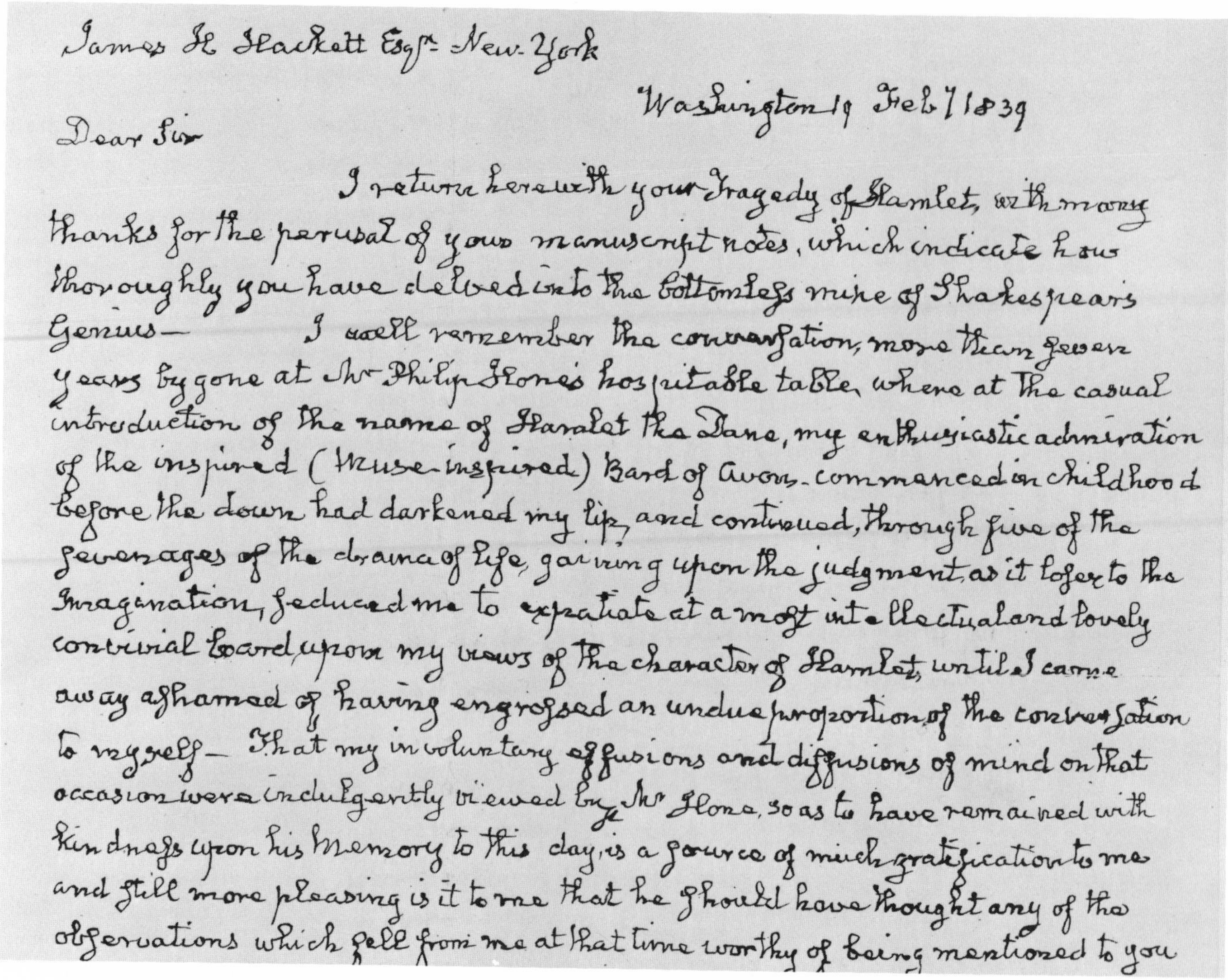

James H. Hackett Esqr. New-York

Washington 19 Feb 1839

Dear Sir

I return herewith your Tragedy of Hamlet, with many thanks for the perusal of your manuscript notes, which indicate how thoroughly you have delved into the bottomless mine of Shakespears Genius— I well remember the conversation, more than seven years by gone at Mr Philip Hone's hospitable table, where at the casual introduction of the name of Hamlet the Dane, my enthusiastic admiration of the inspired (Muse-inspired) Bard of Avon, commenced in childhood before the down had darkened my lip, and continued, through five of the seven ages of the drama of Life, gaining upon the judgment, as it loses to the Imagination, seduced me to expatiate at a most intellectual and lovely convivial board upon my views of the character of Hamlet, until I came away ashamed of having engrossed an undue proportion of the conversation to myself— That my involuntary effusions and diffusions of mind on that occasion were indulgently viewed by Mr Hone, so as to have remained with kindness upon his memory to this day, is a source of much gratification to me and still more pleasing is it to me that he should have thought any of the observations which fell from me at that time worthy of being mentioned to you

Illus. 38. Facsimile of a letter from John Quincy Adams to James Henry Hackett about the role of Hamlet.

In 1863 Hackett collected his papers in a volume called *Notes and Comments upon Certain Plays and Actors of Shakespeare*. Therein we learn about his attempts upon several other Shakespearean roles. He undertook Iago in 1828, but soon dropped it in favor of his growing repertory of American characters. According to the one long review reprinted in *Notes and Comments*, his conception was the enlightened one—no snarling monster but a gay and deceptively honest Iago.[10] He attempted Lear in the autumn of 1840 and played it several times that season. In that year, too, he observed Edwin Forrest's Lear. He disliked it, and *Notes and Comments* preserves his objections to it.[11]

He also played Hamlet in 1840. He had made a study of that role for many years, entering his "new and singular ideas" about it in an interleaved copy of the play. He loaned this copy widely, thus generating much interesting correspondence with John Quincy Adams and others, all of which is included in *Notes and Comments*.[12] He printed a long essay on "To be or not to be" in which he defended the soliloquy against Oliver Goldsmith's opinion that it is "a heap of absurdities."[13] He reprinted a newspaper correspondence in which he argued that Shakespeare was aware of the circulation of blood well before William Harvey "discovered" it.[14] Part 4 of *Notes and Comments* consists of critical analyses of thirteen renditions of Hamlet by actors whom Hackett had seen perform.[15]

But his great Shakespearean enterprise was Falstaff. He first played the Falstaff of *1 Henry IV* in 1828; he added *The Merry Wives of Windsor* to his repertory in 1838 and *2 Henry IV* in 1841.[16] For forty years he played Falstaff throughout the country, from Boston to New Orleans, from New York to San Francisco, in almost every American town that had a proper theatre. In December of 1869 he topped off his long career (in New York, that is) with a month-long stand of Falstaff at Booth's Theatre.

There is very little valuable commentary in the American press on Hackett's early performances of the part, probably because his early critics regarded him only as a purveyor of comic American Originals and did not take him seriously as a Shakespearean. Then, as he went on repeating Falstaff, the time for criticism was past: reviewers would refer to his performance simply as "too well known to be described"—or occasionally, in a flash of impatience, as "a hash of his old dishes that have been done to death."[17]

In defense of those critics who became bored by Hackett's Falstaff, we must recognize that there was a certain dryness in his manner which may well have put them off. His was a didactic Falstaff, schoolmasterly and moralizing. For all the role's surface lustiness and jollification, Hackett intended it as an example of wickedness to be condemned. In his program for *The Merry Wives*, which he subtitled *Falstaff Outwitted by Women*, he taught the audience what to think by explaining that it was a play "wherein the Immortal Bard has contrived to combine the highest diversion with the most salutary moral lesson, and show how a couple of merry honest wives met the impudent advances of a vain old coxcomb, and by an innocent sportive coquetry, misled him to be nearly suffocated in a buck-basket, well ducked in the river, and soundly thrashed in female disguise, and eventually exposed to the laughter and ridicule of all observers."[18] As for the Falstaff of *Henry IV*, it ought indeed, he said, to entertain the audience, but in this play the "always moralizing dramatist Shakespeare" meant to teach *Youth* the danger of "becoming corrupted by intimacy with old and vicious company," and to teach *Courtiers* the danger of "ministering to the vices of great patrons, lest they too, like Falstaff, be left to die in despair."[19]

We can sense the moralizing process at work in any of the well-known portraits of Hackett in the role. His eyes glitter at us; his bony, intelligent face grins toothily and leaps out at us from the obviously laid-on whiskers and costume and paunch. A London critic once observed that "his head did not seem connected with the rest of his body,"[20] and an American critic noted that he "seemed superior to himself, as if he were playing a part."[21]

Hackett, we must remember, was not, from the beginning, a complete and committed *actor*, but rather an impersonator, a satirizing mimic. It appears that the Falstaff which he projected was a partial one, a critique of Falstaff. Hackett the preacher could not quite submit himself to Falstaff the man.

He paid many professional visits to London—he was, in fact, the first important American actor to reverse the westward stream of talent by carrying American stage art to England and winning a sort of acceptance there.[22] When he played Falstaff in London—in 1833, 1839, 1845, and 1851—the critics tried to be tolerant, but plainly they were puzzled. They were, after all, inheritors of the opinions of Maurice Morgann, that whimsical champion of amiability, who had long since proved to the satisfaction of sentimentalists that Falstaff was no *coward*; who

Illus. 39. James Henry Hackett as Falstaff in 1 *Henry IV*.

so loved Falstaff that he was "ready to hug him, guts, lyes and all."[23] William Hazlitt, too, had even more explicitly excused Falstaff from every moral charge—"as a liar, a braggart, a coward, a glutton, etc."—on the grounds that he only "assumes all these characters to shew the humorous part of them."[24] And ever since 1824 London's own Falstaff had been plump and chuckling little William Dowton, who in *The Merry Wives* skipped briskly about the stage embracing now Mrs. Page, now Mrs. Ford, between their verses of the "Cuckoo Song."[25] After Dowton, Hackett seemed heavy-handed, banal. "There is a deficiency in humor—in richness," said the *Times* critic in 1839; "he is merely a laughing old man— nothing more; there is no fine shading; but a little swagger, a wheezing giggle, a nudge in the ribs, and an occasional pant, were all that he contributed towards the embodying of one of Shakspeare's finest creations."[26] Of what use to the London of 1845 (when affection oozed everywhere for Dickens's Mr. Pickwick, Mr. Brownlow, and the Cheeryble Brothers) was a Falstaff with "a kind of mental as well as bodily obesity," ponderous, "touchy, fretful, even serious," even "irascible"[27]—a moralizing Falstaff? Only in far-off, puritanized, dull-spirited America, it seemed—or a long lifetime ago in Dr. Johnson's earnest world—could such a conception of the character be appropriate.

They granted Hackett all that they could. They respected his honesty and his workmanship. In 1851 the *Times* reviewer supposed that

there is, probably, not a more conscientious actor on the stage. He has evidently studied the speeches of the fat knight . . . with a carefulness worthy of a commentator on Sophocles. He has a definite manner of giving every phrase, and of introducing every jest. The finest mosaic work could not be more carefully laid down. And there is not only care, but considerable intelligence evinced in the rendering. The mind of an acute artist has evidently been devoted to a character, with the view of digging everything out of its hidden recesses, and making of it the completest thing in the world.

It lacked only one thing: the *ars celare artem*. However well finished the results, one was always reminded of the artist's labor in arriving at them.[28]

Hackett never let a *Times* reviewer get by without rebutting him point by point in a letter to the editor, accusing his judge of "fine writing," of "pseudo-intelligence," of ignorance of Shakespeare's text, of condescension to

Illus. 40. James Henry Hackett as Falstaff in *The Merry Wives of Windsor.*

Americans, of mere captiousness. He would suggest that he, Hackett, had forgotten more about Falstaff than Sir Oracle had ever known.[29]

They were hard words that Hackett flung in the teeth of the London press. Yet to define his attitude toward the English in a cliché of later vintage, we might call it a love-hate relationship. He genuinely desired, not only for his own sake but for America's sake, to be understood by the English—else he would not have gone to them so often to foist his Jonathans and Nimrod Wildfires, as well as his Falstaff, upon their attention. He wanted the English to accept him, but he insisted sturdily on his own terms. Nor was he by preference so remote from English values as his cranky language might suggest. Within the American scene, during the long-drawn-out contest for cultural control between the so-called "aristocrats" (pro-British effete snobs, as they were regarded by the vulgar) and the "democrats" (uncultivated brutes, in the eyes of high society), Hackett aligned himself with the "aristocrats." Although he made his name first of all as an impersonator of low-caste American Originals, and obviously enjoyed them, he of course did not identify with them, but in the manner of Charles Mathews exhibited them for the fun that could be got out of them—sometimes to be laughed with, more often to be laughed at.

In his personal affairs Hackett plainly regarded himself socially and culturally as a Superior Person, revealing now and then amusing little streaks of vanity. He did not mind the story getting about, when a distant relative died in 1839, that, had he wanted to, he could have assumed the title of Baron Hackett of Hackett's Town in Ireland.[30] He referred to his personal library as "my biblical collection," and to his farm in Illinois as "my landed estate."[31] He loved to associate with affluent and conservative leaders of society, claiming, for instance, to have dined with the patrician Philip Hone, sometime mayor of New York and ardent despiser of Democrats.[32] He was so vain of his friendship with John Quincy Adams, whose feuding with President Jackson pushed him into the social-political camp of extreme conservatives, that he had his correspondence with Adams lithographed in facsimile for distribution to acquaintances. Recipients of this booklet included the Earl of Carlisle; Thomas Noon Talfourd, the distinguished English playwright, jurist, and member of Parliament; John Payne Collier, then at the top of his reputation as a Shakespeare scholar; and Charles Murray, equerry to Prince Albert. Hackett's bid for recognition in the realm of scholarship included publication of notes on certain textual minutiae in Shakespeare. He claimed, too, that in preparing a Shakespearean role he tracked down every use Shakespeare made of every important word in order to establish its exact meaning.[33] Unfortunately this seeming concern for textual authenticity is not borne out by his acting versions: his *Merry Wives*, for instance, was nothing more than Frederic Reynolds's old arrangement of the play as a ballad-opera but with the songs cut out.[34]

When the struggle between "democrats" and "aristocrats" in the theatre exploded into the bloody Astor Place Riot in 1849, Hackett was in the thick of it—the manager,

in fact, of the "aristocratic" Astor Place Opera House, where William Charles Macready was howled down by the "democratic" mob. In the contest between English Macready and American Edwin Forrest, Hackett clearly gave the palm to the Englishman, whom he considered, for all his faults, "the most intellectual and generally effective actor of the time": in his chapter on interpreters of Hamlet he allotted thirty-five pages to thoughtful picking apart of Macready, two pages to a curt dismissal of Forrest.

London was uphill work for Hackett. He could never win from the English critics complete sympathy with his high moral tone. At home, however, his Falstaff rose steadily from critical obscurity to the status of a national institution. By 1855 the *Spirit of the Times* would wonder "how any sane man, with the knowledge that Hackett is going to personate Falstaff, can stay away."[35] In 1867 George William Curtis, the elegant occupant of *Harper's* "Editor's Easy Chair," after rebuking himself for never having seen Hackett's Falstaff before, printed a glowing appreciation of two evenings of it and remarked that Hackett's worth could not be estimated by comparison, "because nobody disputes the representation with him. He has it to himself. It is accorded to him as Lady Macbeth was to Mrs. Siddons."[36] At the end of his career the *New York Herald* would find that "like good wine he improves with age" and would rejoice in the mellow richness of his playing.[37] The *Spirit of the Times*, by way of valedictory, wished to "thank Mr. Hackett devoutly and heartily for this piece of acting; . . . it is something to remember as having seen, when we shall have grown old, and other and worse actors are fretting their brief hour—and the patience of their auditors—upon the stage."[38]

EDWIN FORREST

In an effort to describe the physical and emotional power that Edwin Forrest (1806–72) could lay on when wrath was the issue (the role being the Indian chieftain Metamora), the actor and elocutionist George Vandenhoff invoked comparisons with Niagara Falls and storms at sea:

For power of destructive energy, I never heard anything on the stage so tremendous in its sustained *crescendo* swell, and crashing force of utterance, as his defiance of the Council, in that play. His voice surged and roared like the angry sea,

Illus. 41. Portrait of Edwin Forrest by Thomas Sully. Reproduced by kind permission of the Garrick Club.

lashed into fury by a storm; till, as it reached its boiling, seething climax, in which the serpent hiss of hate was heard, at intervals, amidst its louder, deeper, hoarser tones, it was like the falls of Niagara, in its tremendous down-sweeping cadence: it was a whirlwind, a tornado, a cataract of illimitable rage![39]

Forrest meant all that to Vandenhoff in 1842. Not so for Frances Trollope a decade earlier. She, too, had visited Niagara Falls, like Vandenhoff and every other informed English visitor, and she attempted to record what "wonder, terror, and delight" the sight of it inspired in her. And she saw Edwin Forrest, but when he acted most passionately he reminded her not in the least of Niagara but only of Bottom the Weaver: "He played the part of Damon, and roared, I thought, very unlike a nightingale."[40]

There, in little, is the problem we confront when we attempt to assess Forrest.[41] Unquestionably America's

first important native-born tragedian, he dominated the American stage for thirty years and lasted fifteen years longer. But was he a great actor, or was he only a sort of theatrical frontiersman, a huge, fierce male animal endowed with extraordinary strength of body and voice?

Forrest first went on the stage in Philadelphia in 1820, at the age of fourteen. The role was Young Norval in Home's *Douglas*. He was then, said William Wood, "a well grown young man, with a noble figure, unusually developed for his age"—ready even for such adult roles as Frederick in *Lovers' Vows* and Octavian in *The Mountaineers*.[42] Yet he did not at once catch on, and being "not yet old enough for a man, nor young enough for a boy," he withdrew for a couple of years. At sixteen he left home to resume his theatrical novitiate in the river towns of the West. At eighteen he secured an engagement at James Caldwell's American Theatre in New Orleans. He spent two seasons there, learning his business and developing "manliness." Turning his back on fashionable society, he cultivated associations with waterfront and riverboat toughs; with desperados like James Bowie, inventor of the Bowie knife and the Bowie system of dueling; with a sharper named Gazonac, who initiated him to the vice dens of the old city; with an Indian named Push-ma-ta-ha, who took him into the wilderness for several weeks of primitive living. He worked up a passion for the actress Jane Placide, who seems eventually to have accepted him as a lover.[43] In 1826, at the age of twenty, he returned to the East and appeared in New York, where his success was immediate and immense.

Although he was engaged at the Bowery Theatre for the autumn of 1826, his New York debut actually occurred at the Park in the preceding June, when a Park Theatre actor, Jacob Woodhull, invited him to play Othello for Woodhull's benefit. June 23, 1826, appears to have been one of those magical first nights, when seemingly out of nowhere a phenomenal actor springs full-armed. No Hazlitt was there to record it, else it might have become as famous in the annals as the night of Edmund Kean's debut in London a dozen years earlier. Yet a friend of Forrest's, Charles Durang of Philadelphia, was there and later on took the trouble to write down something of how "He came—we saw—and he conquered!"

Forrest entered with a calm mien and a dignified manner and took the center of the stage. His figure and manner elicited hearty applause at once. His youthful manly form—sym-

Illus. 42. Edwin Forrest as Hamlet.

metrical as the Apollo Belvidere with all that figure's repose —devoid of all superfluous flesh—an expressive youthful face, rather thin in its outline—a flashing hazel eye that foreshadowed vivid intellect—deportment and action naturally graceful and well costumed, made a *tout-ensemble* that at once struck like an electrical chord of harmony from the actor to the audience as he bowed to their warm greetings. The ladies especially threw up their white cambrics in token of heartfelt admiration.[44]

Durang described only Forrest's outsides on that occasion, and said nothing about his Othello. But outsides counted for much. Over the years there was a great deal of tossing up of white cambrics, and sometimes, it is said, women in the audience actually fainted at the sight of him.

All his life Forrest cultivated his body assiduously.[45] He was powerful. At five foot ten, and with his commanding personality, he would in those days pass for a tall man. He was handsome, especially in his youth before he affected mustache and chin whiskers, and the tousle-haired portrait of him by Thomas Sully, painted when he was just past thirty, shows the clean-cut features of a Byronic hero. He did setting up exercises with dumbbells; he boxed, walked on his hands, tossed Indian clubs. He scrubbed his body twice daily, rubbed it down with coarse cloths, flagellated it with rubber balls on the ends of elastic cords. His Spartan diet seems to have been chiefly vegetable—oatmeal, brown bread, cornmeal mush and cream. He drank very little, and after his early years forswore tobacco altogether. The two hundred pounds or more that he ultimately developed was all bone and sinew, and the muscles of his calves and thighs, upper arms, and neck swelled to bull-like strength. In several of his favorite roles he displayed his arms and legs fully (in silk fleshings, of course). His friend and biographer the Reverend William Alger depicted him in sentences almost onomatopoetic in their fervor:

In those happy and glowing years of his prime and of his fresh celebrity, what a glorious image of unperverted manhood, of personified health and strength and beauty, he presented! What a grand form he had! What a grand face! What a grand voice! And, the living base of all, what a grand blood! the rich flowing seed-bed of his human thunder and lightning. As he stepped upon the stage in his naked fighting-trim, his muscular coating unified all over him and quivering with vital power, his skin polished by exercise and friction to a smooth and marble hardness, conscious of his enormous potency, fearless of anything on the earth, proudly aware of the impression he knew his mere appearance, backed by his

fame, would make on the audience who impatiently awaited him—he used to stand and receive the long, tumultuous cheering that greeted him, as immovable as a planted statue of Hercules.[46]

Forrest's superiority over common men was godlike, said Alger, and it could strike terror into "faint ladies, spruce clerks, spindling fops, and perfumed dandies."[47] Fanny Kemble, who was not a faint lady, exclaimed when she first met him, "What a mountain of a man!"[48]

Forrest's vocal powers, too, were extraordinary. At *fortissimo* he could shake the vitals of spectators in the farthest galleries. At normal strength, said John Foster Kirk, his voice "had the fulness and mellowness that belong only to the finest organs."[49] And he could gentle it down to the quietest level. Scattered through the notes which the actor George Becks made of Forrest's Hamlet, we find plentiful testimony to the vocal delicacy he was capable of: "quiet loving tenderness," "half whisper— low determination," "tender loving tones, wonderful," "hoarse whisper," "so low."[50] The mere sound of his "wonderful vocal organ" could bring tears to the eyes of the dancer Fanny Ellsler.[51]

His first regular New York season opened at the new theatre in the Bowery on October 23, 1826—Othello again, and now, with forewarning of his quality, it was even more enthusiastically applauded than it had been in June. Immediately after the curtain fell, the proprietors met him behind the scenes to congratulate him: they raised his salary from twenty-eight to forty dollars a week, reduced his schedule to the three-nights-a-week regularly enjoyed by stars, and allotted him the choicest leading roles. These included such non-Shakespearean characters as Damon in Banim's *Damon and Pythias*, Knowles's Virginius and William Tell, Rolla in *Pizarro*, and Payne's Brutus. His Shakespearean characters were fewer: Othello, Mark Antony, and Lear. In succeeding seasons he would undertake Shylock, Iago, Macbeth, Richard III, Hamlet, and Coriolanus with varying degrees of satisfaction. But the truth which finally emerges is that, except for Othello and Lear, Forrest was temperamentally out of tune with Shakespeare's leading characters; and, except for technical excellencies, he played them mainly because as America's leading tragedian he had to do so. In the great debate between "democrats" and "aristocrats," in which, as we have seen, Hackett sided with the upper class, Forrest planted himself solidly with the "democrats," with the oppressed against the oppressors, with the "common people" against the arrogant rich. And Shakespeare gave him no democrats to work with.

Forrest's friend William Leggett once put the case for him more clearly than he could have done for himself. "I wish," Leggett wrote to him,

Shakspeare, with all his divine attributes, had only had a little of that ennobling love of equal liberty which is now animating the hearts of true patriots all over the world, and is destined, ere long, to effect a great and glorious change in the condition of mankind. What a vast and godlike influence he might have exerted in moulding the public mind and guiding the upward progress of nations, if his great genius had not been dazzled by the false glitter of aristocratic institutions, and blinded to the equal rights of the great family of man![52]

Forrest could identify with Othello and Lear because he could construe them as noble and innocent men, much put upon—true heroes who go down fighting. These two were his Shakespearean favorites. He played Hamlet throughout his career, but not altogether happily, for Hamlet was too dawdling for his strenuous temper; or, as a critic once put it, "Half of him could play it."[53] As an exponent of manly as well as civic virtues, he was uncomfortable with villains of all sorts: he soon abandoned Shylock and Iago—and also, after a single try, Sir Giles Overreach.[54] He retained Macbeth and Richard III, but was never quite right with them. In the one he could not convincingly submit to fear of the supernatural. In the other, though he did well to play up the gaiety of the early scenes, he rather overdid that aspect of the character and in effect he displaced Shakespeare's villain with the historical heroic Richard as rehabilitated by Sir Horace Walpole. Coriolanus—which, as a matter of fact, fitted him like a glove—offended his democratic bias, and his early audiences would have none of it. He came round to it ultimately in the 1860s, when he not only made a special triumph of it but supervised the fashioning of a huge marble statue of himself in the role.[55] Shakespeare provided him great scenes and great language, but no stalwarts at the barricades. So he nursed along his revolutionary passions as Virginius, Damon, Tell, and Rolla until he could stir up native-born American writers to create heroes of his own.

Forrest's democratic bias was accompanied by a flaming patriotism which grew hotter as he grew older, and

Illus. 43. Thomas Ball's statue of Edwin Forrest as Coriolanus. Courtesy of the Edwin Forrest Home, Philadelphia.

the two passions fused into a sort of class hatred. He resented the intelligentsia and sophisticates in American society because they took their values from Europe. He exaggerated the cause and worth of native art and artists. He fomented opposition to actors from abroad, especially intruders from Britain. The focus of his hostility would be the English actor William Charles Macready. In the

Knowles's *William Tell*, a play which Macready himself
had introduced in London a year or two earlier. Forrest's
Tell seemed to Macready vehement but unfeeling, and
he thought that Forrest did not wholly comprehend the
text. He credited him with intelligence, however, and concluded that if the young man would put himself to school
to the better provincial audiences of England and Scot-
land for a few years, he "might make himself a first-rate
actor"; if not, not.[56] Whether Forrest watched Macready
at the Park, we do not know. Probably he would not have
wished to. He was an ardent devotee of Edmund Kean
(lately in Albany he had played Iago to Kean's Othello
and had been praised for it by the great little man) and,
knowing Kean's antipathy to Macready, he may well have
kept away from the Park on party principle.

WILLIAM CHARLES MACREADY

The older actor was, of course, the cynosure of critical attention during that 1826 season—the first of Macready's
three visits to America and the beginning of his contro-
versial involvement in and influence upon the American
theatre.[57] He quite lived up to expectations. His figure
and bearing were approved, and his square-jawed flattish
face, often accounted ugly, was alluded to politely: "His
face, though not technically a first rate stage face, is wonderfully expressive." His voice was described as "peculiarly fine, deep, and mellow."[58] In years to come he would
accumulate a most unpleasant reputation for his treatment of fellow actors. According to Fanny Kemble, "He
was unpopular in the profession, his temper was irritable,
and his want of consideration for the persons working
with him strange in a man of so many fine qualities. His
artistic vanity and selfishness were unworthy of a gentleman, and rendered him an object of dislike and dread to
those who were compelled to encounter them." Besides
the annoyances she herself suffered when acting with him
in London in 1848, she recalled "actors whose eyes had
been all but thrust out by his furious fighting in Macbeth;
. . . others nearly throttled in his paternal vengeance on
Appius Claudius; . . . actresses whose arms had been almost wrenched out of their sockets, and who had been
bruised black and blue, buffeted alike by his rage and his
tenderness."[59] Nothing of this talk, however, floated out
to the American public in 1826. The critics vied with each
other in admiring his art.

Illus. 44. Edwin Forrest.

course of the struggle between these mighty opposites,
the arts of theatre would be sacrificed to mob violence,
and the Emersonian protest against "the courtly muses of
Europe" would come down to bloody brawling in the
streets.

Forrest and Macready approached each other's orbits,
but did not meet, during Forrest's first New York season.
Macready, at thirty-three, was already famous: after a
laborious decade-long rise to the top of the profession in
England, he was making his first starring visit to America. Forrest, at twenty, was hitherto unknown but was
just now exploding into stardom. On one of his off nights
at the Park, Macready went down to the Bowery to see
his old friend William Conway as Shakespeare's Brutus.
Forrest was playing Mark Antony there, and Macready
was sufficiently impressed by his energy, good looks, and
decent reading that he returned to see him again in

The positive qualities of Macready's acting, for which he had already become known, were, first of all, a thorough emotional identification with whatever character he was performing, and, second, in the over-all conception of each character, a unity and continuity and wholeness of design. It was always his ideal, he would one day explain to a friend, "to fathom the depths of [a] character, to trace its latent motives, to feel its finest quiverings of emotion, to comprehend the thoughts that are hidden under words, and thus possess oneself of the actual mind of the individual man."[60] He used many techniques for achieving this deep involvement. Before an angry entrance as Shylock, he would stand in the wings cursing in violent whispers and shaking a ladder fastened to the wall; he would take home from the theatre a suit of armor and wear it all one Sunday in order to feel his way into the person of Henry V;[61] to heighten the emotional reality of his scene with the Ghost in *Hamlet*, he would relive a dream he once had in which he encountered the ghost of a dead friend.[62] "I cannot act Macbeth without *being* Macbeth," he would say, and

my long experience of the stage has convinced me of the necessity of keeping, on the day of exhibition, the mind as intent as possible on the subject of the actor's portraiture, even to the very moment of his entrance on the scene. He meditates himself, as it were, into the very thought and feeling of the being he is about to represent: enwrapt in the idea of the personage he assumes, he moves, and looks, and bears himself as the Roman or the Dane, and thus almost identifies himself with the creature of his imagination.[63]

The American critics at once took notice that Macready sacrificed easy pointmaking in favor of wholeness of characterization. After he opened in Knowles's *Virginius*, the *Mirror* observed, "There seems about Macready that which will not stop for a moment to gain applause by the least uncalled for show of action, or strength of emphasis."[64] This does not mean, by the way, that Macready did not wish for applause within his scenes, or that he did not usually receive it. According to Kirk, in fact, he roused, excited, and moved audiences more than any other actor: "Not Booth in Richard nor Forrest in Metamora drew any such thunders of applause as accompanied and almost interrupted Macready's bursts of fiery passion."[65] Words to notice here are *accompanied* and *almost interrupted*. The pointmaking actor would signal the audience that a point was coming: as the fuse burned down the

Illus. 45. From the portrait of William Charles Macready by Robert Thorburn.

audience would ready itself for the instant of detonation; when the applause broke out, the actor would interrupt his performance until the applause was spent. But another kind of applause, and that which Macready especially sought, was more like the applause one observes at a tennis match, the circus, or the ballet, which rises during a display of remarkable skill, accompanies it, and sustains it. The athlete does not lay down his racket nor the dancer cease to dance while the applause continues, and it appears that Macready, by focusing on continuity, would give the strongest possible impression that he was deep in the character, that he was unaware of the applause, that he would not stop for a moment to gain it.

In Macready's first New York Macbeth in 1826, the *Mirror* reported "such an abandonment of old and hackneyed points, and so much truth and spirit thrown into hitherto unmarked passages" that it seemed a whole new character.[66] The critic may very likely have intended to imply a comparison with Edmund Kean, for Kean had been in and out of New York through the preceding season and was even now, after his return from Canada, about to play one more brief New York engagement before going home. Almost certainly the compliments that the *Mirror* paid to the unity and continuity of Macready's Hamlet would have put readers in mind of Kean's opposite manner: "His acting is not a point, a flash, a flat-scene, and then another point, and flash, and flat again. It is like a finished picture, that does not lay claim to praise on any detached or peculiar merit, but on the general excellence of the execution."[67] The *Albion*'s review of Macready's Macbeth actually mentions Kean, recalling that "the flashes of Kean's genius make us dizzy with the intensity of their blaze": Macready had not achieved that effect, but all the same, the reviewer went on, his Macbeth was the best ever seen in America and "we have never sat out a whole play with more real gratification than we have done with Mr. Macready."[68]

Certain other qualities of Macready's acting, which lay conspicuously on the surface, are less pleasing to contemplate and were less valuable as lessons in the art. Like

Illus. 46. William Charles Macready as Hamlet, with John Stuart as the Ghost.

Kean he practiced and often overdid startling vocal transitions. Such transitions could be histrionic triumphs when for good and sufficient reason the actor effected a total emotional revolution in himself. In the Closet Scene in *Hamlet*, for instance, when the Ghost appears at the climax of Hamlet's raging at his mother, Macready "broke from the most intense and passionate indignation to the lost and bewildered air, and with a voice of unearthly horror and tones of strange awe, tremblingly addressed the spirit."[69] In his own production of *King John* in the 1840s, he not only executed a brilliant transition from chivalric hero to base criminal at the moment when John orders Hubert to commit Prince Arthur to "Death—and a grave" but he could command the services of scene painter, gasman, and a stageful of supernumeraries to underscore the effect as he made it.[70] Too often in his playing, however, he would merely break from a high shrill voice into the "deepest subcolloquial whisper,"[71] or commit other such startling changes for no more reason than to liven up the text. This became an annoying mannerism.

Then there was his lifelong campaign to domesticate tragedy, to treat situation and language so familiarly that the commonest spectator would understand them on his own terms and respond sympathetically. His Lear and Prospero were, above all, family men and loving fathers, provoking tears of joy at their scenes of parental tenderness, tears of grief at their parental anguish. We would not quarrel with the humanizing of these characters, but it appears likely that some of their essential dignity was drowned in the sentimental flood. For the speeches of Hamlet he strove for a "natural standard," for Macbeth a "manly colloquial tone." He broke up lines with pauses *ad libitum* to create an impression of a mind breeding thoughts impromptu. In doing so he flattened the elevating rhythms of blank verse into proselike plain speaking, so that Kirk declared that "the musical flow of the verse was almost utterly lost; the sense alone directed the elocution."[72] The story is told that during a rehearsal of *Virginius* in a provincial theatre, when Macready in his most familiar manner gave the line

> Do you wait for me to lead Virginia in,
> Or will you do it?

the actor of Icilius naturally responded, "Why, really, my dear sir, I don't care; just as you do it in London."[73]

Bulwer-Lytton called Macready "a great metaphysical

Illus. 47. William Charles Macready as Macbeth.

actor," meaning presumably that his acting depended more upon intense thought than upon physical activity.[74] We know that Macready strove tirelessly to achieve this effect, rehearsing impassioned speeches with his hands tied down in order to eliminate needless movement, in whispers to eliminate mere noise, and before mirrors to prevent grimaces and to make sure that the "intense passion should speak from the eyes alone."[75] Lady Juliet Pollock described vividly the "metaphysical" effect of his scene with the witches in Macbeth—how without gesticulation but only through voice and eyes he created a world of mystery:

His wandering, unsettled tone did more than all the efforts of those who played the witches in showing the supernatural at work. In a crowded theatre, Macready had a singular power of looking at nothing; and when he spoke "into the air," we could almost see the hags pass away, and like a wreath of vapour dissolve into the invisible element. Afterwards he was rapt; thick-coming fancies seemed to crowd through his brain—large thoughts, which left no room for lesser perceptions. Scarcely conscious of the presence of Banquo and his friends when once called Thane of Cawdor, his words to them dropped hurriedly and impatiently: it was the sublime of preoccupation.[76]

For such effects as these his detractors belittled him as an "artificial" or a "merely intellectual" actor (Kirk called such talk "much rubbish"), but the example of inward passion and outward restraint which he brought to the American stage was a deserved if premature corrective to the "muscular school." In the national atmosphere of materialism, expansionism, and Manifest Destiny, Macready's example could not stay the popular appetite for histrionic violence. But a few bloodlettings afterward, in the generation of Edwin Booth, Lawrence Barrett, and John McCullough, something like the Macready method would prevail.

FORREST VERSUS MACREADY

When Forrest was invited to sign on for a second season at the Bowery, he named his own salary—not $40 a week but $200 a night—and the management ruefully agreed to it. His eighty nights in the 1827–28 season brought him an income of $16,000, not to mention a few thousands more gleaned from Boston, Baltimore, and Philadelphia.

Illus. 48. William Charles Macready as Shylock.

For the next seven years, as his fame grew, he prospered mightily, or, in the sonorous phrasing of the Reverend William Alger, "Ensphered in the splendid and sounding reputation he had won, he passed in starring engagements from city to city through the land, everywhere welcomed with enthusiastic acclaim and the mark of incessant private attentions."[77]

In the fall of 1828, at the beginning of his third season, Forrest attempted to initiate an American dramatic renaissance: he wanted plays which would express the ideals of democracy in action, plays which would advance the great cause of human liberty. If England could produce a Sheridan Knowles, whose plays sounded a warning to tyrants everywhere, and the poet-playwright Byron, who died at Missolonghi serving the Greek Revolution, surely in America, where modern freedom was born, there must be writers as devoted to freedom as they. The subject matter was at hand, and Forrest prescribed it—the Red Man oppressed by brutal whites: "To the author of the

best Tragedy, in five acts, of which the hero or principal character shall be an aboriginal of this country, the sum of five hundred dollars, and half of the proceeds of the third representation, with my own gratuitous services on that occasion."[78] An actor-playwright, John Augustus Stone, won the competition with a thunderous melodrama called *Metamora; or, The Last of the Wampanoags*. Eight more competitions over the years would bring in as many more celebrations of heroism, patriotism, or resistance to tyranny, and two of these—*The Gladiator* by R. M. Bird and *Jack Cade* by R. T. Conrad—shared with *Metamora* favored place in Forrest's repertory to the end of his days. Forrest got what he wanted out of these competitions—roles exactly tailored to his own physique, temper, and style—but since with his prize money he bought the plays outright, the authors were rewarded very little for having written them. Since he also kept them out of print, no one else could perform them during his lifetime. A few inheritors of his acting methods, such as John Mc-Cullough and D. H. Harkins, preserved them dwindlingly for a decade or so after his death, but by the 1870s the vogue for their style, if not their subject matter, was passing. Thus the dramatic renaissance which he seeded died young.

In the autumn of 1836, after a two-year Grand Tour of Europe, sampling the theatres, museums, and brothels of a half-dozen countries, including Russia, Forrest played a season in London, engaged by Alfred Bunn as feature attraction at Drury Lane. He was generously received. It was a mistake, to be sure, to open with Dr. Bird's *The Gladiator*,[79] which he naively hoped to carry with him to international fame. Most of the critics deplored its crude physical effects or dismissed it as the expectable product of a frontier society. But the first-night audience greeted Forrest's acting with "long-continued cheers" and "overwhelming plaudits." The *Times*, the *Courier*, the *Sun*, the *Atlas*, the *Advertiser*, *John Bull*, the *Globe*, and other journals produced glowing appreciations of his appearance and performing.[80] Many were reminded of the great days of the late Kean. The *Times* rebuked him gently for suggesting in his curtain speech that the audience's response proved their good will toward America and Americans. In England, said the *Times*, no political feelings come between audience and actor: the audience praised him because he deserved to be praised, and they would have praised him as much whether he came from New York or Kamchatka.

Illus. 49. Edwin Forrest as Metamora.

lean figure and Stentor's voice, and at the same time there are copious tributes to his "intellectual endowments," "elevating thought and sentiment," "heartfelt tenderness," "learned and imaginative spirit," "poetic grandeur." Here and there, of course, a sour note was sounded, and according to the *Spectator* his engagement was terminated prematurely because of empty benches in the pit of Drury Lane;[81] but his book of press cuttings proved undebatably that an American actor had triumphed in London's Theatre Royal.

Macready, who was Forrest's principal opposition at Covent Garden and whom he had most to fear from in the way of rivalry, sought him out as soon as he came to town and invited him to dinner. "Liked him much," Macready wrote in his diary, "a noble appearance, and a manly, mild, and interesting demeanour. I welcomed him—wished him success."[82] The words were sincere enough as Macready wrote them, but the gesture must have cost him a mighty effort, for he was constitutionally a jealous man, and in the fall of 1836 almost a frightened one. He was just emerging from what William Archer called "The Doldrums" of his career,[83] a decade of service under unsympathetic managers, without remarkable additions to his store of new vehicles or remarkable advancement in performing the classics. Barely six months earlier he had knocked down and beaten the most unsympathetic of all managers, Alfred Bunn, and all summer had endured burning shame as the assault case dragged through the newspapers and the court. Although generally recognized in literary and artistic circles as first in his profession, Macready as yet held no real command over the general public, and he dwelt in sickly fear that one rival or another would usurp his honors and spoil his means of livelihood. The diary entry in which he recorded the wish for Forrest's success concludes with a timorous qualifier: "This I could *sincerely wish*, while it did no injury to myself; but my home is so dear to me that charity must satisfy itself there before it can range abroad." When he read the *Times*'s opinion that Forrest was "more spirited than any tragic actor now on the stage," he was deeply depressed, his heart "chafed, bruised, and almost crushed." When Forrest played Othello, Macready, being scheduled for it the very next night, was thrown into a fret ("It is of great importance to me to retain my superiority"); and every glowing review that Forrest's Othello got seemed in effect an attack upon his own.

Yet he bottled his spleen and behaved outwardly with

When he played Othello, some thought his Othello greater than Kean's; when he played Lear, some thought he improved over his Othello. Macbeth seemed to some a little tame in comparison to Lear and Othello, yet the *Morning Chronicle* chose the occasion of Macbeth to declare that he "brings to the performance of Shakespeare's heroes an energy and vigor, tempered with a taste and judgment, such as we rarely find combined in any who venture to tread the stage." Shot through the reviews are expressions of amazement and gratification at his Hercu-

absolute propriety—sent Forrest a congratulatory note after his opening; introduced him at dinner to Talfourd the dramatist, Browning the poet, and Blanco White the theologian; toasted Forrest at a banquet in his honor at the Garrick Club. As Forrest reported in a letter home, Macready "has behaved in the handsomest manner to me . . . he has extended to me many delicate courtesies and attentions, all showing the native kindness of his heart, and great refinement and good breeding."[84]

Only one bone would stick in Forrest's throat. Every notice of him which appeared in the *Examiner* was vigorously hostile, and the theatre critic for the *Examiner* was Macready's close friend and adviser John Forster; the story was out that Forster had once said that "no man should succeed as a first actor while Macready was on the stage."[85] Forster was not alone in the opposition, but he was certainly conspicuous; no one could mistake that his intention was to cut Forrest down to size. And Forrest's many associates—Bunn the manager, the American impresario Stephen Price, his personal agent Willis Jones, and countless Macready-haters in the profession—would gleefully affirm the obvious, that Forster wrote at Macready's bidding.

The fact of the matter was that Forster wrote *in spite of* Macready's bidding. Macready anticipated the stand that Forster would take and, fearing the consequences, on October 20 sent him a note "urging him to deal liberally and kindly by Forrest." On the twenty-third, Forster's first review appeared, damning *The Gladiator* and just barely suspending judgment on its executant. On October 27 Macready called on Forster and requested him "not to write in harshness or hostility upon his performance." But Forster had made up his mind—had doubtless already written his *Othello* review—and "was very peremptory and distinct in his expressed resolution to keep his own course." The review was devastating. Macready thought it "ill-natured and not just," and when Forster came in that day "I expressed candidly my dissatisfaction to him." Forster, however, would not sacrifice critical principle to playhouse politics, not even to accommodate his friend, so the reviews of Lear and Damon, which followed in November, adhered to the line of argument he had already laid down. He could not in conscience yield even to Macready's mid-December proposal, at the end of Forrest's run, that he write "a courteous valedictory notice . . . , disclaiming personal feelings and paying a tribute to his private character."

Illus. 50. Drawing of John Forster by Daniel Maclise.

When it had become obvious to Macready in mid-November that he could not dissuade Forster from his course, he caught at a chance meeting with Forrest's agent Willis Jones to establish his credit in the opposing camp. Acknowledging frankly that Forster was his particular friend, he dissociated himself from Forster's doings: "I begged to assure him that . . . I had used all my influence with him—by word of mouth, by writing, and by the mediation of friends, to induce him to abandon his intention of expressing an unfavourable opinion." Jones presumably carried this explanation back to camp, and Forrest must have accepted Macready's word at face value. In the full flush of his London victory he could afford to do so. At any rate, peace prevailed between these opposites, at least on the surface, for another decade.

A close reading of Forster's critiques of Forrest reveals why he would not give in to any pressure to desist.[86] These critiques are by no means the friend-serving or merely political hatchet jobs that Forrest's biographers have always claimed them to be: they are carefully worked-up analyses of "a vicious style in art which the public taste should be carefully guarded against." Forster did not depend upon easy assumptions ("hidden or obscure generalities") to prove his case but offered in evidence dozens of precise examples of what Forrest was actually doing upon the stage. In the earlier pieces Forster expressed regret for taking the hard line against an actor who did at least exhibit *power*; but politeness soon gave way to indignation (to sarcasm and even the spirit of caricature): Forrest ceased to matter as a person and became only a negative example of what the tragic actor ought to do and be.

Forster accused Forrest of the elementary fault of *literalism*—that is, of imposing upon a line or scene some directly illustrative but quite uncalled-for stage business, while completely missing the Shakespearean significance of the matter. Thus when Othello says to Desdemona, "Your napkin is too little," we know that he is speaking distractedly, that his thoughts are far away, fixed on his own shame or on horrid images of adultery but not at all on handkerchiefs. Forrest, however, brought the matter down to insignificant fact: he deliberately thrust the handkerchief from her hand, pointed at it emphatically as he said, "Your napkin," and then ran his finger across his forehead as he said "is too little." When in Othello's death speech his "eyes / Albeit unused to the melting mood / Drops tears," Forrest rubbed his hand over his forearm as if to wipe away tears which had literally fallen there. Similarly when Richard of Gloucester slays King Henry, at "See how my sword weeps for the poor king's death," Forrest shook his sword violently to assure the audience that it was really dripping blood. He had a way of trimming from ironic lines everything except their plain dictionary meaning. Thus when Macbeth, amazed by his Lady's grand scheme to murder Duncan, pays tribute to her boldness with the exclamation, "Bring forth men-children only," Forrest, "by his elaboration of the words, gave them the air of a positive instruction, just as if he were telling her ladyship to go to bed, or to prepare his posset." In Forrest's Lear, Forster detected many such literal readings and many examples of literalizing stage business. The entire conception of Lear, in fact, was an oppressive literalism: "Mr. Forrest played Lear as a 'foolish fond old man.' He expressed weakness tolerably well; he shed an abundance of tears; he made the most of the feeble stare and the cold bewilderment of madness; and he walked as a very old person might be supposed

to walk. But this is not Lear, nor in any way allied to Lear. Lear is old, but the Heavens themselves are old, and in this sublime identification of his own age with theirs, we behold the sublime analogy of his sorrows." As Forster would say in another review, "It is always thus with the poet and his merciless translator into prose. A matter of fact is insisted on . . . while the beauty or grandeur is thrust out of sight."

All of that relentless literalism was part and parcel of the actor's preoccupation with pointmaking. Forster ascribed the worst offenses of this kind partly to Forrest's having borrowed Edmund Kean's "more vulgar and ob-

Illus. 51. Edwin Forrest as Macbeth.

Illus. 52. Edwin Forrest as Othello.

cause of the danger and secrecy of the scene, and because he is listening for mysterious sounds. But first Forrest had to make his point: "As Lady Macbeth waits his entrance in breathless suspense, his back appears at the door of Duncan's chamber, and with outstretched hands holding the bloody daggers, his face still gazing out the door, Mr. Forrest moves over the stage with an elaborately noiseless step, until a touch from the hand of Miss Huddart at the opposite side gives him the opportunity, after a violent start, of throwing his body into one tremendous convulsion—which he does forthwith to the great delight of the injudicious." As Othello, by way of winding up with a striking effect at the close of the great speech "If I do prove her haggard"—having worked his way through outrage, self-pity, hatred, and tenderness, and having brought off the tremendous "I had rather be a toad / And live upon the vapor of a dungeon"—Forrest "literally sprang back with the demivolte of a fencer up the stage, and, catching his glimpse of the coming Desdemona, threw himself into a sort of tenderly gladiatorial position, and waited for the vollies of applause that broke from the stalls and the galleries."

These grander claptraps could be seen at a glance (and were mostly applauded) by anyone. By closer, sharper scanning of Forrest's methods, Forster discovered a more fundamental and more pervasive fault, which in his review of *The Gladiator* he labeled "a want of fusion" or the inability to work "a harmony with differents." The process would begin whenever Forrest would pick out a word from context and lay a heavy emotional reading onto it, whether or not the emotion was called for in the sense of the line. "Where a tender word occurred, it was spoken tenderly," said Forster; "where a fierce word, fiercely." Thus as Othello narrates the course of his wooing, at the line "And often did beguile her of her tears," Forrest put a whine on "her tears" as if sympathetically reenacting Desdemona's pain or pathos. He liked especially to make quick switches between violently contrasting emotions. Thus in "Yield up, O love, thy crown and hearted throne / To tyrannous hate," he would utter the first line in the most affectingly tender way, and the final half-line with sudden fierceness. Or he would give "If thou dost slander her" in a tone of African fierceness, and then "and torture me" in accents of whining self-pity. "Why," said Forster, "in such passages as these, Othello could no more stop the boiling of his blood to indulge in such petty changes, than the path of lightning could be stopped." Every passage

vious points," and partly to Forrest's own laborious invention. A pair of prize specimens in *Macbeth* bracketed the murder of Duncan. Macbeth has just concluded the Dagger soliloquy: "As he steals into the chamber of Duncan, a peal of thunder is heard—he starts back, gasps at the audience, slowly recovers, and disappears in the midst of the applause of galleries and orchestra." A minute later he would top that non-Shakespearean thunder with a spectacularly non-Shakespearean pantomime. Macbeth is supposed to enter from Duncan's chamber and say, "I have done the deed," half-whispering, presumably, be-

of Forrest's Othello throughout the third and fourth acts
"was broken up into little fierce bursts of passion, con-
trasted with heavy drawlings of tenderness," and any
word that could make a point was wrenched from its place
so that the point could have its way. But nothing, Forster
insisted, is less susceptible to pointing than Othello's passion: "It is grand, concentrated, massive. It is a movement of life or death. We can conceive the passion of an
ordinary jealousy full of points and peaks, and running
into narrow nooks or estuaries—but this is not the passion
of Othello's jealousy. His whole being is at issue."

While Forrest was busy with the irrelevancies and the
minutiae of pointmaking, he generally neglected to build
up the greater emotional structures through which his
characters were supposed to work, so that when the climactic explosions came they seemed to come from nowhere. He played Lear's opening scene so slowly that
"we had little of the turbulent greatness or of the royal
impatience of Lear." In the approach to the cursing of
Goneril he was "settled into such comparative calmness,
that the Curse itself, suddenly following, appeared to
have sprung on the instant from a bad and merely violent
impulse of passion." His great final speech in the second
act went for nothing because in the preceding quarrels
with his daughters he blurred his imperial image with
countless touches of pathos, humble begging, and self-
pity. He entered into the Storm Scene by no means "con-
tending with the fretful elements," but walking slowly
and speaking "with a deliberate and stop-watch emphasis
which reminded us of our old exercises at the breaking
up of school." As Othello his emotional build-up toward
the murder of Desdemona was almost nonexistent. As
soon as Desdemona woke, crying, "Who's there?" he left
her bedside, seated himself calmly on a sofa, and conducted his inquiry from that relaxed position. The murder, when it came, seemed quite unmotivated, an Old
Bailey affair.

In reviewing *Macbeth* Forster came to the conclusion
that except for externals Forrest did not see much difference between one tragic hero and another. His Macbeth
"is no more than Richard the Third disguised in tartan.
. . . Not a single ray of the genius of Shakespeare's wonderful Macbeth flickered upon Mr. Forrest from the commencement to the close." It was all too insensitive and
crudely physical. Such meditative, wondering lines as
"The greatest is behind" and "I am the Thane of Cawdor,"
which are in fact buried in soliloquy, Forrest roared out

Illus. 53. Edwin Forrest as King Lear.

exultingly—even, on the second of these, thumping himself on the chest with his truncheon. The Dagger speech was delivered in "a series of gaspings, grimacings, and convulsions." In the Banquet Scene, "We never saw an unhappy ghost so bullied and bellowed at." At "Tomorrow and tomorrow and tomorrow," he stalked about the stage rattling his truncheon. When the Officer drove him to despair with the news that Birnam Wood was moving, he "exhibited a most lusty despair, for . . . he lifted the unfortunate officer bodily from the ground and fairly flung him off the stage." In short, "Will and passion are the sole characteristics of the performance. . . . Everything is sacrificed to a seeking after such coarse effects as may happen to lie on the mere surface of words wrenched from the general text; and what the result may be as a whole, whether to leave the impression of a Macbeth or a Macheath is a matter of no earthly importance." Undoubtedly much of the animus of Forster's half-dozen reviews of Forrest was an indulgence of his own Forrest-like combativeness—his pugilistic instinct to bring down a doughty opponent with a knockout blow. Yet apart from their deliberate one-sidedness, one must acknowledge that these reviews are rooted in critical principle. Furthermore, since Forster had to back his hostile judgments with incontrovertible evidence, he has preserved more exact images of what Forrest actually did upon the stage than dozens of merely encomiastic reviewers.

When Macready made his second trip to America in the autumn of 1843, he had long since worked his way out of "The Doldrums." Veteran now of two famous stands as manager at the two patent theatres—producer of the fashionable new dramas of Talfourd and Bulwer, producer and "restorer" of Shakespeare—he had fairly won the right to be billed as "The Eminent Tragedian." He arrived in New York by way of Boston in a glow of well-being, remembering tenderly the Pilgrim Fathers, those "fervent, stern, resolute, and trusting men, who, in their faith in God, became the authors of all the glorious and happy life I saw about me." He was even charmed by "the natural politeness and hearty, kind feeling" of the customs inspector who went through his luggage.[87]

Forrest welcomed him cordially, repaying every social courtesy Macready had paid to him in London. He called on Macready at least four times at his hotel, took him out to be daguerreotyped, drove him uptown to inspect the city's grand new reservoir, entertained him at dinner with distinguished company, among them the poets Halleck and Bryant and the painter Henry Inman. "I like all I see of Forrest very much," Macready wrote in his diary. "He appears a clear-headed, honest, kind man; what can be better?"[88]

But in Philadelphia on October 21 he saw Forrest act—for the first time since 1826 when he had seen his William Tell. The role was King Lear. In something like dismay he recorded his judgment of Forrest's performance:

I had a very high opinion of his powers of mind when I saw him exactly seventeen years ago; I said then, if he would cultivate those powers and really study, where, as in England, his taste could be formed, he would make one of the very first actors of this or any day. But I thought he would not do so, as his countrymen were, by their extravagant applause, possessing him with the idea . . . that it was unnecessary. I reluctantly, as far as my feelings towards him are interested, record my opinion that my prophetic soul foresaw the consequence. He has great physical power. But I could discern no imagination, no original thought, no poetry at all in his acting.

All muscle. No intellect. No imagination! In Forrest's rendering of Lear's rage Macready acknowledged strength, but neither grandeur nor pathos. Too much of the performance, on the other hand, he found quiet, and the quiet parts were frequently inaudible. The audience applauded often and vehemently, but what were they applauding? "The disgusting trash of Tate!" ("But an actor to speak the words of Tate—with Shakspeare's before him—I think criticizes his own performance.") At this point we must remember Macready's proprietary interest in the play. Only five years earlier he had staged a version of it at Covent Garden, purged of every syllable of the wretched Tate. The fame of his restoration had spread far and wide, and reasonably he might think it laggard of the leading tragedian of America not to have followed suit. "Of Forrest's representation I should like to say that it was like the part—false taste. In fact, I did not think it the performance of an artist. I did not like his curse—it was anything. In the storm . . . he walked on in perfect quietude; there was throughout nothing *on* his mind, fastened *on* and tearing and convulsing it with agony, and certainly his frenzy 'was not like madness.' His recognition of Cordelia the same. *He did not fully comprehend his poet.*" Macready's pen then rambled on to other matters, but haunted by thoughts of Forrest he came back to him. There was much to praise in the evening's perfor-

mance, but "he has not enriched, refined, elevated, and enlarged his *mind*; it is very much where it was, in the
matter of poetry and art, when I last saw him. . . . He
had all the qualifications, all the material out of which to
build up a great artist, an actor for all the world. He is
now only an actor for the less intelligent of the Americans." With that dreadful dismissal the diary entry ends,
except for a dutiful afterthought: "But he is something
better—an upright and well-intentioned man."

It could be argued, of course, in the light of Macready's
ingrained, automatic jealousy, that deep in his heart he
was not at all dismayed, but actually gratified, to discover
faults in a rival. Yet Macready was not writing for publication or even addressing a friend. He was talking to
himself, and for at least a rare moment he genuinely re-
gretted what he had seen.

As the year went on, Macready had reason to wonder
about Forrest's good intentions. Wherever he went to
play, Forrest went also, either simultaneously, if the town
had a second theatre, or else immediately afterward. Then
too, Forrest took to billing himself as "The National Tragedian," so that he seemed not only to be competing with
"The Eminent Tragedian" but to be stirring up hostility
to the "foreigner."[89] One night in Philadelphia he played
Richelieu on the same night that Macready played it, and
later on a Philadelphia manager annoyed Macready by
proposing to engage them both to play the same roles on
alternate nights. When Macready was finishing his run
in far-off New Orleans, Forrest arrived there, too, and he
followed Macready to Mobile, to New Orleans again, and
to Cincinnati. In September of 1844 Forrest rescheduled
his Philadelphia engagement in order to play at the Walnut Street Theatre while Macready was at the Chestnut,
and he put up Hamlet on a night when he knew Macready
was to play it. "This," Macready wrote, "is not the English generosity of rivalry." Through all this professional
jockeying they maintained social relations, exchanged
calls, preserved at least a show of amiability. But under
the surface Macready's temperature was rising: when
Forrest drew a slim house on his Hamlet night, Macready
put it down as a just punishment for "ungentlemanly conduct."[90]

In January of 1845 Forrest went abroad again, and he
acted in England, mainly in the provinces, until September of 1846. His excursion ran into trouble from the first.
He had announced that he would play in Paris, tying his
expected welcome there to the political sympathies of the
two nations. A French paper which called him the "Talma

de l'Amérique" quoted him as believing that "la nation
française n'a point oublié que c'est à l'exemple de l'Amérique qu'elle doit son initiation à la grande cause de la liberté humaine."[91] He was one of the most eloquent spokes-
men of the Democratic party, the paper declared, and had
once been considered as a candidate for Congress. The
public would be especially attracted to his role of the Indian Metamora, "qu'il rend avec tant de l'énergie et de
sauvage vérité."

Unfortunately he had neglected to secure an engagement in advance, and when he arrived in Paris, Col. John
Mitchell, the impresario who handled English-speaking
performers there, declined to receive him. In after years
he would insist that Macready, who was playing under
Mitchell's management at that moment, had prevented
his engagement. The charge was unproved and extremely
doubtful. It is more likely that for reasons of his own
Mitchell preferred not, in the days of Louis Philippe, to
sponsor so well-advertised a champion of "la grande cause
de la liberté humaine."

The theatres of London just then, two years after repeal
of the Theatre Licensing Act, were in sorry disarray.
Alfred Bunn, controlling Drury Lane, rejected the acting
drama and staged nothing but opera. Covent Garden did
not open at all until Boxing Day, and then for thirty
nights only, most of which would be devoted to a semi-
operatic production of *Antigone*. Managers of the minor
houses were not yet ready to subject their regular audiences to the rigors of the Higher Drama. Thus, for instance, when Macready got home from Paris, he spent
the whole winter and spring, from February to mid-June,
in the provinces. But the manager of the Princess's Theatre, J. M. Maddox, caught at the novel notion of presenting two American actors simultaneously. Abandoning for
the moment his established pattern of light entertainment, he announced in mid-February that he would give
a series of tragedies starring the famous Edwin Forrest
and, supporting him, an actress hitherto unknown in
London, Charlotte Cushman.

The engagement, which began on February 17, was a
serious disappointment to Forrest. He got in eighteen
performances—Othello twice, Macbeth five times, Lear
six times, Damon once, Metamora four times—but only
Lear seems to have come off successfully.[92] Something
went wrong with the Othello which he opened with. Although several reviewers praised him for being "more
quiet, chaste, and subdued" than he had been nine years
earlier, the *Times* remarked that his acting "somewhat

took the audience by surprise by its total difference from his former manner," and thought he was perhaps too deliberate, too tame. Did the audience hiss him? According to the Reverend Alger (and all of Forrest's subsequent biographers) they certainly did: "He was saluted with a shower of hisses, proceeding from three solid bodies of claqueurs, packed in three different parts of the house. . . . Beyond any doubt it was a systematic plan arranged in advance under the stimulus of national prejudice and personal interest."[93] Yet, as William Archer reported long ago, diligent search through reviews of that performance fails to discover any mention of even one hiss.[94] The *Times*, indeed, tells us that he was "welcomed heartily" at the beginning of the evening and "cheered heartily" at the end by a crowded house.

But the performance was not the triumph that Forrest expected. The reviews were briefer than usual, and lukewarm. Some of the critics complained of boredom, some of Yankee speech. The *Spectator*, which had never been kind to him, now slashed him without mercy: "His passion is a violent effort of physical vehemence. He bullies Iago, and treats Desdemona with brutal ferocity: even his tenderness is affected, and his smile is like the grin of a wolf showing his fangs. The killing of Desdemona was a cold-blooded butchery."[95] What perhaps nettled Forrest as much as the falling away of his own support was the enthusiasm with which the critics greeted Miss Cushman in the secondary role of Emilia. One declared that any success the engagement might have would be owing to her.

His Macbeth, which followed, was a disaster. The *Times* and various other papers looked the other way and printed nothing. Those who did review it attacked Forrest or tiptoed around him and praised Cushman's Lady Macbeth to the limit. Miss Cushman herself is the witness nearest to the event. As she wrote to her mother, "Susan [her sister] will not be sorry to hear that Forrest has failed most dreadfully. In *Macbeth* they shouted with laughter and hissed him to death. . . . The papers cut him all to pieces."[96] She had to go through with a week of Lady Macbeth while Forrest sulked and behaved rudely toward her, but after that she declined to support him further and worked out her contract with Maddox in Rosalind, Mrs. Haller, and other roles of her own choosing.

If Lear won back some lost ground for Forrest (the *Times* reviewer thought that if he had opened with Lear his whole engagement might have been successful), he

gambled it all away again with his last attempt to convert London taste to original American drama. The critics looked on *Metamora* in stunned amazement. It was far more offensive to them than *The Gladiator* had been. It was "senseless," it was "utter rubbish." In playing it, said the *Spectator*, "he spoke like a braggart beating the air with big words, and only seemed in earnest when butchery was to be done [this refers to the stabbing of his wife Nahmeokee to save her from dishonor]; then, indeed, he nerved his arm and whetted his fangs as if he snuffed blood."[97] And since the role of Metamora was so closely styled to Forrest's own figure, personality, mannerisms, and acting technique, the general distaste for it spread an ugly stain over all the work he had done in better roles. After April 7 he went off to the provinces, where he found more congenial audiences. Particularly among the Irish ("in whom," as he would say, "misrule and tyranny have failed to quench one spark of generous spirit") did his brand of heroic resistance strike sympathetic response.[98]

In after years Forrest would insist that his comparative failure in London in 1845 was brought about by the machinations of Macready and his "toady" John Forster, and he said it so frequently and emphatically that doubtless he came to believe it himself. They were the ones, he declared, who set up the "organized emissaries" who hissed him on his opening night; Forster, he claimed, not only wrote destructive reviews for the *Examiner* but suborned critics on other papers to attack him. It was a remarkable case of paranoia.

In the first place, such behavior would be totally out of character for either of the accused. Although many a hard word was spoken against Macready for his arrogance, cantankerousness, jealousy, and harshness to subordinates, and against Forster for his pugnacity and bullheaded assertiveness, no one could ever lay to them the charge of dishonesty. In the second place, there were no "organized emissaries" hissing on the opening night. Macready was in far-off Newcastle just then, and throughout Forrest's run he was touring in the North. When he did return to London about March 1 in order to celebrate his birthday with his family, he called on the Forrests at their quarters—not, probably, with a heart brimming with affection but as a matter of social decency.[99] Indeed, as he later noted in his diary (November 24, 1848), in subsequent months Forrest "returned mine and my wife's several visits, and met me on friendly terms *outwardly*." The *Examiner* hardly noticed Forrest during this engagement, devoting only a four-sentence squib each to *Othello*, *Macbeth*, and *Metamora*. These squibs were hostile, but Forster did not write them: he was "confined to his bed with a rheumatic fever during the whole period, and some weeks before and after."[100] On this last point the Reverend Alger, perhaps inadvertently, muddied the waters by printing four scraps of hostile criticism and presenting them in such a way that later writers have attributed them to Forster.[101] The Macbeth scrap is from the *Examiner* but was not written by Forster; the Othello and Lear scraps are not from the *Examiner* but from the *Spectator*; the Richard III scrap was indeed written by Forster but as part of his much longer review in the *Examiner* nine years earlier.

Alger could tell the story only as Forrest had told it to him and had been telling it for decades. The truth is that the hostility between Forrest and Macready did not break out into open feud until a year later, on the night of March 2, 1846, in Edinburgh, when Forrest sounded the hiss heard round the world.[102] The paranoiac fiction developed only as a cover-up to that shocking event.

Macready was playing Hamlet that night at the Edinburgh Theatre Royal. Just before the Court gathered for the Play Scene, at "I must be idle," Macready executed his customary expression of indifference by waving a handkerchief about and strutting back and forth across the front of the stage. Suddenly "a man on the right side of the stage—upper boxes or gallery, but said to be upper boxes—hissed!" Macready turned pale at the sound, then livid with rage, bowed derisively toward the hisser, and staggered back to sink into a chair. Someone yelled, "Throw him out!" The hisser rose solemnly, faced the house for a moment, turned, and slowly left his box. "Then Macready like a man possessed, leaped into the breach and took the audience by storm," reported an actor who was present. "Surely he must have been inspired by the ordeal through which he had passed. Such a delirium of excitement for actors and audience as followed that Play Scene and the Closet Scene I have rarely, if ever, witnessed."[103]

The hisser was Forrest. Numerous witnesses guessed that it was he, and the fact was confirmed on April 4 when he published a letter in the *Times* not only claiming the action but affirming the correctness of it: he was simply exercising his right as a spectator to criticize Macready's "fancy dance," which he took to be a desecration of Shakespeare's play.

On his return to America in late summer of 1846 For-

rest received a hero's welcome. He had already gone far toward inventing the past. In a curtain speech to a New York audience he spoke of "that narrow, exclusive, prejudiced, and I may add, anti-American feeling which prescribes geographical limits to the growth of genius and talent."[104] At a public dinner in his honor he told how he had been abused by the London press: how some had threatened him with "critical castigation" before he even arrived there, and how "some of the very journals which, upon my former appearance in London, applauded me to the echo, now assailed me with bitterest denunciations." Yet he had trusted to "the people" to approve him, and finally, indeed, their applause "rebuked the malice of the hireling scribblers, and defeated the machinations of theatrical *cliques* by whom these scribblers were suborned."[105]

The final act of this drama of Forrest versus Macready is an often-told story. In the autumn of 1848, when Macready arrived in the States for his third visit, the popular press was already fanning fires under the brush pile. Some praised Forrest for the "independence" he had exhibited at Edinburgh, others harped on Macready's age and effeteness, his "aristocratic" leanings, his stinginess. One theatre in New York was playing a farce called *Mr. Macgreedy; or, A Star at the Opera House.*

His first run of New York performances, beginning on October 4, was received cordially enough, and at Hamlet's "I must be idle," the business of the handkerchief was greeted with two rounds of applause. Probably he committed a tactical error in his opening-night curtain speech by referring to hostile American journalists and his "unknown accuser," for the insinuations only stung the opposition. When he went to Boston on October 30, the *Boston Mail* published a heavily headlined story by Forrest's press friend James Oakes, rehearsing all the anti-Macready charges that Forrest had made for the past two years and daring Macready to deny them.[106]

After Boston he went to Philadelphia, Forrest's hometown, where Forrest was waiting for him. There at the Arch Street Theatre between November 20 and December 2 Macready played eleven roles; at the Walnut Street, Forrest opposed him on the same nights in six of them. Macready's first audience, for *Macbeth*, spent most of the evening fighting with itself—the greater part applauding, the lesser part yelling, hooting, hissing, and occasionally tossing coins or an egg onto the stage. Macready made the most of such lines as "I dare do all that may become a man," pointing them directly toward whatever knots of

Illus. 54. Edwin Forrest as Richard III.

"scoundrels" he could locate. In his curtain speech he denied every allegation that had appeared in the press and reminded the audience that he himself "had been hissed in a public theatre by an American actor, an act which I believed no other American would have committed, and which I was certain no European actor would have been guilty of."[107] Infuriated by this, Forrest published a "Card" in the *Public Ledger* in which he demanded to know why Macready blamed only "an American actor" for the Edinburgh hiss. "Why not openly charge me with the act? for I *did* it, and publicly avowed it in the *Times* newspaper." His friends in New York, he said, had offered to drive Macready from the stage, but he had advised them to "let the superannuated driveller alone."[108] Macready responded with a Card of his own announcing that he was about to take action for libel. His lawyers dissuaded him from involvement in a court case, but he began to send for defense documents from friends and associates in England.

After Macready's rough opening night in Philadelphia the opposition dwindled. His final Hamlet "went off triumphantly": the audience not only applauded the handkerchief "fancy dance," which had become a test scene for Macready, but followed the applause with "cheers on cheers." His farewell speech to the Philadelphians expressed his gratitude to them for defending him from "the grossest outrage, the grossest injustice."[109] After a week's layover in New York he abandoned the fields of battle and set off on a tour of the South.

New Orleans, just recovered from a cholera epidemic and starved for first-class entertainment, welcomed Macready rapturously. For four solid weeks, from February 12 to March 10, he played to great houses every night, nearly exhausting his repertory (eleven Shakespeares and five non-Shakespeares)—a success which he acknowledged he could not have expected had he all the population of London to draw upon.[110] Although his diary entries for this period are as grumbling as usual, and more than usually sparse, the New Orleans engagement was a golden interlude in this season of outrage, danger, and catastrophe. The *Picayune* and *Delta* reviewers called up superlatives to praise him with, the public chose to swell his benefit by taking their tickets at auction, and on March 20 at the Verandah Hotel a great banquet was given in his honor. Behind the speaker's table hung a huge portrait of the actor; before him at dessert time appeared a model of Shakespeare's house at Stratford and a temple of Thespis done in pastry. It was a rather conspicuously anti-

Forrestian occasion. Toasts were drunk to the three major British playwrights of the day—Knowles, Talfourd, and Bulwer—whose works Macready had first brought upon the stage; to the American actresses Charlotte Cushman and Anna Cora Mowatt, who were just then successfully carrying the torch for American art upon the English stage; and to the everlasting amity of Great Britain and the United States, joined by common language, literature, and theatrical tradition. Macready rose to the occasion with an almost unbelievably euphoric address to the banqueters. The *Picayune*, publishing it verbatim (with the cheers), described it as a "fine effusion of oratory, in which patriotism, philanthropy, and genuine feeling were so forcibly expressed."[111]

As he moved back toward New York the drums of disaster began to rumble. Their first sounding, at his opening night in Cincinnati, was as ridiculous as it was ominous: midway in the Recorders Scene in *Hamlet* a ruffian in the gallery threw onto the stage half of a dead sheep.[112] But the tone deepened then as newspapers hinted that in New York conflict was mounting between the friends of Forrest and the friends of Macready. Word came that Forrest would be acting at the Broadway in opposition to Macready at the Opera House. Forrest began publishing letters "proving" Macready's crimes against him by citing Macready's supposed abusive treatment of other actors—G. V. Brooke and Charles Kean among them.[113] The *New York Herald*, speculating on the impending conflict, concluded its remarks with a cockfighter's cry, "Go it, my chickens!"[114]

On May 7, 1849, New York was invited to three *Macbeth*s. Thomas Hamblin played it to a packed house at the Bowery. Forrest played it at the Broadway "in a style of unsurpassed beauty," and brought his audience to its feet cheering as he underscored the line "What rhubarb, senna, or what purgative drug / Would scour these English hence?" At the Opera House the Bowery b'hoys arrived in great numbers for the *Macbeth* of Macready's opening night. At Macduff's entrance there broke out roars of applause and cheering, opposed by violent whistling and hissing.[115] By the entrance of Macbeth and Banquo the uproar was deafening. A torrent of groans and boos assaulted Macready, and pennies, apples, old shoes, potatoes, lemons, rotten eggs, and even a bottle of asafetida were hurled toward him as he proceeded through his speeches in seeming pantomime. Cries of "Off! Off!" were countered by "Go on! Go on!" Banners were held up proclaiming "You have proved yourself a liar!" and "No apol-

Illus. 55. Edwin Forrest and Charlotte Cushman in *Macbeth*,
Princess's Theatre production.

ogies—it is too late!" The play went on unheard. A mob outside battered at the front doors trying to force entrance. By the third act chairs were flying down from the gallery, making life on the stage and in the orchestra pit altogether too dangerous. Macready finally gave a signal to drop the curtain, while the rioters yelled, "Down with the English hog!" and "Three groans for the codfish aristocracy!" While the storm raged on in the auditorium, Macready's friends spirited him to his quarters through back streets.[116]

Macready would have left New York at once—and should have done so—but a stream of distinguished visitors and a petition signed by a committee of forty-seven prominent citizens, including Mordecai Noah, Evert Duyckinck, Washington Irving, and Herman Melville, insisted that he appear once more, assuring him that the outrages would not be repeated.

Throughout the day on May 10, Macready received assurances from well-wishers, city officials, and fellow actors that it would be "all right at night."[117] At the rehearsal, which Macready insisted on holding lest the excitement of Monday had put the stage business of *Macbeth* out of the actors' heads, all were in good spirits. Observing that the green carpet stunk of asafetida, Macready gave orders that it not be used in that night's performance. Meanwhile, however, outside the theatre the "Workingmen! Freemen!!" of the city were being exhorted by handbills to stand by their lawful rights and "express their

Illus. 56. The Astor Place Riot.

opinion this night at the English Aristocratic Opera House!!"

Near to performance time Macready went cheerfully to the theatre, pleased to observe a Harlem car delivering a load of policemen into Astor Place. When the curtain rose, there was noisy opposition, but not so much as on Monday, and after the fourth scene the police stormed the center of the main floor, hauled the rioters from their places, and locked them in rooms somewhere belowstairs. Still, though, hostile voices in the galleries kept up a din. Meanwhile many hundreds of "Workingmen" had gathered outside the building, and word that their freedom-loving brothers inside were being manhandled by the police maddened them. They stormed the entrances but were unable to force them. Tearing up paving stones, they hurled them at the windows of the building and at the police.

Macready was determined to fight to the end. Since the actors onstage were not physically endangered, he insisted that they continue:

The fourth act passed: louder and more fierce waxed the furious noises . . . ; for whenever a missile did effectual mischief in its discharge, it was hailed with shouts outside; stones came in through the windows, and one struck the chandelier; the audience removed for protection behind the walls; the house was considerably thinned, gaps of unoccupied seats appearing in the audience part. The fifth act was heard, and in the very spirit of resistance I flung my whole soul into every word I uttered, acting my very best and exciting the audience to a sympathy even with the glowing words of fiction, whilst these dreadful deeds of real crime and outrage were roaring at intervals in our ears and rising to madness all round us. The death of Macbeth was loudly cheered, and on being lifted up and told that I was called, I went on, and, with action earnestly and most emphatically expressive of my sympathy with them and my feelings of gratefulness to them, I quitted the New York stage amid the acclamations of those before me.

He did not know until he was dressing that the military had arrived.

From about nine o'clock a detachment of cavalry with sabers and infantry with guns confronted the mob but could not persuade them to disperse. Not even the first round of gunfire convinced them, and they began to shout that the cartridges were blank and to pelt the soldiers with stones. One image fixed in the records of that night catches the madness of the occasion and links it to the climax of a hundred melodramas and scenes from the barricades: "A grimed and burly ruffian with a huge stone between his knees, exposing with both hands his bare breast covered with a red flannel shirt, cried: 'Fire into this. Take the life out of a free-born American for a bloody British actor! Do it. Ay, You darsn't.'" Some say the soldiers fired three volleys, some say four. Thirty-one persons were killed, and no one knows how many more were wounded in that night's work.

Forrest continued to act, except when gout and other ailments prevented him, for nearly a quarter of a century longer, and to the end he could find admiring audiences across the country; yet early in the second half of the century his leadership and influence in the theatre began to decline. The Astor Place Riot lowered his credit with cultivated and genteel folk, who, to be sure, had never been quite at ease with him. Although no one could accuse him of directing the riot, he obviously did nothing to prevent it. Although he could not alone have infected the whole nation with the xenophobia which was rampant in the late 1840s, he contributed to it. His hatred of Macready was on public record; it fueled and sparked the local passions out of which the riot grew.

In 1851 came Forrest's wretched divorce case, which blighted his public image further. When he attempted to divorce his wife on grounds of adultery, her lawyers turned the case around and sued *him* for divorce on the same grounds. He lost. Blown up by his own petard and condemned as an adulterer, he was ordered by the court to pay his wife $3,000 a year alimony. This he bullishly refused to do and insisted on carrying his case to "the people." Thereafter certain of his principal roles became briefs for the defense. Othello's fancied wrongs became his real ones, and he underscored every line in the play which conveyed that message. As for Lear, "By God, I *am* King Lear"—a man more sinned against than sinning. His audiences roared their approval, but there was no turning back the court's judgment. In the long run he lost the alimony and a good deal of esteem in quarters that mattered, too.

As early as the mid-fifties a young avant-garde critic

named Adam Badeau would be dismissing Forrest as passé, a rather vulgar giant outside the charmed circle of "artists." Breathing the heady perfume of neoromanticism—of Louis Gottschalk's music and Tennyson's lyrics, of Dumas, Verdi, and the Brontës, of Turner's paintings

Illus. 57. Catherine Sinclair Forrest. Courtesy of the Harvard Theatre Collection.

and the rise of the Hudson River School—Badeau had no stomach for Forrest's muscle and thunder. He moves us, Badeau said, but he does not inspire us. He excites horror but not the sublime terror which is the end of tragedy.[118] The future of tragic acting lay with a beautiful young man with great dark eyes, a musical voice, and gentle manners, whose name was Edwin Booth.

In 1857 "rheumatic inflammability" (the gout) drove Forrest into a three-year retirement, but in 1860 he returned to the stage, where his box-office appeal suffered no abatement. Amid the rising social angers and through the war years the Forrestian brand of heroics was quite to the taste of a vast public craving release in vicarious action. One balmy evening in the autumn of 1863, George William Curtis was asked by a friend from the country for a tour of the town. First they visited a political meeting at the Cooper Institute, then Forrest at Niblo's Garden. Forrest was not playing Shakespeare that evening, but *Damon and Pythias*, yet Curtis's genre painting of Forrest playing before the admiring throng tells us as much about Forrest's kind of Shakespeare as we can read anywhere.

We paid our money at the little hole, where the strange being within must have a marvelous opportunity for studying the human hand, and entered the theatre hall at Niblo's. It was crammed with people. All the seats were full, and the aisles, and the steps. And the people sat upon the stairs that ascend to the second tier, and they hung upon the balustrade, and they peeped over shoulders and between heads, and everything wore the aspect of a first night, of a *début*. And yet it was the thirty or forty somethingth night of the engagement. And every year he plays how many hundred nights? And people are grandfathers now who used to see him play in their youth. Yet there he is—the neck, the immemorial legs —the *ah-h-h-h-h*, in the same hopeless depth of guttural gloom. . . . But the crowd is the perennial amazement. For it is not to be explained upon the theory of deadheads. The crowd comes every night to behold Metamora, and Damon, and Richelieu, because it delights in the representation, and shouts at it, and cries for more, and hastens and squeezes the next night to enjoy it all over again. Certainly there was never a more genuine or permanent success than the acting of Forrest. We may crack our jokes at it. We may call it the muscular school; the brawny art; the biceps aesthetics; the tragic calves; the bovine drama; rant, roar, and rigmarole; but what then? Metamora folds his mighty arms and plants his mighty legs, and with his mighty voice sneers at us "Look there!" until the very ground thrills and trembles under our feet. For there is the great, the eager, the delighted crowd. He has found his πού στῶ.[119] And he moves his world nightly.

Illus. 58. Edwin Forrest reading Shakespeare in Steinway Hall in the last year of his life. Courtesy of the Harvard Theatre Collection.

One should no more criticize this as acting, Curtis said, than one criticizes the stories of Mary Elizabeth Braddon. No human beings ever talked or acted as they do in the Forrest drama or the Braddon novel. It is only a boundless exaggeration of all the conventions of the stage.

You have seen and heard exactly the same thing a hundred times, with more or less excellence. I say excellence, because it is certainly very complete in its way. The life of "the stage" was never more adequately depicted. It is the sock-and-buskin view of nature and emotion. And it has a palpable physical effect. There were a great many young women around us crying in the tender passages between Damon and his wife. They were not refined nor intellectual women. They were, perhaps, rather coarse. But they cried good hearty tears. And when, upon the temptation to escape, Pythias slapped his breast, and, pushing open the prison-door with what may be turned "a theatrical air," roared out, "Never, never!—death before dishonor!" the audience broke out into a storm of applause.[120]

When Curtis and his friend had had enough of this, they walked a little way up the street into another generation: at the Winter Garden they caught a few scenes of Edwin Booth's Iago. The house there was filled, but not crowded, by a polite audience. The actor—pale, thin, intellectual, with long black hair and dark eyes, looking exactly like Thomas Hicks's masterly portrait of him in the part— was playing the subtle Iago admirably. The audience, paying quiet attention, seemed to be both expecting and appreciating his fine points. With sophisticated theatre-goers like these, the Forrestian mode of massive over-statement was steadily passing out of fashion.

CHARLOTTE CUSHMAN

Charlotte Cushman (1816–76), commonly held to be the greatest American actress of the nineteenth century and the only American of her generation to achieve a thoroughgoing success in theatres abroad, became a Shakespearean only by accident.[121] She had meant to be an opera singer. During her Boston girlhood, or tomboy-hood, she developed a strong contralto voice. Unfortunately the teacher-director to whose training she committed herself forced her into soprano roles, which she could not manage, and in her first professional engagement, at the St. Charles Theatre in New Orleans in the winter of 1835–36, she failed abysmally. The critics deplored her Countess Almaviva in *The Marriage of Figaro* and ridiculed or ignored her further operatic efforts. She persisted relentlessly, however, through what must have been a spirit-killing four months, in the course of which she damaged her voice so badly that a career as a singer was out of the question.

The manager of the St. Charles, James Caldwell, did not dismiss her, as a merely sensible manager would have done; he advised her to abandon opera in favor of straight acting, turned her over for coaching to James Barton, an old-style tragedian in the St. Charles company, and set her on course for a proper dramatic debut as Lady Macbeth. Barton, who had known Sarah Siddons, evidently recognized in the nineteen-year-old novice the potential

of Siddonian power. She was tall and big-boned, almost mannish; her face, though flat and homely, was expressive; her voice, having been "ruined," was still a powerful speaking instrument, and it was fascinatingly husky —James Murdoch referred to its "woody or veiled tone . . . being Nature's mode of utterance for the evil passions."[122] She was fiercely determined. All that she seemed to lack as they rehearsed Lady Macbeth was emotional commitment. Naturally reserved and driven back upon herself during months of heckling by the New Orleans critics, she was afraid to expose herself in the full dimensions of the character. But Barton hit upon a device to set free the passion in her and at the same time to deliver one of the most important lessons in acting that she would ever learn: he made her forget herself. In a practice session one day he took to belittling her—sneered at her efforts, denied she could ever amount to anything, insulted her in every way he could think of.[123] Shocked, weeping, and furious, she let fly a storm of rage at him. A few moments later she realized that he had played a trick on her, understood why he had done so, and knew that it was a trick she could at any time play upon herself. She never lacked power again.

"And thus I essayed for the first time the part of Lady Macbeth, fortunately to the satisfaction of the audience, the manager, and all the members of the company."[124] It was on Shakespeare's birthday—April 23, 1836—that Miss Cushman began at the top, so to speak, by succeeding in the Shakespearean role with which she is most often identified to this day.

The success was only local and temporary, however. Her next eight years were a heavy struggle in the profession—a steady but unspectacular progress upward—in New York, Philadelphia, and other northern cities.[125] For three seasons, from 1837 to 1840, she served as "walking lady" at the Park; that is to say, she was regularly employed but without starring status, required to play anything the management put her into and to act in support of whatever greater actors came along. From time to time she was allowed to repeat Lady Macbeth, and she added such heavy roles as Bianca in *Fazio*, Mrs. Haller in *The Stranger*, and Romeo—the most important of her many transvestite creations. But among the more than a hundred assignments during those three seasons, one notes such indignities as Paul in *The Pet of the Petticoats* and Zuzu in *Zazezizozu*. She picked up whatever pointers she could by watching the great ones as they passed through—Ellen Tree and Josephine Clifton among

Illus. 59. Portrait of Charlotte Cushman by Thomas Sully.

the ladies, and Edwin Forrest, fresh home from triumphs in London, whom she had been taught to reverence as a national hero. Forrest's remarkably vigorous handling of language inspired her to deeper study of stage diction, and his gigantic voice and physique taught her something about the farther limits of power. As Goneril to his Lear she stood in the eye of the storm while his curses swirled about her. As Volumnia she stood up to his arrogant Coriolanus.

She played Meg Merrilies in *Guy Mannering* as early as May 15, 1837.[126] This small but dominant role of gypsy witchwoman would in later years be reckoned her masterpiece of pathos and mad grandeur, but many other actresses had played it before her and in 1837 no one seems to have regarded her performance as extraordinary. Her Nancy Sykes in *Oliver Twist*, however, which she created two seasons later, carried earth-bound realism and physical horror about as far as a Zola of another generation would wish to see it. She prepared for the role by disguising herself in rags and spending several days in the worst slums of the city, mingling with whores and beggar-women in order to acquire their coarsest manners. Her Nancy was a full-length study of life in the lower depths, and her death scene was unbearably agonizing. According to Lawrence Barrett's account, after her off-stage scream when Bill Sykes dealt her the fatal blow, "she dragged herself on to the stage in a wonderful manner, and, keeping her face away from her audience, produced a feeling of chilly horror by the management of her voice as she called for Bill, and begged of him to kiss her. . . . It sounded as if she *spoke through blood.*"[127]

In 1840–41 William Burton engaged Miss Cushman as leading lady at the new National Theatre in Philadelphia—not an enjoyable or profitable season but technically a professional advancement. The next season she was back at the Park to play a remarkable variety of roles in comedy. On August 30, 1841, she was Oberon in a rare production of *A Midsummer Night's Dream.* With her sister Susan she shared the leads in revivals of *The Beaux' Stratagem* and *The Rivals.* She was Lady Teazle in *The School for Scandal* and Dorinda in *The Suspicious Husband.* She created leading roles in the American premières of the two most successful new comedies of the decade—Lady Gay Spanker in Boucicault's *London Assurance* and Clara Douglas in Bulwer's *Money.* For the moment at least she throve in these roles, but, in the long run, comedy was not her métier. When William

Charles Macready came to America in the autumn of 1843, she being then engaged at the Chestnut in Philadelphia, he sent word that he required her Lady Macbeth to support his Philadelphia opening.

Flattered and elated at being thus singled out by the actor-producer who stood at the head of his profession in England—whom indeed she had admired ever since childhood when she had seen him act in Boston—and terrified, too, by his reputation for harshness to fellow-actors and underlings, she took extraordinary pains to live up to his expectations. She succeeded. Throughout the *Macbeth* of October 23 she pleased him as few other actresses had. He paid her the ultimate compliment in his vocabulary: she must act on *English* stages. He wrote in his diary that she "interested me very much. She has to learn her art, but she showed mind and sympathy with me; a novelty so refreshing to me on the stage."[128] On subsequent evenings he so approved her Gertrude and Emilia that he invited her to support him in his forthcoming engagement in Boston. He even paid the expenses of her journey there.

The plan for Boston went awry, however. Manager Pelby declined to engage Miss Cushman and put up his daughter for the female leads instead. Macready was furious at being discommoded (the Pelby girl was "reported to be drunken, and . . . does not understand one word of what she says");[129] but for Miss Cushman the contretemps was the most fortunate thing that could have happened to her. With nothing else to do she stayed on for ten days, attending the theatre nightly and learning all she could from close observation of Macready's acting.

It was time for such lessons. After seven years of playing anything and everything, relying mainly on strength and gusto, she needed above all to investigate the higher mysteries of histrionic technique, to measure her own instinctive, largely self-taught methods against those of a polished artist. Macready's observation that she still had to learn her art would be seconded by George Vandenhoff, who had performed with her a year earlier: "Charlotte Cushman . . . was by no means, then, the actress which she afterwards became. She displayed at that day, a rude, strong, uncultivated talent; it was not till after she had seen and acted with Mr. Macready . . . that she really brought artistic study and finish to her performances. At this time, she was frequently careless in the text, and negligent of rehearsals." When she played Gertrude to Vandenhoff's Hamlet, he was shocked to hear her say "What wilt thou do? thou wilt not *kill* me?" instead of "What wilt thou do? thou wilt not *murder* me?" "She was much annoyed at her error when I told her of it; but confessed that she had always so read the line, unconscious of being wrong."[130] Although she committed no gaffs quite comparable to this when playing with Macready, he did have to scold her once for coming to rehearsal without knowing the words or business of a new part which he had assigned her a month earlier: "How can there be artists when this lady, one of the most intelligent and ambitious, so entirely disregards the duties of her calling?"[131]

From listening to Macready, Miss Cushman learned that her own sometime "ruined" voice was capable of effects she had never thought to try for. She found that on occasion she could sharpen its veiled and husky timbre into clear ringing tones. Unimagined variations of pitch and speed became available to her, and she could achieve shifts of volume from contralto thunderings, through lullaby gentlenesses, to penetrating whispers. She learned, too, to think before she gestured and to gesture before she spoke. Many of Macready's poses and movements could be adapted to her own uses. Most important of all, Macready taught her the necessity of analyzing deeply any role she would undertake so that the emergent character would be a coherent entity from beginning to end, utterly distinct from any other character and by no means a haphazard collection of histrionic points.[132]

For these recognitions Miss Cushman expressed her gratitude with unrestrained enthusiasm. She entertained him on several occasions at her Boston hotel, praised his performances without stint, sent him flowers, showed him poems she had been writing—even, at their last meeting in Boston, reverently kissed his hand. In the January *Anglo-American* magazine there appeared an extended sonnet to him which she must have composed during this Boston experience. After apologizing for her own inadequacies, her lines declared:

Long after thou hast left us, men will speak
Of thine all matchless skill, thy well stored mind . . .
Then will thy name be in all hearts enshrined
Thy genius well-remembered; and thy name
Placed among those wondrous teachers of mankind,
Who ever may a world's high reverence claim
And e'en midst change of time be still revered the same.[133]

He had opened to her "a mine of depth and power."

Macready was alarmed by her approaches, mistaking her pupil-master worship for another of those crushes by amorous females which he frequently had to fend off. "I am in a strange country," he wrote, "and I think it is only a duty to myself to be strictly circumspect." He would visit her, as she requested, but in the hotel common room, not in her private room.[134] His fears are understandable, as a matter of fact, for at twenty-seven Miss Cushman had arrived at a splendid peak of physical development. Her face, to be sure, was quite unbeautiful; she referred to it as "my unfortunate Mug,"[135] and in its breadth and flatness it astonishingly resembled Macready's own face, which he referred to as "il mio brutto volto."[136] But her figure at that time was magnificent. An Italian sculptor once proposed to use her (face excepted) as a model of the Goddess of Beauty, and at the far end of the century the actor John Coleman would still be celebrating her physical charms in such leering phrases as her "breasts' superb abundance."[137] Had Macready known her better, however, he need not have worried, for her "affections did not that way tend." Her temperament, like her face, was strongly masculine, and her deepest longings drew her into sentimental relationships only with women. At the moment she seems to have been in love with Rosalie Sully, daughter of the portrait painter Thomas Sully. A year or two later, in England, she took up with the poet Eliza Cook. That affair provoked so much gossip that she had difficulty persuading Rosalie, left behind in Philadelphia, that her love for her remained constant. After Rosalie's death she entered into a "female marriage" with an English girl named Matilda Hays. Later she took the young sculptor Harriet Hosmer to Rome with her as a protégé, and for many years the sculptor Emma Stebbins was her constant companion.[138]

She expected nothing from the relationship with Macready except a continuation of the encouragement he had offered from the beginning, but she did not get it. Because of his egoism and suspiciousness the relationship soured. Angered by her failure to prepare her role in *The Bridal*, he claimed that she cut him up in the performance; at a rehearsal of *Much Ado* he decided that she lacked "the *first* qualification of an artist"; he resented the applause she got and her curtain calls; he suspected she was persuading friends on the press to write notices for her which she did not deserve; having laid down a rule for this American tour not to contribute his services to other actors' benefits (lest at every stop he be inundated with requests), he refused to make an exception and act in hers.[139] At this point she wrote him a rather sharp note, citing certain disparaging comments which had come back to her and demanding an explanation. He denied flatly that he had ever "by word or act been wanting to you in delicacy and consideration, nor in manifestation of kindly feeling"; but in his diary he exclaimed, "I do not like thee, Dr. Fell!"[140] She supported him again in New York in May of 1844 (when rather surprisingly he once more praised her and urged her to go to England) and again in Philadelphia, New York, and Boston in the autumn of that year. His second refusal to act for her benefit taught her to depend on him no further, and so, borrowing money to eke out her small savings, she crossed the ocean to brave London on her own.[141]

London made a star of her. Edwin Forrest, already there when she arrived and confidently preparing for his second success in London, persuaded Manager Maddox of the Princess's Theatre to hire her to act in his support. But she had not undertaken a transatlantic crossing to play second string to anyone, and she insisted on making a first impression in a role of her own. Maddox, though annoyed, allowed her to open on February 13, 1845, as Bianca in *Fazio*—a romantic claptrap of betrayed love, madness, and death which she knew from long experience would afford her the broadest possible range of emotional effects. The critics—and Maddox—were astounded by her performance. Those with long memories could compare her authoritatively to Sarah Siddons or Eliza O'Neill, but younger spectators had never seen anything like her. Tragic actresses of the present generation, of whom the lovely Helen Faucit was the most eminent, aimed for sentiment and gentility. None of them could match Miss Cushman's raw power or emotional variety. "From jealousy dropping back into tenderness, from hate passing to love," said the *Times* critic, "she gave an equal intensity to each successive passion, as if her whole soul were for the moment absorbed in that only."[142] Here and there a hypercritical writer, like the reviewer for the *Spectator* or John Forster's stand-in at the *Examiner*, harped on her angular movements, her inelegant attitudes, or her unprepossessing appearance ("Her face is a feminine caricature of Mr. Macready's physiognomy"); but having hedged thus much the writer had to acknowledge her energy, earnestness, and intelligence and to allow that with some polishing of rough edges she was bound to succeed.[143] The *Sun* called her "the very first actress that we have."[144]

She "supported" Forrest in only two roles. After her

Illus. 60. Charlotte Cushman as Lady Macbeth.

Emilia had outacted his Othello and her Lady Macbeth had won golden opinions while his Macbeth was being hissed and laughed at, she refused to share the platform with him any longer, preferring to do her own plays on the off nights. When he gave up in early April and went to the country, she remained at the Princess's as Maddox's star attraction, carrying on deep into the summer for a total of eighty-four nights. At the end of May there appeared in the New York *Spirit of the Times* an amusing letter from a "London English Gentleman," twitting Brother Jonathan for his inability to recognize native genius when he saw it. Very ordinary English actors and actresses, or even quite bad ones, the Gentleman pointed out, were received in America as extraordinary luminaries, but Miss Cushman had to cross the ocean to be acknowledged as a theatrical wonder of the age.[145]

It appears to have been Miss Cushman's "masculinity" —her decisiveness, forthrightness, and vigor—that won the day. Her Emilia was better than any other actress's, as John Forster would point out during a later season, because she conceived Emilia correctly—not, as the standard acting edition suggested, a delicate handmaiden to the heroine, but as Shakespeare displayed her in her entirety—"a knowing, loud-speaking, self-willed, unscrupulous woman; very clever, and very conscious of what is going on."[146] Her Lady Macbeth, according to George Vandenhoff, was tougher than her master: she positively bullied Macbeth, got him into a corner, and "pitched into him," suggesting that if other arguments failed she would resort to blows.[147] Early in her London run she startled the town, who had put her down as an exclusively tragic actress, by coming out as Rosalind, and startled them even more when she put on Ganymede's dress. Never mind that Rosalind protests she has no doublet and hose in her disposition: Miss Cushman "looks in every inch a man; and a man she is in voice and manner also, and gesture, so long as she retains these outward and visible symbols of the stronger sex. . . . Her mind became masculine as well as her outward semblance; and on the assumption of her manly garb she would seem to have doffed all the constraint of her sex." Thus she avoided that coy squeamishness which other Victorian Rosalinds affected when they had to speak certain naughty words. Her motto was *"Honi soit qui mal y pense,"* said the *Observer.* "She spoke her speeches 'trippingly,' and seeming to see nothing equivocal in the meaning of the words she uttered, and nothing obnoxious to good taste in the dialogue as set down by the author."[148]

At the end of her first year in London, by then engaged with Ben Webster at the Haymarket, she struck a double blow for recognition, both as actor and as producer. If London liked her "breeches part" acting as Rosalind, she would go all the way and show them her transvestite Romeo. And in the fashion of the day, set by Macready, Madame Vestris, Samuel Phelps, and others, she would restore the "true text." For nearly a hundred years the only version of *Romeo and Juliet* known in the theatre was the one cobbled up by David Garrick, who had trimmed the language of the play to accommodate it to modern taste, suppressed all reference to Romeo's Rosaline, transferred Mercutio's Queen Mab speech from a torchlit scene in the streets to a woodland scene by daylight, inserted a long-drawn-out funeral procession after Juliet's supposed death, and heightened the pathos of the ending with a *liebestod* colloquy between the lovers

Illus. 61. Charlotte and Susan Cushman as Romeo and Juliet.

just before Romeo's poison takes effect. To cast out all these foolish "improvements" was indeed a major accomplishment, and Miss Cushman was the first American to contribute significantly to the cause of textual integrity in the staging of Shakespeare.[149]

With her sister Susan as Juliet, she opened the production at the Haymarket on December 29, intending only a brief run of it and even a little worried about its reception. In America her Romeo, together with other male impersonations, had long since been taken for granted, but London might reject it as an impropriety. When she had tested the play in the provinces during the autumn it had mainly gone well, but in Puritan Edinburgh there had been unpleasant whisperings about the indecency of sister making love to sister.[150] Luckily, however, London was not yet quite so finicking. The *Spectator* critic, never to be counted among her advocates, declared her "the best Romeo that has appeared on the stage these thirty years."[151] The *Times* praised her earnestness and intensity and her skill in knitting together the fragments of the part into "a living, breathing, animated, ardent human being"; and dwelt, too, on her appearance: "Miss Cushman looks Romeo exceedingly well. Her deportment is frank and easy, she walks the stage with an air of command—her eye beams with animation."[152] The *Athenaeum*, where the critical department had always somewhat perversely cried up the delicacy, the charm, the tenderness in her acting, now protested that her playing Romeo was a "mistake," on the grounds that it might weaken her "feminine attraction." But then it declared her performance to be "one of the most extraordinary pieces of acting, perhaps, ever exhibited by a woman," and showered it with superlatives: "Never was courtship more fervent, more apparently sincere, more reverential, and yet more impetuously passionate, than that which on the silent air of night ascended to Juliet's window."[153] The playwright Westland Marston agreed that the ardor of her lovemaking exceeded that of any male Romeo he had ever seen,[154] and John Coleman declared that no man would dare express such eroticism in public.[155]

As a matter of fact, she had no serious competition in the role, for not since the famous rivalry of Garrick and Barry in the 1750s had first-rate tragedians been eager to play it. The old New Orleans manager Noah Ludlow pretty well expressed the nineteenth-century male actors' attitude toward Romeo when he declared that it requires a boy, not a man, to express Romeo's passion—"or rather a youth who begins to imagine he is a man because he has some hair on his upper lip; for none but such can feel and utter such sweet nonsense."[156] The regular actor of Macbeth and Othello would find embarrassingly womanish that passage in Friar Lawrence's cell where Romeo is called upon to tear his hair in grief and throw himself upon the ground. But Miss Cushman could unblushingly make this scene the very high point of her performance. Sheridan Knowles reported it in fine Irish enthusiasm:

I witnessed with astonishment the Romeo of Miss Cushman. Unanimous and lavish as were the encomiums of the London press, I was not prepared for such a triumph of pure genius. You recollect, perhaps, Kean's third act of Othello. Did you ever expect to see anything like it again? I never did, and yet I saw as great a thing last Wednesday night in Romeo's scene

Illus. 62. Charlotte Cushman as Meg Merrilies.

Illus. 63. Torchlight procession for Charlotte Cushman's farewell in New York, 1874.

with the Friar, after the sentence of banishment, quite as great! I am almost tempted to go further. It was a scene of topmost passion; not simulated passion—no such thing; real, palpably real; the genuine heart-storm was on—on in the wildest fitfulness of fury; and I listened and gazed and held my breath, while my blood ran hot and cold. I am sure it must have been the case with everyone in the house; but I was all absorbed in Romeo, till a thunder of applause recalled me to myself.[157]

That it was indeed "the case with everyone in the house" was confirmed by Westland Marston, who said the audience was roused to wildest excitement as if witnessing a tragic event in actual life, and that it waited, stunned, until it could recollect that Romeo's misery was but a triumph of acting, and then would "thank the impassioned performer in volley after volley of applause."[158]

In the autumn of 1847 Miss Cushman played a long engagement with Macready at the Princess's, during which she shared the stage with him in *Othello*, *Macbeth*, and *Hamlet* and added to her repertory Queen Katherine in *Henry VIII*. This role, of which Sarah Siddons's rendition was still a glorious memory, would become one of Miss Cushman's mainstays in the years ahead. At her first approach to it, however, she seems to have brought

insufficient rhetorical drive to the Trial Scene and perhaps a touch too much of Nancy Sykes to the Death Scene. According to the *Times*, "she did all she could to give reality to the death bed; she gazed with feverish anxiety after the fleeting visions; she lay in her chair in a position most indicative of utter weakness; she gave many symptoms of physical pain. All this was wrought out with great care and talent, but surely the situation ought to be more idealized to prevent the death of Katharine from being an unpleasant spectacle."[159]

The long remainder of her career was a succession of working (and money-making) times in America and England divided by times of retirement in Rome, where at 38 Via Gregoriana, above the Spanish Steps, she kept open house to the dozens of English and American artists, literati, and other choice spirits who lived in or passed through the Holy City in the 1850s and 1860s.[160] Her tours of duty in America, where admiration of her art passed almost into personal worship, were in the years 1849–52, 1857–58, 1860–61, 1863, and 1870–74. On November 7, 1874, after a valedictory Lady Macbeth at Booth's Theatre in New York, she was accorded the most spectacular farewell ceremony in the history of the American theatre, surrounded by civic, literary, and theatrical notables, with an address by William Cullen Bryant, the reading of an ode composed by Richard Henry Stoddard, the presentation of a laurel crown, a torchlight escort with band music through the streets, and fireworks over Madison Square.

It is difficult to assess Miss Cushman as a Shakespearean actress, for in the long run her size, voice, face, and disposition limited her to very few Shakespearean roles, and even these often took second place in popular and critical favor to her melodramatic Meg Merrilies. Her finest, according to William Winter, was her Queen Katherine in *Henry VIII*—"the consummate image of sovereignty and noble womanhood, austere and yet sweetly patient, in circumstances of cruel injustice and bitter affliction."[161] Winter's sentences glow with appreciation of her magnificent speaking, her dignity and grace throughout the trial, and the pathos of her Death Scene, its sentiment augmented by Handelian music and the hymn of "Angels Ever Bright and Fair." Such unrelieved moral exaltation, however, seems rather a lesson in piety than the development of a dramatic character, and, like the play itself, it stands at the periphery of our concern for Shakespeareanism.

One would genuinely want to see Miss Cushman's Lady Macbeth, although even William Winter thought her conception mistaken. She imagined Macbeth a great burly bullying fellow ("the grandfather of all the Bowery ruffians," she told Edwin Booth),[162] and her Lady had to be stronger still. She seems to have told Winter also that because of the amount of wine drinking in the play both the Macbeths ought to appear half-intoxicated.[163] It annoyed her that most of the actors of Macbeth that she had to play with (except, presumably, Forrest) were such "*little*" men," and Booth, who was indeed slight and small, wanted to say to her as she urged him to the murder, "Why don't you kill him? You're a great deal bigger than I am." What her Lady Macbeth lacked was the subtlety achieved by the actress who can draw Macbeth on, in part at least, by sex appeal. As someone said, she was a plain prose actor. "She caught the facts of a character," said James Murdoch, "but its conceits were beyond her reach."[164] Her understanding was perfect, but she lacked imagination. Having caught the obvious quality of Lady Macbeth—her strength—and found it compatible with her own ability, she was content to drive home that fact alone. Yet, as Winter said, her personation, "in grandeur, intensity, and magnificent grace, had no parallel on the

Illus. 64. Charlotte Cushman near the end of her life.

stage of her time and has had no equal since. Her figure, towering above Macbeth and pointing beyond him to the coming Duncan who 'must be provided for,' or crouching against the door-post of the chamber in which the midnight murder is afoot, was indescribably awful, and it has not passed from the memory of persons who saw it, nor will it pass from the most glowing page of the annals of our Theatre."[165]

Desperate to extend her dramatis personae, and prevented by nature from the whole range of delicate and physically beautiful women characters, she broke across the sex barrier to play not only Romeo but occasionally (and less successfully) Hamlet and Cardinal Wolsey also. She hated the fact that "with an outlandish dress and a trick or two, I can bring much more money to the theatre than when I give the public my heart's blood in my finest characters."[166] But that was what the public cared most for: Meg Merrilies.

Proof.

Illus. 65. Charles Kemble as Hamlet.

CHAPTER IV

Fresh Fashions from Abroad

IN THE SECOND THIRD of the nineteenth century, while Americans were breaking the plains and pioneering through the dangerous western territories, the attributes popularly held in highest regard were raw energy, muscle, and dauntless physical courage. And since every generation sees its own image in the plays of Shakespeare (or refashions those plays to mirror itself), it is not surprising that in one powerful actor of the time Othello and Lear shared attention and attributes with Jack Cade, Spartacus the Gladiator, and the noble savage Metamora; that in the repertory of another, Lady Macbeth and mad Meg Merrilies stood side by side.

Yet no generation is all of one mind. In the cities of the East the upper class of playgoers, fashionable and sophisticated, gradually drew away from what they came to regard as the vulgar crudity of Forrest and his followers. A good many intellectuals drew away from the theatre altogether, for as editions of Shakespeare became increasingly accessible they preferred to read the plays in the comfort of their armchairs rather than sit among rough company to see them melodramatically performed. Visitors from England were often offended by what they encountered in the theatre; visiting actors were put off by the ignorance and inefficiency of resident companies; visiting spectators took exception to the coarseness of American acting and even more to rowdyism in the house. Frances Trollope complained repeatedly that men in the audience wore their hats, took off their coats and rolled up their sleeves, sprawled on the benches, presented their backsides over the box fronts, smelled of onions and whiskey, chewed tobacco incessantly, and spat, spat, spat. On one occasion she was shocked to observe a lady in the forefront of a box "performing the most maternal office possible."[1]

Mrs. Trollope's own book about American manners, which appeared in 1832, drew fire from touchy chauvinists but helped greatly in eliminating the offenses of which she complained. Her name itself became a call to

order. A visitor who arrived a few years later observed that when certain gentlemen in the boxes assumed "an indelicate posture" during the entr'acte, "several voices in the pit called out 'A Trollope, a Trollope,' and a general hissing and hooting from the same quarter had the effect of inducing the offenders speedily to withdraw."[2]

Further civilizing of the theatre was accomplished by Charles and Fanny Kemble in the early 1830s: their refined acting, together with the reputation for excellence which for half a century had accrued to the family name, drew sophisticates to the box office again. Next came Ellen Tree, whose decorous femininity charmed even leaders of fashion. Intellectuals were gratified by Macready's second visit in the early 1840s. In 1846 Charles Kean offered New Yorkers the delights of full-fashioned historically accurate scenery, and although his efforts failed to take, he planted ideas which others after him would make grow.

Meanwhile, too, American actors were recognizing the uses of literary study and at least a show of erudition. James Hackett began publicizing his concern for the true text and bringing out his correspondence with distinguished persons on other Shakespearean matters. Charlotte Cushman investigated Shakespeare's own version of *Romeo and Juliet*, found it better than Garrick's, and restored a good deal of it to the stage. Edwin Forrest acquired a copy of the First Folio. In the 1850s William Burton, author and bibliophile as well as comedian and theatre manager, assembled at his New York residence a truly magnificent library of theatrical, Shakespearean, and classic literature and drew about him a company of the best Shakespeare scholars of the day.

CHARLES AND FANNY KEMBLE

In the late summer of 1832 the "better sort" of New York playgoers were alerted by the news that for the first time since the departure of Macready five years earlier, London's finest were coming to call. On September 4, Philip Hone—philanthropist, socialite, patron of the arts—noted in his diary that the packet ship *Pacific* had just brought "Charles Kemble, the celebrated comedian, and his highly gifted daughter, Miss Fanny Kemble, who has lately created by her fine acting a great sensation in the theatrical circles of Great Britain. . . . There is no doubt that we shall be furnished with a theatrical treat of the highest order."[3]

Hone did not know that the Kembles' visit was a desperate attempt to retrieve financial stability. Charles Kemble (1755–1854) had long been manager of Covent Garden Theatre, and for years its sagging fortunes had been dragging him down toward bankruptcy.[4] The success of his daughter Fanny (Frances Anne; 1809–93) in the autumn of 1829—first as Juliet, then as Belvidera, Portia, Lady Townly, Beatrice, Bianca, and in other leading roles—saved his situation, or barely saved it, for three seasons. But in the autumn of 1831 his health collapsed, and though he recovered by spring and even enjoyed one last triumph in management when Fanny created Julia in Sheridan Knowles's *The Hunchback*, his only practical course was to accept an invitation from Stephen Price to make a two-year stand in America.

Friends of his later years wished that Charles Kemble could wear knee breeches, silk stockings, diamond buckles on his shoes, and powdered hair, for he seemed to them "the express image of the English gentleman of the past generation—of the gentlemen whom Reynolds painted."[5] Tall, handsome, urbane, he moved about easily in the best society. He was widely traveled, spoke several languages, was well read in modern literature and the classics, was an amateur appreciator of painting and sculpture. His interest in antiquities spawned the nineteenth-century movement of historical accuracy in the staging of Shakespeare: in 1823, with the assistance of the antiquarian James Robinson Planché, he produced *King John* in costumes of the thirteenth century, and subsequently he dressed *Henry IV*, *Hamlet*, *As You Like It*, and *Cymbeline* in styles appropriate to the times and places of their fables.

The youngest member of the great Kemble family, he was perhaps the most finely tuned as an actor. He played well, if not universally so, a great many more roles, both comic and tragic, than any of the others. Macready, who disliked him personally, put him down as a first-rate actor of second-rate parts;[6] but William Robson, the "Old Play-Goer," accounted it fortunate that the senior brother, John, was the Macbeth, the Othello, the King John, the Brutus, the Lear of the family, for nothing could have been more brilliant than Charles's Macduff, Cassio, Faulconbridge, Antony, and Edgar, and nothing could be more delightful than to see the "noble rivalry" of these brothers, "each stimulated by the fine acting of the other to play up to his best."[7]

His opening role at the Park Theatre in New York, on September 17, 1832, was Hamlet, and "Oh, what a fine and delicate piece of work this is!" wrote daughter Fanny in her journal that evening. "There is not one sentence, line, or word of this part which my father has not sifted grain by grain; there is not one scene or passage to which he does not give its fullest and most entire substance, together with a variety that relieves the intense study of the whole with wonderful effect."[8] William Bodham Donne would declare that Hamlet was Charles Kemble's highest achievement as an actor.[9] And so it was—in the sense that it was the most complex role upon which he exercised his finest intellectual discriminations. Yet it was not vastly successful on stages. It was lapidary work, true to a minim under a jeweler's glass but theatrically not quite visible to vast audiences. Even Hone, disposed as he was to admire the performance, found at the end of the evening that he had not got as much pleasure from this Hamlet as from others: "The part was deeply studied and well understood; his reading is critically correct, his elocution distinct, and his manner dignified; but he is too formal, even for Hamlet. His pauses are too long and too frequent, so much so as to make the representation fatiguing."[10]

Fanny herself discovered this at the opening in Philadelphia a month later. She watched her father narrowly on that occasion, with fatiguing (like Hone, she invoked the word *fatiguing*) attention, "and the conclusion I have come to is this: that though his workmanship may be, and is, far finer *in the hand*, than that of any other artist I ever saw, yet its very minute accuracy and refinement renders it unfit for the frame in which it is exhibited." He lacked, she recognized, the particular qualifications of Edmund Kean in his better days: "an eye like an orb of light, a voice exquisitely touching and melodious in its tenderness, and in the harsh dissonance of vehement passion terribly true," plus vigor, intensity, and an ability to concentrate his effects. She would not by any means advocate Kean's careless method of exerting himself only in detached passages and leaving the character as a whole destitute of unity and consistency. Yet she saw clearly that her father's refined and perfected method, lacking power, could not bring off "those startling and tremendous bursts of passion, which belong to the highest walks of tragedy." He was not so much the tragic actor as the perfect gentleman. "There is one thing in which I do not believe my father ever has been, or ever will be, excelled; his high and noble bearing, his gallant, graceful, courteous deportment; his perfect good-breeding on the stage. . . . He appears to me the beau ideal of the courtly, thorough-bred chivalrous gentleman from the days of the Admirable Crichton down to those of George the Fourth."[11] The autumn of 1832 was a time of national elections in America—the tumultuous struggle between Andrew Jackson's Democrats and the Whig party of Henry Clay, Unionists versus Secessionists, the Bank faction and the anti-Bank faction. Against the passions raging in the streets, not to mention the theatrical rivalry of Edwin Forrest roaring through *The Gladiator* and *Metamora*, Kemble's genteel Hamlet may have sounded faint indeed.

During this first stand in New York, he could not exhibit his Mercutio, which for buoyancy, wit, and grace was among his masterworks. The utter wretchedness of the Park Theatre's leading actor, one W. H. Keppel, who had already failed as Romeo in London, forced Kemble to stand in as lover to his daughter's Juliet. At fifty-seven he could hardly pass for "the youngest of that name," yet in the eyes of Philip Hone "the difficulty was overcome, by his perfect conception of the character, the grace of his elocution, and the eloquence of his deportment."[12]

The Park management undertook on October 1 to display Kemble's celebrated Faulconbridge in *King John*, only to shame itself by the total incompetence of its company to deliver the text of the play. As Faulconbridge, Westland Marston would write, "the secret of his superiority lay, perhaps, in the fulness of life which seemed to radiate from him—to make war a gay pastime, diplomacy a play of wit, and to clothe worldliness itself with a glow of bright, genial satire."[13] So, for over three decades, his Faulconbridge had delighted London audiences, but all this was lost in the shambles of an evening at the Park. In the very first scene, Fanny reported, the impersonator of King John was stuck for words, "and there he stood, shifting his truncheon from hand to hand, rolling his eyes, gasping for breath . . . like a man in a nightmare." In the scene before the gates of Angiers, when the herald was supposed to summon the French citizens to

Illus. 66. Charles Kemble as Mercutio.

the walls with a trumpet call, though he puffed out his cheeks, no sound came; then just as he lowered his instrument and looked into the wings indignantly, the offstage trumpeter issued a blast that would wake the dead—to the vast amusement of the audience. Cardinal Pandulph, being greeted by derisive yells (extradramatic antipapistry), lost his lines altogether and stood thumping his breast and twitching his scarlet skirts. Fanny, who was playing Lady Constance, thought to save the situation by going on with her own speeches, but Pandulph suddenly remembered his final speech and pitched it in where it made no sense at all. In Constance's last scene, "king gazed at cardinal, and cardinal gazed at king; king nodded and winked at the prompter, spread out his hands, and remained with his mouth open: cardinal nodded and

Illus. 67. Portrait of Fanny Kemble by Peter Frederick Rothermel. Courtesy of the American Shakespeare Theatre, Stratford, Connecticut.

winked at the prompter, crossed his hands on his breast, and remained with his mouth open; neither of them uttering a syllable! What a scene! O, what a glorious scene!" Fanny left the theatre after her last exit, went home, supped, and waited for her father's account of the rest of the evening. "What a cast! What a play! What botchers! What butchers!"[14]

Kemble was much admired by New York audiences, of course. "We think Mr. Kemble's appearance in America will do a service to the art," said the critic of the *Evening Post*; "that it will raise and refine its style."[15] And Hone maintained that he was "a good study for the younger men, and his visit to this country ought to improve the American stage." But what New York was hungering after was Fanny—for three seasons past the toast of London, the most exciting actress to emerge since

Eliza O'Neill, and, as some would have it, the inheritor of the talents of her aunt, the late Sarah Siddons.[16]

Juliet was the role in which she had been most adored, but cunningly (as Charlotte Cushman would do in London a dozen years later) she exhibited herself first as Bianca in Milman's *Fazio*; for whatever her faults, faintness was not one of them, and in Bianca she could bombard the audience with salvos of emotion which even the stubbornest Yankee spectators must submit to. Hone was beside himself with delight:

It is a fine part, well calculated for a display of the strongest passions of the female heart—love, hate, and jealousy. . . . I have never witnessed an audience so moved, astonished, and delighted. Her display of the strong feelings which belong to the part was great beyond description, and the expression of her wonderful face would have been a rich treat if her tongue had uttered no sound. The fifth act was such an exhibition of female powers as we have never before witnessed, and the curtain fell amidst the deafening shouts and plaudits of an astonished audience.[17]

A writer for the *Mirror* was much taken by Miss Kemble's expression of sardonic hatred ("Kean-like," he called it), her impassioned and tender love scenes ("all bashful girlishness, and full of exquisitely graceful touches—*full* of them"), her fixed look of despair, her silent glance of scorn: "This is, indeed, *acting.*"[18]

There were faults though. In certain unemotional passages she would lapse into monotony; at certain ordinary remarks she would strike a pose and overdo the emphasis; or she would pitch her voice too low to be clearly heard. A much debated question was, "Is she beautiful?" Apparently not, in the ordinary sense, for as Hone observed when he entertained her at dinner, "Her features separately are not good."[19] And this was puzzling, for the face that preceded her across the ocean in Sir Thomas Lawrence's sketch of her was exquisite—one more image (the very last of them, as it happened) in Sir Thomas's lifelong dream of fair women. Fanny loved the sketch herself and was much touched and pleased when someone told her that a peddler had carried a copy of it far across the Alleghenies and auctioned it at high price to young engineers constructing the western railroads.[20] "The people here make me mad by abusing Lawrence's drawing of me," she exclaimed. Yet she knew that it was a charming lie, that she only wished she looked like that: "If ever there was a refined and intellectual work, where the might

Illus. 68. Portrait of Fanny Kemble by Sir Thomas Lawrence.

of genius triumphing over every material impediment has enshrined and embodied spirit itself, it is that."[21]

What mattered on the stage, of course, was the marvelous expressiveness of her face in action. "The great peculiarity of her acting is *mind*," declared the *Mirror* critic. "You cannot, even for a moment, withdraw your gaze, without losing some look or gesture, full of thought and meaning."

There are times . . . when her countenance is overspread with a perfect loveliness. Her features are not regular, and in her most violent efforts they undergo a slight distortion; but her smile is winning, her hair long and dark, and her low forehead charmingly redeemed . . . by a pair of eyes which some-

times assume force and splendor almost intense, and are again subdued to a most feminine and lustrous softness. Then the play of her features has seldom been equalled on our stage,—blending the transient gleamings of Clara Fisher's light comedy, with the depth and glancing fire of Edmund Kean. When the spell of a passion is on her, mind and soul break out over her face like actual light.[22]

It was not truly a Kemble face, large featured and masklike. She was, in fact, of a new breed of Kemble—nervous, vivacious, and impulsive—qualities unexpectable when one contemplates the monumental elders of the tribe, Sarah and John Philip, Elizabeth and Stephen. From her father's bright spirit and from the Gallic temperament of her mother, Theresa De Camp, she inherited a mercurial intelligence, quick responses, deep and unsatisfiable longings, and a vigorously independent judgment. By these qualities she mastered her art almost instantly and arrived almost effortlessly at the top of the profession. But before she was twenty-five these same qualities, together with pride, fastidiousness, and romantic idealism, drove her out of the profession.

She hated the profession. She had to go on with it because her father depended on her to recoup his fortunes, but she dreaded the prospect of dreary years "devoted to labor that I dislike and despise."[23] Acting, she maintained, is the lowest of the arts, if indeed it is an art at all. It creates nothing. The actor only fills up the outline designed by another, expounds what another has set down; "a fine piece of acting is at best, in my opinion, a fine translation." Her own success was proof of the cheapness of the art, for she had got her reputation "without time or pains of any sort."[24]

"How I do loathe the stage!" she exclaimed in her journal after a disconcerting performance of Juliet opposite some bumbling local Romeo.

What a mass of wretched mumming mimicry acting is! Pasteboard and paint, for the thick breathing orange groves of the south; green silk and oiled parchment, for the solemn splendour of her noon of night; wooden platforms and canvas curtains, for the solid marble balconies, and rich dark draperies of Juliet's sleeping chamber, that shrine of love and beauty; rouge, for the startled life-blood in the cheek of that young passionate woman; an actress, a mimicker, a sham creature, me, in fact, or any other one, for that loveliest and most wonderful conception, in which all that is true in nature, and all that is exquisite in fancy, are moulded into a living form. To *act* this! to *act* Romeo and Juliet! horror! horror! how I do loathe my most impotent and unpoetical craft![25]

In Boston once, when she was not needed for Ophelia and thus could watch her father's Hamlet straight through, she momentarily overcame her "absolute feeling of contempt for the profession." Her father's acting, the result of a lifetime of care and labor, did indeed seem the work of an artist, and "I certainly respect acting more while I am seeing him act than at any other time." Yet even as she penned these words, gazing out her hotel room window into a churchyard, her thoughts took a bitter turn: "Yet surely, after all, acting *is* nonsense, and as I sit here opposite the churchyard, it seems to me strange to think, that when I come down into that darkness, I shall have eaten bread, during my life, earned by such means."[26]

She allowed herself to be worshiped on American stages for two seasons—as Juliet, Beatrice, and Portia among her Shakespearean roles; as Bianca, Julia, Lady Teazle, Belvidera, and in a dozen other roles of modern authorship. And she was lionized. When she went to Washington, Daniel Webster and Chief Justice Marshall, ex-President Adams and Dolly Madison attended her performances, and she was received by President Jackson at the White House. In Boston the young men of Harvard, including Charles Sumner and Wendell Phillips, came to the theatre nightly, and among her social connections were the novelist Catharine Sedgwick and the Reverend William Ellery Channing. One of the least conspicuous members of her New York audience was the thirteen-year-old Walt Whitman, who would one day credit her with some part of the inspiration for *Leaves of Grass*. When she and her father made their trip to Niagara Falls, the famous world wanderer Edward Trelawny was their

Illus. 69. Fanny Kemble as Juliet, with the Nurse.

Illus. 70. Fanny Kemble as Isabella.

tinguished company she kept and by her further claims upon public attention. She wrote several plays and three collections of poems, admired in their day. A year into her marriage, much to the annoyance of her husband, she published her *Journal*—a sparkling and often indiscreet selection from diaries she had kept between the day she sailed from Liverpool and the day of her marriage. It fascinated and often shocked the dozens of proper persons who recognized themselves under the blanks that stood for their names. Headstrong and reckless in its criticism, it is often as revealing and even more amusing than Frances Trollope's *Domestic Manners*. The Butler marriage eventually disintegrated, and in 1849 it ended in long-drawn-out, much-publicized divorce proceedings. Meanwhile in London she had made a brief return to the stage, and after that she began a very successful career as a dramatic reader, with nearly half the Shakespeare canon in her repertory. Midway through the Civil War she published her long-withheld *Journal of a Residence on a Georgian Plantation*, a factual account of a season she had once spent with her husband amid his slave population on Butler's Island—so shaking a book that it is said to have done much to reverse the pro-Southern affinities of the English press and people. In the 1870s and 1880s she published two volumes of her *Records*—hundreds of letters she had written during her girlhood and middle years. A superb letter writer, she has preserved an invaluable mass of information about men and women, art, theatre, books, and society in England and America down to the mid-century. Fanny Kemble's passage through the American theatre was as brief as the flight of a comet, and cometlike it was unforgettable.

guide and companion. Wherever she went a well-to-do young Philadelphian named Pierce Butler followed her—his purpose, marriage. In the spring of 1834, she left the stage, gave her earnings to her father, married Butler, and turned to what she expected to be a happy social life in Philadelphia.

It is amazing that in so brief a career on the American stage Fanny (and her father) achieved so much. As Francis Wemyss put it, "That she revived the prostrate fortunes of the drama in the United States, admits not of a doubt; her popularity, and the name of Kemble, made the theatres once more a fashionable place of amusement."[27] Whether or not so embracing a claim is quite defensible, certainly a legend about her sprang up and grew, fed and freshened from time to time by the dis-

Mr. and Mrs. Charles Kean

Historians of the theatre generally agree with the verdict passed upon Charles Kean (1811–68) by impartial observers in his own time—that as a Shakespearean actor he was a second-rater. George Henry Lewes's summing up is clear and fair enough: "He began by being a very bad actor; he has ended by forcing even such of his critics as have least sympathy with him to admit that in certain parts he is without a rival on our stage. . . . The stamping, spluttering, ranting, tricky actor, who in his 'sallet days' excited so much mirth and so much blame, has become remarkable for the naturalness and forcible quietness with

Illus. 71. Charles Kean as Hamlet.

which he plays certain parts."[28] Those parts, in Lewes's judgment, would include no Shakespearean tragic heroes but a number of melodrama roles—the Corsican brothers, Louis XI, and the like. Kean's stolid, expressionless face, his inflexible voice, and his lack of sympathetic imagination exactly qualified him for such roles. He could make big points, bring off broad, striking effects. Sometimes, too, by a sort of underacting—a dead-level, deadpan non-playing—he could achieve that peculiar effect of iron strength concealed behind a mask. Thus, Westland Marston tells us, as Louis XI, while laying out plans for a murder, he would hear the Angelus bell, remove his cap, utter a prayer, put on his cap, and resume the murder plans without the slightest change of voice. Probably this was nothing more than what we have learned to expect, since the invention of Hawkshaw and Sherlock Holmes, of every theatrical detective or underworld chieftain, but for Marston in the 1850s it was a thrilling novelty.[29] In some quarters (not all) Kean's Hamlet was held in high regard, and his success in it perhaps depended upon well-planned alternation between outbreaks of passion and passages of stony-faced, still brooding.

Lewes allowed that Kean made an excellent Ford in *The Merry Wives of Windsor*, for his very limitations were admirably suited to express "the puzzled, wondering stolidity of the jealous, bamboozled husband."[30] The same limitations doubtless served his vengeful Shylock and his sullen King John. It is less easy to imagine his Benedick in such terms, and he must have brought to that role not only bafflement but sharpness in repartee, for it was widely praised through several decades.

When he first went on the stage in 1827 at the age of sixteen—tempted there by the entrepreneur Stephen Price, who saw in him the chance of quick commercial profit—he knew little more about acting than how to imitate the methods of his famous father. He had no training, and he lacked his father's face, voice, and mimetic imagination. His voice was often affected by bronchial disturbances, and his blocked nasal passages prevented the pure sounding of certain consonants. *Punch* once twitted him for his inadvertent commentary on Shylock's diet:

> You take my life
> When you do take the *beans* whereby I live.[31]

The London audiences and critics would have little to do with him, and he soon withdrew to the provinces. In

1830, at the age of nineteen, he crossed to America, where he remained for nearly three seasons.[32]

The American critics generally were kind to the youngster. His shortcomings in comparison with his father were obvious enough, and he was frequently bested in competition with his father's old rival Junius Brutus Booth—or even, alas, in competition with the newest Infant Wonder, the eleven-year-old Master Joseph Burke—but still in a modest way he prospered. The critics, having for the most part no fond attachment to the elder Kean, encouraged the younger in his Hamlet, Romeo, Othello, and assorted non-Shakespearean roles. Philip Hone in 1831 thought his Hamlet "a chaste classical performance . . . without rant and bombast."[33] Years later, however, a more professional American observer, James Hackett, would rule otherwise, declaring his Hamlet "a tissue of bustle, rant, and posturing," full of "false emphases, bad cadences, and misplaced pauses," and "remarkable also for claptrap effects with which it superabounds."[34] Very likely his playing of the part coarsened and case-hardened with the passing of time.

In January of 1842 Kean married Ellen Tree (1806?–80), an actress several years older than he, and by several degrees a better performer. She too had spent three seasons in America, where between 1836 and 1839 she enjoyed enormous popularity and prosperity: in spite of the great financial panic of 1837 she was able to take home a fortune of some £12,000.[35] Among her Shakespearean roles she was especially admired as Rosalind, Viola, and Beatrice, and on either side of the Atlantic she was recognized as exactly the right kind of actress for the oncoming generation: her characterizations were impeccably pure and decorous in the proper Victorian manner. J. W. Cole in his biography of Kean recalled a conversation with a septuagenarian who had assured him that Dora Jordan's Viola (by all sound accounts the finest Viola of the eighteenth or early nineteenth century) was much inferior to Mrs. Kean's. Of course, the old man allowed, Mrs. Jordan had greater breadth, higher coloring, more exuberant spirits, and "a broad-wheeled laugh peculiar to herself," but she would appear only "coarse and vulgar to modern ideas of refinement."[36] The American journalist William Leggett once wrote of Miss Tree's Beatrice, "Feminine delicacy is one of the attributes of woman's character which Miss Tree is not willing to dispense with; and while other actresses give the utmost sharpness and acerbity to every sarcasm and jest that Beatrice utters, we find Miss

Illus. 72. From a portrait of Ellen Tree Kean by Sir William Charles Ross.

Tree occasionally delivering a repartee with a downcast air and softened tone, that shows her innate sense of the propriety of Shakespeare's admonition, not to overstep the modesty of nature."[37] Being tall as well as handsome, she occasionally played male roles—Romeo, to the great delight of Fanny Kemble who once was her Juliet,[38] and frequently in the middle thirties the hero of T. N. Talfourd's pseudo-Greek tragedy of *Ion*. Speaking of her Ion a writer for the *New York Mirror* repeatedly invoked the word *charming* and underscored her femininity. "She has woman's energy, and woman's passion, and woman's tenderness, and woman's weakness. She cannot unsex herself. In Ion, for instance, she is not a whit masculine. She becomes not Ion, but Ion becomes Ellen Tree."[39]

For all her personal drawing power, however, once she married Kean she conscientiously dwindled into a wife. No longer Ellen Tree, she was henceforth Mrs. Kean, subordinating her interests to his, playing such roles as supported his roles, promoting his reputation, health, wealth, professional programs, and ambitions in every way possible to a wifely collaborating assistant.

In the autumn of 1845 the Keans began a two-season visit to America, their main purpose being to produce on this side of the Atlantic a grand series of classic English plays according to the principles of historical accuracy. Although ultimately frustrated in their endeavor, their significant contribution to Shakespeare in America was to initiate this typically Victorian staging practice. Whatever else Shakespeare's plays might be worth, they were also becoming instruments of popular education, illustrated lessons in European history, ancient and modern. This was not new in England. Over twenty years earlier, as we have seen, Charles Kemble had commissioned James Robinson Planché to create historically accurate costumes for *King John* and other plays. In the 1837–39 seasons at Covent Garden, William Charles Macready had offered well-researched historical reconstructions of both costumes and scenery for *King Lear, Coriolanus, Henry V*, and others, and between 1841 and 1843 at Drury Lane he had added to his list *As You Like It, King John, Cymbeline*, and others. Kean himself had been involved in the movement in a minor way. At Drury Lane in 1838, as a countercheck to Macready's endeavors, Manager Alfred Bunn had presented Kean in an elaborately historicized revival of *Richard III* (the Cibber version); and again in January 1844 Bunn and Kean had revived (and improved?) this same production.

When the Keans came to the Park Theatre in New York in 1845, they brought some of the paraphernalia of the Drury Lane production with them, and while they played two short engagements in their standard repertory pieces—*The Gamester, Much Ado, As You Like It, Money, Hamlet, The Stranger*, etc.—the scene painters, costumers, and machinists began preparing for a revival of *Richard III*.[40] It took place on January 7, 1846, and, as Philip Hone had been told, it was intended as the first in "a series of Shakespearean plays which Mr. Kean has undertaken to get up in a style of unusual magnificence." Everything about it came off splendidly—except perhaps the acting. Hone thought that Mrs. Kean made something interesting of the small part of Queen Elizabeth, "but her husband cannot play Gloster."[41] The reviewer for the *Spirit of the Times* suggested that "Mrs. Kean could play the part much better than her husband."[42] Nonetheless it enjoyed packed houses every night for three weeks and could have run longer but for engagements elsewhere which the Keans were committed to.

Illus. 73. Charles Kean as Richard III.

The New York audiences were properly dazzled by the staging. In Hone's opinion, "The scenery is beautiful, representing the actual places where the events took place; the costumes of all the characters, from the king in his royal tent to the sentinel walking his lonely round, the armor, standards, music all are strictly correct and derived with antiquarian diligence from the most authentic historical records, so that the spectator seems carried back to the times of the white and red roses, and transported on one of Professor Morse's copper wires to Bosworth Field and Tamworth."[43] The critic of the *Albion* described the production at vast length (most of the *Albion* review is reprinted in Odell's *Annals*), mentioning every one of the twenty-two scenes and noting many details of the dresses, music, and heraldic effects.[44] With the *Albion*'s words, supplemented by watercolors and

Illus. 74. Charles and Ellen Kean in *King John*.

drawings in later Kean promptbooks,[45] we can envision the production scene by scene: the garden of the Tower of London with the White Tower in the background; the funeral procession of Henry VI through the cloisters of Old St. Paul's with a view of the churchyard and the Gothic cathedral; the city gates of London with a distant view of London Bridge; and many landscape, tented camp, and battlefield scenes of the final act.

Exactly when Kean first engaged in serious historical and archaeological researches, for which he would win monumental reputation at the Princess's Theatre in the 1850s, it is impossible to say; but for these first practical ventures in historical staging in America it appears that he simply took the eftest way. He engaged the service of one George Cressall Ellis, prompter at Drury Lane Theatre (later to become Kean's own stage manager at the Princess's), to transcribe for him out of the Drury Lane Library the promptbooks of the Macready productions.[46] Whenever he could find them Ellis was also to send Macready's costume and scene designs. In December of 1845 he sent the promptbook of *The Two Gentlemen of Verona*, with ink sketches of eight scenes; Kean staged it at the Park on October 6, 1846. Ellis sent the promptbook of *King John*, together with William Telbin's fourteen watercolor scene designs, in March 1846; Kean staged it at the Park on November 16, 1846. Ellis sent the promptbook of Milton's *Comus* in January 1846, and *Macbeth* in July 1846; Kean announced production of these two to follow *King John*, but with the failure of *King John* he abandoned his program altogether. The unstoppable Ellis continued to prepare other books, complete with costume and scene designs—*The Merchant of Venice*, *Othello*, and *Cymbeline*—while Kean was still in America, and in the following years yet others, which Kean would keep for future reference.

Kean's *Two Gentlemen* was the first production of that play in America, but otherwise it was not remarkable; it disappeared after three nights. *King John*, heavily publicized, was supposed to surpass *Richard III* in attractiveness. It cost $12,000 to produce; at least 176 costumes were made new for it, and in one scene alone 150 persons were on the stage; the scenes were painted on more than 15,000 square feet of canvas. One fact not mentioned in the advertising, but which should nonetheless have improved the play's chances, was that the fourteen scenes were closely adapted from Telbin's splendid designs. In fine dedication to a noble cause, the *Albion* reviewed *King John*, or at least noticed it, after every one of its eighteen performances (most of the *Albion*'s account of the scenery, published on November 21, is reprinted in Odell's *Annals*), but the play simply did not draw.[47] Nothing could overcome the public's indifference to an unpopular play. Houses of $600 to $800 could not pay off the huge expense. Kean's first impulse, restrained only out of consideration for Manager Simpson, was to vent his wrath on the audience and withdraw the piece. Then for reasons unknown he took offense at Simpson, too, and at the end of the third week he seceded from the Park and went off for a tour of the South and Middle West to recoup his losses. What was achieved by this expensive disaster is that it set a high level of productional splendor for the future Shakespearean theatre of America.

WILLIAM EVANS BURTON

The first actor-manager in America to take up the cause of full stage production of Shakespeare, as Kean had demonstrated it, was not a tragedian but a specialist in low comedy and eccentric character roles, William Evans Burton (1804–60).[48] Burton was the son of a London printer and bookseller. Intended for the ministry, he began his classical education at St. Paul's School and proceeded to Cambridge, but when he was eighteen his father died and he had to withdraw from school to run his father's business. In 1825, after dabbling in amateur theatricals, he left business for the stage. For some nine years—most of them in the provinces—he developed his broad comic style, studying and imitating the methods of John Reeve, John Liston (whom he replaced for one season at the Haymarket), Edward Knight, and others. In 1834 he emigrated and joined the Arch Street Theatre in Philadelphia. For the next quarter of a century he would prosper as actor and manager in cities along the eastern seaboard, his finest years being those between 1848 and 1856 in New York when he conducted a company of first-rate comedians at Burton's Theatre in Chambers Street.

In his offstage portraits Burton does not look the least bit actorish. His handsome head, with large clear features, sits low on the shoulders of a stocky if not fat body. His thick dark hair is brushed at the sides in a style fashionable at mid-century. According to William Keese, his biographer, "He seemed in general aspect to blend the suave respectability of a bank president with the easy

Illus. 75. King John, Act I, scene 1, as staged by Macready in 1842 and restaged by Kean in New York, 1846.

going air of an English country squire."[49] He was in fact a genial, generous host at two houses—a four-story city house in Hudson Street and a country mansion on Long Island Sound. During the years when he must have been busiest establishing his theatrical career in America he worked hard also at writing and publishing, and he was a famous bibliophile and collector. In Philadelphia in the later 1830s he published the *Gentleman's Magazine* (Edgar Allan Poe assisted him as editor) and two volumes of the *Literary Souvenir*. He contributed stories and articles to these and essays on theatrical subjects to the *Knickerbocker Magazine*. In the 1850s he compiled a four-volume *Cyclopedia of Wit and Humor* that went through numerous editions. In New York in 1852 he promoted and was first president of a Shakespeare society, which included not only a number of actors but such well-known writers and men of affairs as Richard Grant White, George William Curtis, Charles Dana, Gulian Verplanck, Charles Daly, and Parke Godwin.[50] He assembled a library of some 20,000 volumes, containing the finest collection of dramatic and theatrical literature in America, and built a three-story fireproof building outside his Hudson Street residence to house it.[51] He owned all four of the Shakespeare Folios, many of the early Quartos, numerous Shakespearean source and background books, the eighteenth-century and modern editions, and a folio set of the plays divided into thirty-seven parts and extra-illustrated with pictorial items which he had personally collected. He owned hundreds of other Elizabethan and seventeenth-century English plays and countless biographies of actors, histories of the theatre, and cognate items. His interests, however, reached far beyond those of the profession. As Keese said, "He loved learning for its own sake." He collected dictionaries, Bibles, Americana, travel books, wit and humor. He owned all the earliest printings of Chaucer, a 1497 Dante, a rare sixteenth-century Plautus, a vast lot of English Renaissance poetry, and many early editions of the Latin classics. And he knew and used his books. He loved to spend Sundays in the library with his three daughters, promoting their education. He would often adjourn a social gathering to the library, where he would lay out and explain his treasures. White, Verplanck, and many another scholar of the day depended upon his collection for their research.

However learned, however dignified he was in private, Burton's business was to make people laugh. Once onstage, his handsome, well-composed features could ex-

Illus. 76. William Evans Burton.

press utter absurdities, and he hardly needed the words of an author to sustain the merriment. As Francis Wemyss once wrote, "We have seen Burton keep an audience in roars of inextinguishable laughter, for minutes in succession, while an expression of ludicrous bewilderment, of blank confusion, or pompous inflation, settled upon his countenance."[52] As a comedian he apparently stood somewhere between *actor*, who conceals himself in the character he is playing, and *clown*, who stands beside the character, laughing at it and flattering the audience by inviting them to share in his fun.

James Murdoch, who for some reason did not like Burton, accused him of using artistically indefensible techniques in order to get away with indecencies. Given an "objectional expression" to utter, "he winked his eye at the audience without reserve, and wriggled and grimaced . . . , rolling the precious morsel under his tongue, and actually smacking his lips, as it were, with unction at a questionable joke"; what the author had only remotely hinted at, Burton would paint "with a copious daubing of unmistakable grossness."[53] Probably a fair specimen of what, in hypersensitive niceness, Murdoch took exception to is contained in a passage of a farce called *The Mummy*. Burton played Toby Tramp, a down-at-heels actor, who is persuaded to impersonate a mummy which a sharper has promised to deliver to an antiquarian. The scene is the antiquarian's museum, and the mummy is brought in. As William Keese told it,

After the necessary raptures . . . the professor withdraws and the stage is left alone. There lies the mummy in his case, and a pause succeeds. The intent audience observe a slight movement in the box. Slowly the head of Burton is raised, and he glances warily around the room. Raising himself to a sitting posture in the case, he turns toward the audience his marvellous face, on which rests an expression of doleful humiliation. We shall never forget how, finally, he rose to his feet, stepped out of the case, walked abjectly to the foot-lights, looked his disguise all over with intense concern, and then turned to the house—by this time scarcely able to contain itself—and said, with the accent of self-reproach and mortification—"I'm [damned] if I'm not ashamed of myself!"[54]

Murdoch, perhaps, would "never use a big, big D——" (which even Keese conventionally suppressed from print), but the word on Burton's lips must have had much the effect of Eliza Doolittle's *bloody* half a century afterward. The audience laughed but the nation did not fall.

The character of Toby Tramp was nothing, of course; but whatever character Burton played—Nick Bottom or Paul Pry, Micawber or Autolycus—he brought to it "this native faculty of rising superior to the part assumed, and investing it with undreamed-of humorous interest . . . the felicitous interpretation, the by-play, the way of saying a thing, the facial expression—his own and no other man's—the Burtonian touch and treatment."[55]

The theatre which Burton converted into his own in 1848 had been Palmo's Opera House, built near City Hall Park four years earlier by an Italian restaurant keeper who wished (but failed) to provide a permanent home for Italian opera. It was an intimate house, seating about eight hundred in its parquet, dress circle, and family circle; and after Burton installed a new proscenium with private boxes at either side, new carpeting, new chandeliers, and gold decorations, it was often referred to as a jewel of a theatre. The size was certainly appropriate to

the program of comedy that Burton projected and to the controlled and often delicate acting of such performers as John Brougham, Henry Placide, William Rufus Blake, and Charles Fisher, Mary Taylor, Lizzie Weston, Fanny Wallack, and Mrs. Hoey, who in various seasons were featured in his bills.[56]

Burton did not come to Shakespeare until his fourth season, and then perhaps only because in the autumn of 1851 he brought in for a brief engagement the famous London star Mary Amelia Warner, who had been one of Macready's leading ladies, then partner of Samuel Phelps at Sadler's Wells, and more recently manageress of the Marylebone Theatre. Among the plays Burton staged for her were *The Winter's Tale* and *Macbeth*. Presumably he resorted to stock scenery for these, and we may well wonder how effectively his stable of comedians supported the visitor in such heavy drama; but all that mattered to the New York audiences was the opportunity to see Mrs. Warner in her two most celebrated Shakespearean roles. Of her Hermione in the Statue Scene, the *Albion* declared "that such a bit of stage illusion was never seen in New York, and that no professed model artist ever came near it in a 'living statue.'"[57]

Busy as he was with producing old and new comedies, farces, extravaganzas, and adaptations from Dickens, Burton was alerted to the challenge and the usefulness of Shakespearean comedy. In March of 1852 he staged *Twelfth Night*, again without any special getting up of scenery, but with a cast which thirty-five years later Joe Jefferson would claim had never yet been equaled.[58] Reviewers on the spot, to be sure, found things to complain about.[59] William Blake seems to have altogether missed the ridiculous arrogance of Malvolio and to have played him almost like a man of sense and breeding; Henry Placide (perhaps too old for the part) offered a very grave, sententious, unamusing Feste. Burton, though, won an instant triumph as Toby Belch. According to the *Albion* he "was admirably made up, and revelled and rollicked with infinite gusto through the fun set down for him"; and the contrast between his fat-bellied self and the Aguecheek of Mr. Lester (Lester Wallack), "who was the very essence of feebleness and thread-paperism, was exquisitely droll." Most attractive on the romantic side was Lizzie Weston's Viola. She alone was huzzaed and called before the curtain at the end. "Her Viola," said one critic, "was remarkable for its simplicity of conception, its delicacy of feeling, and the easy, natural way in which the points were taken up." A week or two later the reviewer for the *Spirit of the Times* marveled that one so young as she could outact "the best and (alas!) the oldest actors in the profession. Well, well, we old boys have little chance by the side of a young and pretty girl. The eyes and ears are more quickly acted on than the brain, and beauty is a sure card all the world over. Success attend all pretty girls, say we."[60]

From Toby Belch to John Falstaff would seem a natural transition, and a year later, on March 14, 1853, Burton brought out *The Merry Wives of Windsor*, promising to follow it with Part I of *Henry IV*. The text was Shakespearean: that is to say, it was a reduced (and of course bowdlerized) version of the original, stripped too of the dozen and more songs and other additions laid on it at Drury Lane in the 1820s when Frederic Reynolds made it into a comic opera. For the first time Burton attempted

Illus. 77. Mr. and Mrs. Burton as Sir Toby Belch and Maria.

a "full" production of Shakespeare. Nine new sets by his scene painter, Mr. Hielge, represented Windsor Town, Windsor Castle, and environs "exactly" as they appeared during the reign of Henry IV. The wardrobe for the play, constructed by Mr. Keyser, was derived from models of the early fifteenth century. In all this well-advertised historicity and textual fidelity, Burton was directly following the lead of Charles Kean, who in the autumn of 1851 had staged the play in London, together with *Henry IV*, in the very same manner. Unfortunately Burton's production did not please.[61] Except for the Dame Quickly of Mrs. Hughes and the Dr. Caius of Henry Placide (whose comic Frenchmen in any play were a delight), none of the actors made much of an impression. Burton's Falstaff, which should easily have topped his joyous Toby Belch, was a failure. Perversely he restrained his natural exuberance, withheld his winks, his leers, his chuckles, his wriggles: to the bafflement of his audience, he presented Falstaff as *Sir* John—a gentleman! Having committed himself to that strategic error, he could not afford to go on with it, and he quietly dropped his plans for *Henry IV*.

On February 3, 1854, Burton achieved a chef d'oeuvre with his production of *A Midsummer Night's Dream*.[62] In his curtain speech that evening he was careful to point out that he had never seen the *Dream* in performance, and thus all the stage business and all the spectacular effects that the audience had just been enjoying were entirely new and original. Why did he feel called on to make such a declaration of artistic independence? Because, as everyone knew, the inspiration for his production had been the news and reviews of Samuel Phelps's glorious staging of the play at Sadler's Wells in London only four months earlier. Indeed, the Broadway Theatre, too, had caught Phelps-fever and would reveal its version of the *Dream* three nights later. Phelps was already famous for his masterly rendition of Nick Bottom and even more for his magical scenic effects: by cunning use of moving panoramas (in place of the customary wing-and-shutter system of scene changing), of lighting, and of gauze curtains softening the contours, his scenes melted dreamlike one into another.[63]

Burton's efforts at scenic magic were limited by the size and equipment of his stage, but there were other claims he could put forward.[64] The text, for the first time in America, was purely Shakespearean, cleansed of the operatic additions Reynolds had made in 1816. During the course of the evening the entire Felix Mendelssohn

Illus. 78. William Burton as Bottom.

Dream music would be performed—for the first time in any theatre. The corps de ballet, composed of pretty little girls as fairies and satyrs who really looked like satyrs, would execute appropriate dances. And the scenery and dresses would be historically correct. Early in the run, Burton published a twenty-four-page pamphlet listing the cast, summarizing the play, reprinting a number of the reviews, describing the scenes, and whenever relevant citing the scholarly authorities from which the physical staging was derived. The play opened grandly in "A courtyard of the Palace of Theseus, with the entry of the Duke of Athens and his warriors and the Queen of Amazons and her Guard." The warriors were "attired in the correct costume of old Greece, as pictured by Willemin, in his *Costumes des Peuples d'Antiquité.*" The Athenian civilians wore "rich tunics given on the authority of Hope in his *Ancient Costume,* with the cothurnus or buskin and Attic fillet on the head." Hermia and Helena wore "the long sleeveless tunic, the caladris or stole, with the rich and varied peplum over the bust, and the crepida sandal." The next scene, where Peter Quince was at home, was no mere peasant's hut pulled from the scene dock, but "a plain room in the severe simplicity of the earliest Doric." For once a New York audience was served as fulsomely with erudition as Charles Kean served his audiences at the Princess's in London.

Other scenes, less loaded down with "authority," sound rather more inviting. The second act opened in "The Wood by Moonlight," into which Oberon and Titania descended in aerial cars. The fourth act opened with a fairy dance in Titania's bower at sunrise: "The mist rises from the valleys and the God of Day rises in powerful splendor." The final scene took place in the great hall of Theseus's Palace, with a stage erected for the Pyramus and Thisbe play. This stage, we know, was a genuine theatre-within-a-theatre, with proscenium arch, draw curtains, and prompter's bell and whistle; and when Pyramus died he of course rolled off the front of the mock stage and had to roll himself back onto it.

The acting seems generally to have been satisfactory. Burton properly cast Puck—too often in those days played by a pretty woman—to Master C. T. Parsloe, who acted the role not sentimentally but as a juvenile satyr—rascally, grinning, mischievous, rude. And Burton recovered whatever credit he may have lost with his misguided Falstaff by delivering an authentic Nick Bottom—no dull, heavy-witted clown, but a merry, conceited fellow, nat-

urally admired by his simple companions for his pretensions to knowledge, skill, and authority. And if Burton was inclined in some roles to "speak more than was set down for him," in Bottom he restrained himself. "He follows his author," said the *Albion*; "he refuses almost all temptations to run riot."

Those critics who objected that Burton's stage was not broad or deep enough for "the right setting forth of the dainty imagination of the great poet" were better pleased with the more expansive staging at the Broadway, where they even found moving panoramas. Otherwise, however, the Broadway *Dream* fell short of Burton's.[65] The orchestra played Mendelssohn only "scraggily"; W. Davidge misconceived Bottom and fell into public dispute with his critics; Puck was played prettily by a girl child billed as "La Petite Viola," but as one critic complained, she was got up according to the ideas of Kenny Meadows (a popular Shakespeare illustrator), not according to the ideas of Shakespeare. And for no reason easily discernible the Broadway production brought down severe attacks on the play itself. The *Herald* critic found himself tired of Bottom, thought Puck merely wearisome, dismissed the lovers as positive bores. "Who on earth cares about any of them?" he exclaimed. As for their language, "We have picked the diamonds out long before the actors have waded through the trash." The *Tribune* critic, buzzing with socialism, pitched into Shakespeare for always telling lies about the Working-Man. Why was it that he could never "produce one ray of genius or polish except in courtly Hamlets and gallant Petruchios"? Why were his honest laborers always greasy, dirty, stupid, and slavish?[66]

Heartened by the triumph of *A Midsummer Night's Dream*, Burton two months later (April 11) introduced his second Shakespeare of the season, a spectacular production of *The Tempest.*[67] Again he could boast that here at last the play could be seen in America "more nearly as Shakespeare wrote it"—that is to say, without the Dryden-Davenant additions which had displaced the original for nearly two centuries. Macready had "restored" the text in his Covent Garden production in 1838, and Burton's stage manager, the Irishman John Moore, had brought from England a transcription of Macready's promptbook: thus Burton had before him a well-worked version upon which to found his own.[68]

In his curtain speech Burton likened the task of staging so big a play in so small a theatre to "raising a tempest

in a teapot." Yet he seems not to have shirked any of the indicated technical effects, and most of them worked well enough. In the opening scene, while lightning flashed and devils flew through the air, a ship tossed amid frothy waves until it broke to pieces. This, said the *Tribune* (easily satisfied), "may be commended as one of the most artistic scenic interpretations yet rendered on our re-formed stage." Prospero, wanting a bench to rest upon, waved his wand and caused a tree to fall just where he needed it. A winged Ariel flew in and out of the scenes, though on all-too-visible ropes instead of neat wires. Iris appeared in her rainbow, Juno with a pair of mechanical peacocks which dutifully spread their tails. Besides their wonderment at these pantomimic gimmicks, the critics generally reported the acting as excellent. Mrs. C. B. Hill sang sweetly as Ariel, Charles Fisher delivered Prospero's verse in a "dignified, impressive manner," and George Jordan's Ferdinand was clear, sensible, and distinct. Burton forsook comedy for once and played a threatening Caliban. He was shaggy, misshapen, half-human in appearance, with long talons on his hands and feet, his utterance "half snarl, half hiss," his manner a kind of "dull fiendish malice or besotted merriment." William Keese, who was a boy when he saw this Caliban, tried to forget it: "It terrified us and made us dream bad dreams."[69]

The *Tribune* reviewer on February 14, 1856, observed that "Mr. Burton is deservedly earning for his house the title of Shakespeare's theater, and we begin to look forward to these yearly revivals with the same pleasure as to the coming of Spring." Unfortunately, *The Winter's Tale*, which the critic had just seen, was to be Burton's last Shakespearean creation.[70] He would presently leave Chambers Street for a larger theatre, undertake there a program of visiting stars (Edwin Booth, Charlotte Cushman, the Davenports, and others), lose that theatre, and go on the road. Early in 1860 he died. But *The Winter's Tale* made a fine period to his career as a Shakespearean producer. Once again he brought his erudition to bear upon a re-creation of life in classical antiquity; and though his program notes are nothing compared to those of Charles Kean, whose own *Winter's Tale* would appear in London two months later, yet the delight which his

Illus. 79. Playbill for Burton's *Midsummer Night's Dream*, 1854.

reviewers took in the play, the acting, and the *mise-en-scène* suggests that this was indeed a masterwork. The first act took place in the Vestibule of a Sicilian Palace, with a view of Mount Aetna, and in the course of it was featured a Pyrrhic Dance by sixteen youths "embodying many beautiful and graceful tableaux." The third act showed the Theatre at Syracuse prepared for the trial of Queen Hermione, "a correct and classical representation of the administration of justice in ancient Greece." The passing of sixteen years between acts three and four was represented by a "Classical Allegory" of the Four Seasons in transit, followed by the retreat of the Goddess of Night before the ascent of Phoebus in the Chariot of the Sun. Perdita's home in Bohemia, in the fourth act, was a pastoral scene in mountain country of great beauty, suffused with roseate sunlight. The Statue Scene of the fifth act was staged in the peristyle of Leontes's palace in Sicily.[71]

In John Moore's workbook for running the show we discover a bit of useful information about the "Classical Allegory": immediately after the passage of the Four Seasons, the figure of Time (a bald-headed old man in sandals and slate-colored robes bearing a scythe and an hourglass) emerged from among "Working Clouds," spoke his piece, and disappeared again. But elsewhere Moore complicated matters by suggestions for improving the Allegory. In his promptbook he pinned slips of paper bearing the following prescriptions:

Temple of Jupiter Ammon on top of Globe (see Martin's picture of Lucifer [the reference is to John Martin's engraving of Lucifer at Book 2, Line 1, "High on a throne of royal state," of *Paradise Lost*]).[72] Painted gigantic Jupiter with sceptre &c, signifying, or intended to signify Universal Sovereignty.

Jupiter descends slowly shewing Time behind him. Temple and Globe descend leaving Time discovered on back of (*Republican*) eagle—comes forward to speak with an American flag in his hands delicately hinting at Manifest Destiny, which will enable Time to carry the Stars and Stripes all over the Earth and adjacent planets.

Times goes off, and back clouds rise shewing Phoebus in his chariot of day drawn by the hours (*all painted*). As this works up, Landscape is discovered behind.

Then Autolycus enters, singing, "When daffodils begin to peer."

We must assume that Moore was joking, although as a matter of fact the expressions of patriotism which he seems to be making fun of are not much more extravagant

Illus. 80. William Burton as Autolycus.

than what audiences of those days, fired up by the Mexican War or the Oregon Question (Fifty-four Forty or Fight!), might have expected to see in the theatre. But the notion of carrying the American flag into outer space was *too* farfetched: in 1856 only an Irishman concocting a leg-pull could have dreamed up such an absurdity.

Burton's actors were generally praised for their command over the often difficult text. The critic for the *Spirit of the Times* was so in love with Miss Thorne's Perdita that he longed for a painter's skill to immortalize her on canvas. The *Herald* declared Mrs. Parker's Hermione quite the equal of Mrs. Warner's, and found Mrs. Hughes's Paulina a valuable advocate for women's rights. The editor of the *Tribune* evidently engaged a special writer—perhaps one of Burton's scholar friends—to cover the event, for the *Tribune* review is a remarkably long, carefully composed essay which not only judiciously discusses the work of the actors but recounts the origin of the play and its early stage history, analyzes the art of its construction, and discusses the significance of the principal characters. Happily in its last long section it comes to focus in a glowing tribute to Burton's rendering of Autolycus, which was "the great feature of the night."

Burton was in prime order. When entering with his careless jollity of air and greasy swagger, he might have stood for a picture of Rembrandt. He absolutely reveled in the geniality of the character as if it was his own. Mirth seemed indigenous to his nature, and shot out with an unchecked luxuriance. Nothing was stunted. He appeared to run riot in mirth. Yet the relish did not interfere with the exquisite delicacy in which he touched off a shade or pictured a quaint humor, or described a beautiful image. . . . We have never seen the fun cream up more exuberantly, and its flow was full of racy flavor. The audience were in high spirits. The sly humor of the rogue oozed out so quaintly that if it were not for the recognition he gives to the audience in the shape of a nod or a wink—which points the fun like a poke in the ribs—one would think it equally unconscious as spontaneous. Never did an actor admit an audience more confidentially and unreservedly into his secrets. The whole audience seemed to him one person; his wink seemed directed to each particular person, and it was only the universal roar which disturbed each one's delusion that he was himself the special confidante. Even the victims seemed half gammoned with their own consent, so oily was his deception. What stiff, formal, artificial and exaggerated imitators of human nature do all other actors appear beside him.

From time to time Burton played other of Shakespeare's clowns—Dromio and Touchstone, for instance—but only in stock productions. On September 6, 1852, he joined the Castle Garden company to celebrate the centenary of the Hallams' first performance in America: the play was *The Merchant of Venice*, of course, and Burton stood in for Lewis Hallam as Launcelot Gobbo.

Chapter V

Masters of the Craft

DURING THE THIRD QUARTER of the nineteenth century one can perceive a certain coming-of-age of Shakespeare in the American theatre. Without breaking the lines of interest and influence running from England, the American Shakespeareans achieved a measure of independence and developed initiatives of their own. Incidentally, American scholarship in Shakespeare was also well under way. Gulian Verplanck's three-volume edition of the *Works* had come out in 1844–47. H. N. Hudson was delivering his famous Shakespeare lectures in the 1840s, and his popular eleven-volume edition, graced with these lectures, began to appear in 1851. The brightest of the early American editors, Richard Grant White, whose injunction to the reader was to read the plays—"Throw the commentators and editors to the dogs. Don't read any man's notes, or essays, or introductions. . . . Don't read mine"—brought out his edition in twelve volumes between 1857 and 1865. In 1871 Horace Howard Furness issued *Romeo and Juliet*, the first item in the great New Variorum Edition upon which we still depend. Several other American editions and many reprints of English editions were available, so that every American reader had easy access to Shakespeare's own texts.

As we have seen in the last chapter, William Burton discovered the uses of "production" and presented several Shakespeare comedies in newly designed mountings. In E. L. Davenport we find an actor of remarkable versatility whose art was sufficiently refined and effective to win approval on both sides of the Atlantic. John McCullough, associate of Edwin Forrest and his artistic heir, succeeded in humanizing and civilizing the greater roles of his master—in projecting Othello and Lear, for instance, in their full dimensions yet stripped clean of the Forrestian self-serving interpretation and melodramatic excess. Finally, in Edwin Booth there emerged an actor remembered to this day as his century's finest, who moreover looked be-

yond his art as an actor to attempt (however he failed) to create a total theatre, where the best plays would be best mounted and acted to the best of audiences—total in every way.

EDWARD LOOMIS DAVENPORT

It has long been a subject of wonder that Edward Loomis Davenport (1815–77), who could and did perform every sort of role extremely well, should not be counted among the foremost actors of his generation.[1] Even he wondered about this. Late in life he would boast that once upon a time he had played in one evening "an act from *Hamlet*, one from *Black-Eyed Susan*, and sung *A Yankee Ship and a Yankee Crew*, and danced a hornpipe, and wound up with a nigger part"; and he would demand somewhat truculently whether anyone in the profession nowadays could equal such a feat.[2] It probably did not occur to him that no one then eminent in the profession would wish to do so. From Richard Burbage to Edwin Booth many a great actor's reputation had been heightened by versatility; but from Hamlet to hornpipes is a long leap downward, and the gentlemanly Hamlets of the 1870s could not afford such antics.

In any case, by the 1870s Davenport seemed to have outlived his day. He had been all things without becoming identified with anything distinctive or permanently marketable. First-class managers no longer cared to engage him, and their response to his applications was everywhere the same: "A devilish good actor, but don't draw."[3]

The son of a Boston tavern keeper, Davenport was stage-struck from early youth, and in 1836, at the age of twenty-one, he mounted the bottom step of the professional ladder, playing small parts in stock companies along the eastern seaboard. His progress, though steady, was slow. Ten years later, having won commendations

Illus. 81. Edward Loomis Davenport.

from the elder Booth, Edwin Forrest, and other touring stars for his work in supporting roles, he accepted the position of leading man with Anna Cora Mowatt, the young society matron and playwright turned actress.[4] In those days no ambitious actor in his thirty-first year would submit to second billing under a woman (a near amateur at that), but the advantage for Davenport was that with Mrs. Mowatt he could play certain leading roles hitherto outside his range: he could drop Macduff and take on Romeo, could substitute Benedick for Laertes and Richmond, and could add to his repertory certain heavy roles of modern vintage. He toured America with Mrs. Mowatt for one season and accompanied her to England for two seasons more. He found an English wife—the actress Fanny Vining—and stayed on in England for a total of seven years, touring the provinces as an American tragedian and sometimes playing support to such English stars as G. V. Brooke and William Charles Macready.

Davenport approached the English theatre somewhat gingerly, for the late forties was a time of considerable political strain between England and America, and he vigorously insisted upon his "Americanism." As he put it jocularly in a letter home early in 1848, "It will take us some little time to get our posts well bedded in the soil of their beef-eating, porter-guzzling hearts, but when we do, 'git out of the way, old Dan Tucker.' . . . Tell Ayling I have seen nothing here of my size, age, looks, and weight that I fear."[5] Or in a spirit of playful jingoism, early in 1849—about the time the Forrest-Macready quarrel in America was building toward its bloody catastrophe: "Well, we are still here in John Bulldom, and are still better Yankees than ever; our last success has raised us in our own estimation several feet, and per cent. to match. We feel thanks. Yankees are some 'punkins,' and dear old America in the dim distance looms up like the seventy-four-gun ship of nations amidst a whole squadron of Baltimore clippers. We are a great people and bound to be greater, and to any fool who dares to squint at us we will prove we are nutmeg graters of the greatest sort."[6] Meanwhile, however, his professional competence and his amiable personality were persuading British audiences to sink national differences in easy enjoyment of his acting.

The English critics, who in Davenport's words were "loth to allow that Yankees have talent," received him surprisingly well. The *Times* of February 10, 1848, spoke of his "good person and gentlemanlike bearing," acknowledged the genuinely pathetic effects he achieved in *The Stranger,* and allowed him to be "an actor of considerable talent." The *Examiner* of April 1 thought him "one of the most sensible American actors we have seen," and on May 20, reviewing his joint performance with G. V. Brooke in a play called *The Lords of Ellingham,* found him to be the better of the two: "He is not always Sir Termagant. He speaks often sensibly and unaffectedly, is easy and self-possessed in manner, and during Edith's dying scene showed a real tenderness. . . . Mr. Brooke is violent throughout."

In the season of 1850–51, hired by Ben Webster at the Haymarket to support Macready in his long series of farewells, he ran afoul of "The Eminent Tragedian's" bad temper. On one occasion, after he had played with especial energy, Macready asked him rather cuttingly not to "*act* quite so much." At their next performance Davenport folded his arms and merely walked his part, so that Macready had to reverse himself: "You will oblige me, Mr. Davenport, by throwing a little more animation into your acting." Thus, as Davenport remembered it, he had taught the great man a lesson, and the episode ended "to the satisfaction of both sides."[7] Perhaps that was all that occurred on the surface, but inwardly Macready raged.[8] When he played Iago he wrote in his diary that Davenport was "very feeble and inefficient in Othello." When they exchanged these roles, he was upset by the "wretched bad acting and *imperfectness*" of Davenport's Iago. Again he labeled the Iago "an atrocious stick . . . really and utterly devoid of all meaning"; and one night (echoes from Astor Place!) he was convinced that Davenport was being applauded by "a parcel of Yankee claqueurs." Davenport never knew how thoroughly Macready disliked him, for these ugly remarks were suppressed from the only edition of Macready's diaries that appeared during Davenport's lifetime. Meanwhile he must have been gratified by what the critics said about his part in the engagement: they flattered his "good natural qualifications," his "judgment and feeling," his "force and intelligence"—and even prophesied his success in the tragic line.[9]

Unfortunately he did not adhere to the tragic line. At

Illus. 83. E. L. Davenport as Othello.

the end of the Macready plays in which for two months he had been admired by the best audiences in London in such roles as Brutus, Laertes, Macduff, and Othello, he let himself be drawn into one of those displays which, as we surmise from hindsight, served to diminish his reputation as a serious actor. From time to time, though not conspicuously, he had been playing William the Sailor, the hero of Douglas Jerrold's melodrama *Black-Eyed Susan* —a piece so crudely comical in its exploitation of nautical jargon and so blatantly absurd in character, situation, and action that it seems to us nowadays little more than a far-off promise of *H.M.S. Pinafore*. To Davenport, however, it was neither crude nor absurd, and when, at the request of the author and for the pleasure of Dickens, Thackeray, and others of the literary set,[10] Webster put him up for William at the Haymarket, he played it in deadly earnest, by no means parodistically. The first night was a grand occasion. The box of eminent authors laughed and wept

Illus. 82. E. L. Davenport as Benedick.

with all the rest. According to the *Times*, Davenport's "hilarity is hearty and unaffected, his pathos is manly and genuine. . . . From the beginning to the end of the piece he was applauded not only by the hands, but by the audible mirth and visible tears of his public, and when it was ascertained that the model sailor was not to be strung from the yard-arm the delight expressed was as if he had been a personal friend of everybody present."[11] Davenport's identification with William was so easy, complete, and satisfying that, as Laurence Hutton would say on a later occasion, "we can only account for it as being a true artist's handling of an impressive part."[12] William Winter would call it "acting of a high order."[13]

While in England, Davenport studied to improve his acting of the classics, of course, and what he learned of especial value was the importance of organization, discipline, and company collaboration. He was confident that American actors of the day—Miss Cushman, Mrs. Mowatt, John Gilbert, he himself—were individually talented enough to hold their own with the best of the British; but what the American theatre lacked was "system."

> We can play Shakspere almost *without* a rehearsal. Not so here. The actors and all know and feel their responsibility (I am speaking of the greatest theatres), and for their own credit's sake are alive to all. Stage appointments are also here more attended to, effects of scenery more studied, the artist being for a period the director for his own purpose; then the machinist, and then, with good acting, regulated by a stage manager who knows his business, you see things done well.[14]

How much these recognitions contributed to his managerial practices in years to come is moot. One notes that as a sign of good intention he brought home a transcription of Macready's promptbook of the "restored" *King Lear* —but probably he never used it.[15] And he abandoned the impulse to coach or correct his fellow actors. Clara Morris reported that long before the 1860s he had vowed "never again to volunteer any advice, any suggestion, any hint as to reading, or business, or make-up to man or woman in any play of mine." Crushed by the weight of what he called that "lump of stupid self-satisfaction we call the 'profession,' " he seems to have given up early any hope of bringing the American theatre up to scratch.[16]

In 1854, then in his thirty-ninth year, Davenport reentered the American theatre and made his bid for recognition as a star. His physical qualifications were splendid:

a strong-framed, well-proportioned body; large, handsome, expressive facial features, eminently visible from the stage; a voice often described as soft and melodious, yet powerful enough in climaxes, and in moments of excitement, said William Winter, "characterized by a ringing quality which was singularly affecting."[17] He performed the standard Shakespearean roles—Othello, Hamlet, Shylock, Richard III, Macbeth, and Brutus—and the critics who thought of him only as a respectable actor of character parts and roles in melodramas were astonished by his self-control, good taste, and what someone called a triumph of intelligence over physique. During his long apprenticeship and years abroad he had become a master of histrionic technique and a precisionist rather than an overwhelmer in performance. Of his Othello, in which he opened on September 11, 1854, the *New York Herald* critic wrote, "In his natural and truthful rendering of those delicate and sensitive qualities of the Moor's character which are in general lost in the effort to give an *ad captandum* effect to it, and in his entire avoidance of those violent exaggerations which, however they may please the multitude, are as offensive to good taste as they are false to the spirit of the text, and in the concentration and intensity of his emotions, he approaches nearer the French school of tragedy than any actor we have as yet seen."[18] In whatever role he played, Henry Dickinson Stone tells us, "the various parts appear so duly balanced that the impression left upon the mind is precisely that produced by a well-drawn, well-grouped, and well-colored picture."[19]

Davenport's Shylock, which he did not play often, perhaps fell short of the smooth-blended perfection which Stone claimed for him. According to William Winter, he read into Shylock three modes of being which he could not fit together.[20] In the early scenes he was an evil schemer, with emphasis on craftiness, apparently creating an effect of saturnine comedy. In the middle scenes he rose to what Winter called the tragic mood (but which we should probably call the melodramatic), expressing unqualified murderous hatred. Finally in the Trial Scene he bid for admiration and sympathy as the majestic Hebrew, the ordained avenger of an abused race. "The portrayal, accordingly," said Winter, "while full of professional talent, exemplified only a fruitless effort to blend and unify opposed and irreconcilable attributes."

His Hamlet, which until the emergence of Edwin Booth's Hamlet many critics considered the finest in

Illus. 84. E. L. Davenport as Hamlet.

America, was technically beautiful—melodious, noble, imposing. With extraordinary clarity he exhibited the sorrowing son, the gentle lover, the scholar, the soldier, the unimpassioned but capable avenger.[21] Yet it was a curiously unmoving Hamlet. "He had a certain intellectual following," as Clara Morris remembered it, "who delighted in the beautiful precision and distinctness of his reading of the royal Dane. He always seemed to me a Hamlet cut in crystal—so clear and pure, so cold and hard he was. The tender heart, the dread imaginings, the wounded pride and love, the fits and starts, the pain and passion that tortures Hamlet each in turn, were utterly incompatible with the fair, high-browed, princely philosopher Mr. Davenport presented to his followers."[22] "It never once excited any real emotion in the audience," said Adam Badeau; "it never made us feel."[23] William Winter said, "It did not satisfy the sense of soul."

If, as Miss Morris suggested, Davenport sometimes alienated his common hearers by playing over their heads, he seems likewise to have alienated intellectuals by trading in vulgar stuff. Now and again in the fifties and sixties he took up theatre management (usually unsuccessfully), and it was his policy to produce and act in whatever came to hand, so long as it carried some topical interest or would provoke a shudder or a smile. Such titles as *The Scalp Hunters, Our Country's Sinews, The Man with the Red Beard, A Struggle for Gold,* and *The Mormons; or, Life in Salt Lake City* suggest the levels of taste to which he was willing to descend for the sake of box office.

He is even said to have damaged his place in public esteem by miscalculating the worth and effect of one of his major classic roles. His Sir Giles Overreach was unquestionably a superb performance, probably surpassing in power the Sir Giles of the elder Kean or of the elder Booth.[24] He played it over five hundred times, and he once told William Winter that he would make it as popular as Joe Jefferson made Rip Van Winkle. But the more brilliantly he worked up the viciousness of the character and the horror of the ending, the more it was disliked. He foamed at the mouth, cursed his daughter Margaret in choked tones as if from a throat bleeding internally, struggled to lay murdering hands upon her, was felled by a stroke of apoplexy—in short, he threw histrionic temperance to the winds in an effort, for once, to be "overwhelming." But Sir Giles's day was past. The display of raw evil which had thrilled the contemporaries of Lord Byron was simply abhorrent to the sentimental and practical

audiences of the mid-century and after. "Everybody admired it," said William Winter, "and everybody refrained as much as possible from seeing it."[25]

By the 1870s Davenport's personal appeal had abated so far that in the minds of most younger theatregoers he was regarded only as the father of the vivacious Fanny Davenport, who had lately emerged at Daly's Theatre, or of other of his offspring who were then taking to the stage. His audiences dwindled, even for *Black-Eyed Susan,* and Clara Morris remembered a shameful night in Cleveland when, on taking a curtain call, he delivered a bitter tirade against the taste of the public. If they would not come to see him act, he declared to them, he would learn to swallow swords and play the banjo. He was an old dog now, but he could learn their tricks. "Oh, it was dreadful taste," said Miss Morris, "and so unjust, too, to abuse those who

Illus. 85. E. L. Davenport as Sir Giles Overreach in Philip Massinger's *A New Way to Pay Old Debts.*

Illus. 86. E. L. Davenport as Brutus.

Illus. 87. Lawrence Barrett as Cassius.

were there for the fault of those who remained away."[26]

His very finest Shakespearean role had been Brutus in *Julius Caesar*, and by great good luck he was summoned to play it once more very near the end of his life in a New York production which set a world record of 103 performances. Counting the road engagements that followed he played it altogether 222 times in the run—a grand capping of his career.[27]

This revival of *Caesar* was staged in 1875 by Henry Jarrett and Henry Palmer, who had got control of Booth's Theatre after Edwin Booth's bankruptcy, and they based

their staging on the magnificent scenery and other productional materials which Booth had created for his own staging of the play four years earlier.[28] They engaged Davenport for Brutus, pairing him with Lawrence Barrett, whose characterization of Cassius was unsurpassable. It was an ideal team. A comment by Edward Tuckerman Mason, who recorded the stage business of all their scenes, reads as follows: "E. L. Davenport's *Brutus* and Lawrence Barrett's *Cassius*—worthy companion pictures. Somewhat difficult to consider separately—as each performance owes much of its effectiveness to the perfect

124

artistic harmony existing between both actors."[29] Davenport's figure was massive, Barrett's slight and gaunt; Davenport's face was open, thoughtful, kindly, Barrett's drawn and pale; Davenport's sixty-year-old voice had become slightly husky, Barrett's was incisive, demanding, clear. Davenport moved little, and his movements were steady and purposeful; Barrett's pacing—nervous, quick, irregular—betokened frustrated energy, impatience, and instability. Barrett-Cassius initiated plans and actions and drove them forward; Davenport-Brutus, though slow to respond, took control of actions once they were agreed upon and governed their timing and direction.

Professional observers admired most the great quarrel and reconciliation scene (the Tent Scene in the fourth act), and several accounts preserve for us the details of Barrett's angry storming about and Davenport's patient waiting and slow mastery over the other's rages. It is difficult to appreciate Davenport's effectiveness since his power lay in doing as little as possible—like a rock against which waves beat, or, as a whimsical commentator then put it, "like some grand St. Bernard listening to the snarling of *Cassius*—Barrett."[30] Typical of Davenport's business and the effectiveness of his restraint are these notes of Mason's:

Brutus seats himself at the council table, front. He quietly takes off his helmet, and lays it on the table, carelessly passing his hand through his hair. His whole bearing denotes calm self-possession.

Brutus, during these speeches, stands quietly, right center, partially turned away from Cassius.

During this speech, Brutus returns to the table, and again sits, rather wearily.

Partially turning, semi-contemptuously, & takes paper as if to resume his business.

Brutus quietly looks over his shoulder at Cassius; his face, devoid of any anger or rage, instantly checks Cassius' movement.

Brutus goes to Cassius, gently placing his hands on his shoulders, & speaks.

William Winter, for many years an admirer of Davenport, welcomed his return from obscurity: "It is long since we have seen him so like the artist of old whom we love to remember—thoughtful, stately, gentle, gracious, and tender, secure in the treasures and resources of his professional scholarship, and at ease amidst surroundings worthy of his powers and his fame."[31]

Illus. 88. John Edward McCullough.

JOHN EDWARD McCULLOUGH

Three years after the death of John McCullough (1832–85), a company of his friends gathered in Philadelphia's Mount Moriah Cemetery to dedicate a monument to his memory.[32] This was no mere engraved slab, but a shrine—an elegantly designed granite tower rising nearly forty feet to the tip of its granite "eternal flame," and displaying under its canopy a colossal bronze bust of McCullough in the role of Sheridan Knowles's Virginius. Never before or since has a play actor been honored by so grand a monument (word got about that it cost over $9,000), and no one there could have doubted that McCullough would be remembered as one of America's greatest actors—or one of the greatest actors that ever lived. It is ironic that they chose to memorialize him as Virginius rather than as Othello or Coriolanus or Lear: a century afterward his reputation is almost as dust-covered as Sheridan Knowles's play.

A heroic actor, McCullough worked within a narrow range. Unlike Davenport, whose strength was versatility and whose weakness was the profligate expenditure of talent in too many directions, McCullough confined himself mainly to characters conspicuous for manliness and nobility. Virginius—the Roman centurion who defies corrupt authority, stabs to death his beloved daughter to save her from sexual violation, goes mad and slays her would-be violator—was indeed the role in which he was most admired, and several other exemplars of heroic virtue (many of them wearers of the toga) were prominent in his repertory—Payne's Brutus, Banim's Damon, Kotzebue's Rolla, and Spartacus (Forrest's favorite) in *The Gladiator*. He was the last actor of consequence to play these old-fashioned roles, and his immense popularity in them well into the 1880s is, incidentally, a register of the moral myopia in America during the Brown Decades.[33] During a time when the nation was ruthlessly expanding its territories, its resources, and the bank accounts of unscrupulous financiers, simple-minded manliness, uncriticized and sentimentalized, continued to be exhibited in the theatre and in the books of Horatio Alger, not only as the national ideal but as a true reflection of the national way of life. In some quarters the delusion persisted much longer. As late as 1913, William Winter, who had won his laurels in the Brown Decades, was still describing McCullough's performance of these heroes in sentences like ropes of sand. He never doubted, as the sweet phrases flowed off his nib, that the values he was celebrating would endure as theatrical staples forever:

He was the manly friend, to whom life and all the possessions of the world are nothing when weighed in the balance against fidelity to love. He was the fond and tender father, whose great strength became a sweet and yielding feebleness in the presence of his gentle daughter. He was the simple, truthful, affectionate, high-minded man, whose soul could exist only in honor. To ideals of that kind he gave perfect expression, and for an essential nobleness and manliness such as stimulate human hearts to a renewed devotion to duty and a fervid allegiance to high ideals of character and conduct he will be remembered as long as anything is remembered in the history of the Stage.[34]

McCullough was a perfect figure to hang such sentences upon. A large, handsome, uncomplicated, gentle, generous, loving man, called Genial John by hundreds of friends (he seems to have had no foes), he combined power with pathos in his acting and exuded an irresistible appeal for the affection of his audiences.

McCullough's career was a rags-to-riches story, though geared to slow tempo: he did not arrive at national fame until he was in his forties, and his death at fifty-three was a dismaying anticlimax. Born in northern Ireland the son of a poor farmer, he crossed the ocean alone at the age of fifteen to seek his fortune in the New World. He settled in Philadelphia, married at seventeen, and supported himself by various kinds of manual labor (in a chair factory, at the gasworks) for about a dozen years. Never having enjoyed formal schooling, but being ambitious and quickminded, he taught himself to read and write and to speak without "the brogue." He memorized vast amounts of poetry and literary history out of Chambers's *Encyclopedia of English Literature*, was introduced to Shakespeare's plays by an Irish workman who could recite long passages from them, and, after some years of practice with a group of theatrical amateurs, joined the profession at the Arch Street Theatre to play small parts for four dollars a week. Soon thereafter he separated from his wife, who disapproved of his going on the stage. They were never divorced. His wife and two sons, all of whom outlived him, are buried with him at Mount Moriah.

In 1860 E. L. Davenport gave him a somewhat stronger line to play at the Howard Athenaeum in Boston, and there on one occasion he distinguished himself by a remarkable feat of quick study: Davenport, being ill one morning, sent word to the theatre that McCullough should read Davenport's role in *The Dead Heart* that night; beginning about noon McCullough memorized the whole of it by curtain time—an extraordinarily long role—and played it letter-perfect without book.

He found his proper master in 1861 when Edwin Forrest, impressed by his handsome face, strong build, strong voice, and reputation for actorship and devotion, hired him as leading man. For six years he toured the country with Forrest, supporting him as Macduff, Richmond, Edgar, Iago, and in other roles, and winning such respect from the older actor that occasionally, as in *Othello*, they exchanged roles like equal players on a well-practiced team. Inevitably he modeled his acting upon Forrest's compelling style, and, indeed, when they parted company in California in 1866, Forrest's emphatic advice was to develop a style of his own: "Stay here. Leave off imitating me. Blank!—Blank!—Blank! A lot of infernal fools are doing that, all over the country. Build yourself up here, and you will do well."[35]

After such long indoctrination, however, McCullough could not easily effect a radical change of style; nor, in fact, was change just then to be desired, because for the

Illus. 89. John McCullough as Richard III.

next ten years he was for the most part tied to San Francisco and the West, where theatregoers still preferred their tragic actors to show muscle, make points, and deliver rousing rants. The San Franciscans made much of him. He was probably the first actor to be inducted into the exclusive Bohemian Club; and one W. C. Ralston, a bank president, joining with other of McCullough's wealthy admirers, built a handsome new theatre called the California and turned it over to him to operate. Doubtless the cares of management distracted him from cultivation of his art as a tragedian, and he often had to act in plays which, though essential to repertory, were quite out of his line—such modern comedies as *Money, The Marble Heart,* and *London Assurance,* in which "the free, swinging gestures of the classic school accord illy with broadcloth and social cigars."[36]

In 1873 he undertook a starring tour as far east as Saint

Louis, and he starred in New York for the first time in 1874. Everyone in the East recognized his affinity to Forrest (who had died in 1872), and when he introduced himself to New York audiences in the role of Spartacus he seemed to invite comparison with the old lion. Some put him down as merely a weak copy; others found that the differences between him and Forrest were not shortcomings but, rather, promises that heroic acting was moving into a new and more civilized phase. As Spartacus, according to the *Spirit of the Times,* McCullough was like a David against Forrest's Goliath—a Coeur de Lion rather than a Thracian savage. He was gentle where Forrest had been rude; he repressed passion where Forrest had unbridled it; he won audiences by appealing to them where Forrest had only excited them by violence. He was, in short, a hero, where Forrest had been a brute.[37] In the *Tribune,* William Winter, who could never quite stomach Forrest, found sharper terms in which to state the case. According to him McCullough did not resemble Forrest at all. If he fell short of Forrest in "muscular force," in volume of voice, and in "animal exaltation," on the other hand he avoided Forrest's ugliest mannerisms: "He does not spend half-an-hour in saying the word 'boy,' so that his auditors may spend another half-an-hour in applauding him for saying it. He does not use his fist as a trip-hammer and his chest as an anvil. And he neither snorts nor howls."[38] Winter and the critic for the *Spirit* appear to have been as much interested in pulling down the reputation of their bête noire Forrest as in defining the art of McCullough. At the *Herald,* however, where the proprietors (the James Gordon Bennetts, father and son) had long admired Forrest and championed him, the first reviewer of Forrest's successor, while praising him warmly enough, was careful to preserve Forrest's credit, too, in a temperate and judicious statement of the case: "Forrest was a magnificent type of manhood, but his face naturally expressed the fiercer and more terrible passions. McCullough, like Forrest, has the comely grace of perfect manhood—of athletic stature and mould, with the thews and sinews of the gladiator. More than this, he has a fineness of touch, a glad expressiveness of feature, a bright, genuine, winning quality which Forrest never succeeded in expressing, . . . an intense beauty of feeling, which Forrest never surpassed."[39] Then this *Herald* reviewer (neatly ruling out of court any claims to greatness by his own especial bête noire, who was Edwin Booth) concluded with the flat assertion that such a success as Mc-

Cullough's "has not been achieved in New York by any tragedian for a long time."

Except for short runs of Hamlet and Faulconbridge, he held back Shakespeare on this first visit to New York, and it was not until he came again in 1877 that as Richard III, Lear, and Othello he submitted his best Shakespearean work to the examination of the metropolitan critics. In that year he had taken instruction from Steele Mac-Kaye, whose Delsartean teaching seems to have freed him from the more harmful effects of Forrest's influence. No longer tempted to blast out points for the amazement of gallery gods, he achieved a markedly more thoughtful, disciplined, and coherent approach to his roles. "That teacher, MacKaye, has taught me more in three months than I could have learned otherwise in twenty years," he explained to A. C. Wheeler (the critic Nym Crinkle); and Wheeler, along with other expert observers, was amazed at McCullough's improvement:

His Othello and Richelieu astonished me by being entirely unlike his former impersonations of those characters. The native vigour, resonance, and fire were there, but they were *disciplined and controlled*. A nicer balance of faculty was apparent. The intelligibility of the subtler emotions had been made sharper and clearer. There were noble climaxes of passion, less waste of energy in making himself felt, a cleaner adaptation of tone and gesture to the exigent thought—more repose, more dignity, more grace.[40]

During the half-dozen seasons after 1877 McCullough appeared in many cities of the South and East, achieving everywhere enormous popular success. "The public like McCullough," said the *Spirit of the Times* on one occasion. "Let him play what he will, the houses increase every night."[41] Given a stage and a crowd to cheer him, Genial John could do no wrong.

But unfortunately, when he was at the very peak of his development, his mind began to give way. Throughout 1883 and 1884, though continuing to take engagements, he suffered bouts of depression and the terror of knowing that he was going mad. In June of 1884 he went to Carlsbad in Germany to try the fashionable water cure —to no avail. On September 29, 1884, during a performance of *The Gladiator* at McVicker's in Chicago, his memory failed altogether. He retired from the stage, and for many months he lived in New York or drifted about to other cities in a half-lunatic condition. In June of 1885 he was committed to the Bloomingdale asylum. Med-

Illus. 90. John McCullough as Coriolanus.

ical treatment was useless. His disease was paresis—the destruction of the brain caused by the advance of syphilis into the central nervous system.[42] He died at his wife's home in Philadelphia on November 8, 1885.

As a Shakespearean, McCullough followed much the same paths that Forrest had trod before him. He chose or avoided nearly the same roles that Forrest had done, and for similar reasons. His successes and failures stood in close parallel to Forrest's. In general style, however, and in the quality of his major successes, he refined and improved upon the work of his master. This very considerable achievement of McCullough's has largely been forgotten.

With his imposing physical stature (less muscular than Forrest's but better proportioned), his resonant voice, and his practiced elocution, he could sustain the mightiest passions and the grandest rhetorical structures in Shakespeare as well as Forrest had and yet have power to spare. No one ever made the complaint, so often charged against the Keans or the Booths or Macready, that McCullough was not "big enough" for Othello or Brutus, Macbeth or Lear. A reviewer of one of his infrequent revivals of *Coriolanus* declared that Caius Marcius could not have had a more fitting representative than McCullough: "In appearance he realizes the rugged grandeur of the personality—the noblest Roman of them all —his massive head and face, his stalwart and manly form, clad in the classic robes, his rich, powerful voice and broad, grand style of acting."[43]

His engaging personality was, of course, an invaluable asset in any role he played. Where Forrest was typically on the attack—in deadly earnest, growling, and humorless—Genial John would exhibit graciousness and affection, would find occasion for some gentleness or loving tenderness which stirred sympathetic response. And finally, after his lessons with Steele MacKaye, he improved his technique: he spoke better, moved better, and above all learned to regard the performance of a tragic character as something better than a string of histrionic firecrackers—learned to relate the beginning of a role to its ending, to integrate the parts of a character, scene by scene, into a dramatically meaningful whole.

Like Forrest he rarely played Shylock. As William Winter said, he required parts "which implicate the heart"; noble himself, he cared only to exhibit "the noble, the manly, the heroic, the magnanimous conditions and aspects of human nature."[44] He understood Shylock to be a figure of evil, and therefore the role did not interest him. Macbeth eluded him, too, probably because his imagination could not find the hero behind the murdering usurper, and in his occasional performances of it he brought little more than fine elocution to his characterization.[45] Iago, which he played often in the early days when supporting Forrest, disappeared from his repertory thereafter.

If he wanted to display nobility and magnanimity on the stage, one would expect him to have made much of Hamlet, and it is true that, like Forrest, he played Ham-

let often over the years; but most of the critics felt that he understood it little better than Forrest did. Winter thought his performance often too "robustious," and accounted for his comparative failure in it on the grounds that it "did not touch his heart"—as King Lear did.[46] One quite clear reading of his performance (an approving one, too) appeared in a Saint Louis review in 1874. The critic of the *Republican* declared that he preferred McCullough's Hamlet over that of Edwin Booth. "His Hamlet is a flesh and blood man, and not a philosophic abstraction; his Hamlet has his five senses and his perfect mental poise, his normal affection, his sound philosophy and his vigorous manhood. He places himself in a strong and no ambiguous light. Nothing in his nature is misty or obscure, and he behaves himself like almost any young man of twenty-eight, in his surroundings, would do. He really loves Ophelia and meant to do honestly by her."[47] But this would be regarded as heresy (or vulgar ignorance) in a generation whose conception of Hamlet was grounded in the romantic interpretations of Goethe, Coleridge, or Hazlitt. By the 1870s in America it was agreed among sensitive and sophisticated observers that Hamlet was weak-willed, irresolute; deterred from action by moral scruples, by sensibility, by preference for dream over reality or for thought over action—the hero who sinks beneath a burden he cannot bear and must not cast away. McCullough's "flesh and blood" Hamlet did not "take on the poetry and grace of the personage Shakespeare drew"—so declared the *New York Times* critic in 1874. And again in 1882 the *Times* remarked that McCullough lacked "that sensuous poetic imagination which is a conspicuous element in Hamlet's effeminate nature."[48] (Of course McCullough would never have accepted the premise of Hamlet's "effeminate nature".) In the *Tribune*, Winter complained that McCullough's Hamlet was too much in control of circumstances and of himself, and later suggested that McCullough (perhaps like Forrest) could not submit to or reckon with the supernatural: "In situations that are haunted and weird, involving mystery and dread, McCullough was impeded by insuperable obstacles, both physical and spiritual."

If he avoided the murderous Macbeth, one would expect him to have shunned Richard III, but, again like Forrest, he kept that monster (the Cibber version) in his repertory. He even made a reasonably complex character of it. Winter, in fact, chose this role to prove McCullough's versatility, arguing that while he was nearest to his noble self in Knowles's Virginius, and farthest from himself in Richard, yet he acted the one as truly as the other.[49] Not all his critics were readily convinced, however. At the *Herald*, where his reception was usually cordial, his Richard of 1877 was judged to be too gross a hypocrite, and though by 1880 the *Herald* was approving the "virile heartiness" which distinguished his Richard from the "wrinkled Richards" commonly on display, it continued to grumble at his use of the Cibber version.[50] In 1880 the *Times* critic thought the Richard role outside the range of McCullough's talent, which was "essentially robust, sincere, and direct," and outside his method, which was "a combination of simplicity and sturdiness guided by a broad, healthy intelligence which is but faintly tinged with either imagination or subtlety."[51]

But in Winter's view, McCullough's Richard was "nothing less than a prodigy of structural power," skillfully combining disparate qualities and building to a tremendous climax. The instant he walked on the stage, Winter said, one recognized in his deeply lined face that he was "a consummate type of malignant force"; yet as he played along he exhibited "off-hand good nature" and bore himself with "the bluff manner of a winning man of the world." Thus, the Wooing Scene was completely credible: he was so much a man of flesh and blood, ardent and remorseful, that "no spectator could marvel at the widow's surrender." Meanwhile, too, he managed from the earliest scenes to foreshadow the agonies of the fifth act, suggesting that remorse was already gnawing at him. The night and dream scenes were horrifying: "No actor can ever have done more with the delirium of the awakening. Its action and the almost inarticulate cries curdled the blood of many a listener." In earlier days, according to Winter, McCullough's only interest in the role was to "play for points," imitating the points that Forrest made, but in the long run "friendly counsel" (Steele MacKaye?) persuaded him to attend to the "entire drawing" of the character.

His two most impressive Shakespearean creations had been Forrest's best ones also—Othello and Lear. For each of these roles he developed a distinctive structure, and that structure defined and intensified the force of his performance. Other actors of Lear would open with a display of regal authority and, as the critic of the *Dramatic Mirror* observed, would remain strong in mind long after the denunciation of Cordelia;[52] but almost from the rise of the curtain McCullough's audience was aware that this

Lear was in the first stages of mental decay. He was not yet mad, as William Winter put it, "but ready, *and certain*, to become so."[53] McCullough called attention at once not so much to Lear's authority but to his excessive and irrational vehemence, creating a sense of impending danger, a foreshadowing of the madness to come. From then on, in scene after scene through three acts, he gradually drove the King into dementia. According to Winter, McCullough was the first actor who clearly discriminated between the agony of a man who knows he is going mad and the vacant, heedless, even at certain moments cheerful condition of one who has slipped over the edge into total madness. Thus he carried his spectators through a series of palpably shifting emotional experiences: from the beginning through the storm scenes an increasingly painful witnessing of (almost a sharing in) the King's decline and fall; in the fourth-act Mad Scene a relaxing into pathos almost free of pain, followed by a kind of heartbreaking joy when the King wakes in Cordelia's tent; and finally a resumption of the tragic mood as the action drives toward the catastrophe. This structure of McCullough's, to be sure, was no more or less than Shakespeare's own structure, but it is to McCullough's credit that he revealed it. Here it should be noted that, along with Lawrence Barrett and Edwin Booth, McCullough was one of the first important actors in America to disembarrass himself of every vestige of Nahum Tate's perversion of the play and work from a purely Shakespearean, if trimmed and bowdlerized, text.[54]

His structuring of Othello almost reversed that of his Lear. From the beginning Othello was all health and joy —"like a grand tower bathed in sunrise" was William Winter's apt metaphor—giving not the slightest hint that here was a man about to be torn to pieces in the tragic machine.[55] He was serene, confident, firmly in command during Brabantio's attack in the streets, eloquent without affectation in his address to the Senate, exuberant in his love and his good fortune. Euphoria deepened throughout his reunion with Desdemona at Cyprus—was hardly diminished even by the riot of the night watch and the demotion of Cassio. But in the third act, almost from Iago's "Ha! I like not that," the spectators' apprehensions were awakened, and from then on, as Othello's jealousy rose like a slow flood to engulf him, terror mounted almost without abatement to the tragedy's end. The working of this structure was not, like that in *King Lear*, a foreshadowing of tragedy and an early growth of the tragic

Illus. 91. John McCullough as Othello.

mood but a deliberate postponing of danger until it blows in like a sudden summer storm. The shock of it and the steady intensification of passion until the last curtain's fall worked a sharper and more concentrated dramatic effect than the other. Again one might observe that it was Shakespeare, not McCullough, who invented this structure; but evidently McCullough was one of the few Othellos of his time who did not make his first entrance "grand, gloomy, and peculiar," as the *Times* critic once put it, and did not give the show away before it had properly begun.[56]

McCullough raised the emotional temperature of both plays by his ability to create moments of irresistible pathos. Lear's four tiny words, "I did her wrong," emerging abruptly while the King is half listening to the Fool's helpless attempts at fooling, suddenly exposed the inner agony Lear is suffering—his guilt, remorse, and grief. Lines like "We'll no more meet, no more see one another," "O Fool, I shall go mad," "I have one part in my heart that's sorry yet for thee," and many another, coming often in the midst of or just after some terrible burst of passion, realized the systole-diastole rhythm of the play's emotional flow. Having once viewed McCullough's Lear, the *Spirit of the Times* critic recognized that the romantic theorists were quite wrong to declare the play unactable: by reason of its stronger passions and livelier rhythm it is much more dramatic than *Hamlet*.[57]

The especial warmth of McCullough's Othello arose from the fact that he never let the audience forget that he was deeply, tenderly, and reverently in love with Desdemona. When the great Italian Tommaso Salvini brought his Othello to America, audiences knew even through the veil of a foreign language that once he suspected Desdemona of unfaithfulness he positively loathed her, and they sat transfixed while the play stormed on to a murder and a suicide that were raw butcheries.[58] Forrest, too, once he came to use the play almost as a part of the case against his divorced wife, was moved by black hatred: in his slaying of Desdemona he believed he was exterminating evil—destroying a wanton who, if allowed to live, would betray more men. When Othello only hates, as the *Herald* critic once observed, the effect is hideous.[59] McCullough, however, retained the sympathy and affection of his audience to the very end. They rejoiced in his inherent nobility. They trusted his desperate desire to believe in Desdemona's innocence. They respected the sacrificial spirit in which he conducted the killing. They sympathized with his almost crazed grief when he learned the final truth about his wife, his lieutenant, and himself.

Incidentally, Othello was the only Shakespearean role that McCullough offered in London when he played a brief engagement at Drury Lane in 1881, so that English opinions of him as a Shakespearean are too limited to be conclusive. The critics were at least as cordial as protocol demanded. Most of them respected his physique, his discretion, and his convincing soldierliness. The *Times*, to be sure, thought him "too fierce and noisy," "loud but not touching the heart."[60] According to the critic at the *Theatre* magazine, "He is an actor of the people, rough, it is true, unequal, old-fashioned, as we now express it, but there is a boldness of treatment, a firmness of grasp, and a hold upon the multitude that can be distinguished from trickiness, claptrap, and rant. We can conceive an actor like Mr. McCullough taking his Virginius, his Othello, and his Mark Antony to the Far West, among the rough toilers, the hewers of wood and the drawers of water, and making more effect there than anything short of genius."[61] The *Athenaeum* critic convicted him of a peculiarly American lapse of judgment and taste. In the Lodovico Scene in the fourth act, he refrained from striking Desdemona. Presumably this omission (certainly a wrongheaded one) was dictated by his persistent tenderness toward Desdemona. At the *Athenaeum*, however, the motive assigned was that American audiences simply could not endure the sight of a "coloured gentleman" striking a woman who was white.[62]

Meanwhile his Drury Lane audiences applauded him "abundantly, even tumultuously," and he was honored at a reception given by the Duke of Manchester with Prince Edward and Princess Alexandra in attendance. London was becoming hospitable to American actors in the 1880s, and McCullough probably seemed as good as could be expected from a land where, it was commonly assumed, art and manners lagged at least a generation behind those of the civilized world.

Edwin Booth

Edwin Booth (1833–93) was not physically the most powerful American actor of his time; a rather small man (five foot seven), slight and lithe, he was by no means of the heroic school. In point of technique, however, he was probably the finest of his time, and certainly he was the most celebrated and the best loved.[63] How he managed to attract almost universal affection is something of a mystery, for he was not an outgoing or glad-handing person, but shy, quiet, retiring in company, recessive—in short, a very private person. He had hundreds of acquaintances, few intimates, and very few enemies.

Other actors were more versatile than he. Booth had no sense for genial comedy so that he was not comfortable in Benedick. He hated to play lovers. His lack of inches somewhat diminished his effectiveness as Othello, Macbeth, and other characters commonly thought of as "big men." His long suits were earnestness and intellectuality, which served him especially well in Hamlet; a capacity for sardonic, biting humor, which sustained his Iago, Richard III, Bertuccio in *The Fool's Revenge*, Payne's Brutus, and Bulwer's Richelieu; emotional intensity, by which he could bring off climaxes of rage or agony in any role; a rich (though not loud) voice, superb elocution, beauty of face, and astonishingly expressive eyes, which served him everywhere.

But it was not only as an actor that he achieved eminence. For ten years of his career (1864–74), emulating the major figures in English stage history, he undertook theatre management, first at the Winter Garden, then at the theatre which he built and which bore his name. He conducted these theatres on what he took to be the highest artistic principles, giving the best possible production to the "best" plays of Shakespeare and to those modern masterpieces, like *Richelieu* and *The Fool's Revenge*, which were in those days deemed worthy to be joined with Shakespeare in the repertory. Management ruined him financially, but that is another story.

On February 3, 1869, Booth inaugurated his milliondollar New York theatre with a scenically stunning production of *Romeo and Juliet*. The event was heralded as the beginning of a new era in the production of Shakespeare and the "higher drama," and it was recognized that never before had such a theatre been erected "solely by the individual enterprise and sagacity of one actor."[64] Tickets for the opening were sold at auction. The governor of the state and the mayor of the city occupied proscenium boxes, and among the audience were hundreds of New York's social and professional elite.

The building itself, which Booth had planned and which had been rising for nearly a year at the southeast corner of Twenty-third Street and Sixth Avenue, was the object of intense curiosity, wonder, and delight. Within

Illus. 92. Edwin Booth.

Illus. 93. Exterior of Booth's Theatre.

and without, it was as ornate as high Victorian fashion would dictate and money could buy. The facade along Twenty-third Street (which was in fact not the front of the theatre but the stage-right *side* of it) was an elaborate composition of Italian and French Renaissance motifs: arched doorways flanked by rusticated stone at the first level; at the second level a row of niches, some of them containing statues; the whole crowned by a deep mansard roof and three broad towers.[65] Several Italian artists (G. G. Gariboldi, C. Brumidi, and G. Turini) decorated the interior with marble and scagliola, with bas-reliefs and statues, with fresco painting of literary and mythological scenes. At the front and center of the proscenium arch was the Shakespeare family coat of arms, above that a statue of Shakespeare in the act of composition, and at either side of him portrait busts of famous actors. The act drop, a lovely Italian landscape, was the work of the then well known painter Russel Smith.

The audience could hardly settle themselves for the play, so eager were they to take in all this gorgeous decoration.

They swarmed into the blazing lobbies, breathing sighs of astonishment at the wealth of color and perfection of lux-

Illus. 94. Interior of Booth's Theatre.

uriant decoration; they commended the Pompeiian tiles and panels, and praised the antique figures and fittings; they roamed through the lighted dressing-rooms, where medallion carpet and voluptuous furniture invited them in vain to linger; they poured into the auditorium, stood up in all the empty spaces and sat down in all the distant seats to get new views of the ceiling and new lights on the statuary, and to stun themselves pleasantly with a fresh *coup d'oeil*; and everywhere, in corridor, aisle, parquette, and box, the warm glow of Gariboldi's pencil tinted everything.[66]

Finally Edward Mollenhauer's orchestra struck up "Hail, Columbia" to call them to their seats.

More important than decoration, however, were the many technical features conducive to audience comfort. Sight lines and acoustics proved to be excellent in every part of the house. The gas jets, which illuminated the house from wall lamps and from a great central chandelier, were ignited by electric spark: this meant that the house lights, controlled at the gas table backstage, could

be taken out completely when the play began and instantly ignited and brought up again when the act drop fell for the intermission. Seats were separated by chair arms, thus preventing crowding. Ventilation and heating (the best in any American theatre of the day) were controlled by a huge fan mounted between the ceiling of the auditorium and the outside roof; this fan sucked up warmed or cooled air through apertures under the seats, and expelled stale air and gas fumes through an open skylight. A fire-warning bell behind the proscenium, spray systems in the walls, and trained bucket brigades made fire protection almost absolute. The orchestra pit was sunk deep enough so that the conductor, the players, and the fiddle bows did not obtrude between the spectators and the actors.

Behind the curtain line Booth introduced a technique of sceneshifting that was revolutionary. Abandoning the centuries-old split-scene method, whereby wings and shutters slid on and off stage in lateral grooves, he instituted the rise-and-sink method. His stage house was so tall that rigidly framed back scenes could be lifted entirely out of sight, and the cellarage under the stage was so deep that scenic pieces thirty feet tall could be thrust up through slits in the stage floor. The subterranean lifts which raised and lowered these pieces were driven by hydraulic rams, the weight of the water bearing down from huge storage tanks at roof level. The movement of the scenic pieces, visible to the audience, was swift, smooth, silent, and astonishing.

Booth had long dreamed of such a "Temple to the Muses," where he could realize what his generation taught him was proper service to Shakespeare and serious modern drama. Even in the 1850s he would have known about Charles Kean's historically accurate and spectacular stagings at the Princess's Theatre in London—not to mention the lingering reputation of Kean's *Richard III* and *King John* at the Park Theatre in 1846. When he read J. W. Cole's 1859 biography of Kean, and when he visited London in 1861, he was immensely impressed by the fame of Kean's accomplishment. In 1864, in a three-way partnership with the comedian John Sleeper Clarke (his brother-in-law) and William Stuart, Booth took on the management of the run-down Winter Garden Theatre, refurbished it, and set about to emulate Kean.[67] As he wrote to a friend in Boston, it was his wish "to bring out several of the Shaksperian plays in a superior manner."[68] The first would be *Hamlet*, in which he had already won

Illus. 95. Setting the scene, Booth's Theatre.

high reputation for his performance of the hero. Together with his scene painters, John Thorne and Charles Witham, he would re-create the tenth-century royal Court at Elsinore. "Every scene, every dress, every chair and table—and nearly all the actors will be new," he told his friend Adam Badeau. "Some of the pictures in the play will be what has never been used on any stage in America & I doubt if Kean did anything like it."[69]

The result of this effort was his famous "Hundred Nights *Hamlet*," which ran from November 26, 1864, to March 22, 1865. Three weeks afterward, when his brother John assassinated President Lincoln, it appeared that his career was ended, but in January of 1866 the public welcomed his return to the stage and he proceeded with his long since formulated plans. In February of 1866, with Charles Witham in charge of the scenic department, he brought off a handsome production of Bulwer's *Richelieu*. In January of 1867 he revived *The Merchant of Venice* with scenery which Witham derived from Venetian scenes sketched by the well-known painter Emanuel Leutze. His

WINTER GARDEN THEATRE,

1854-55. *(Inaugurated Monday, September 18, 1854.)* 1864-65.

No. 624 BROADWAY, OPPOSITE BOND STREET.

11TH SEASON. 32D WEEK.

MANAGER, - - - - - - Mr. WILLIAM STUART.

WEDNESDAY EVENING, MARCH 22, 1865.

BENEFIT OF Mr. EDWIN BOOTH.

SOUVENIR PROGRAMME.

One Hundredth Night of "Hamlet."

This Evening, for the Final and One Hundredth Consecutive Night Performance,

"HAMLET,"

A TRAGEDY IN FIVE ACTS BY WILLIAM SHAKESPEARE.

CAST OF CHARACTERS.

HAMLET	**Mr. EDWIN BOOTH**
CLAUDIUS, King of Denmark	S. K. CHESTER
GHOST OF HAMLET'S FATHER	CHARLES KEMBLE MASON
POLONIUS, Lord Chamberlain	G. H. ANDREWS
LAERTES, Son to Polonius	J. G. HANLEY
HORATIO, Friend to Hamlet	CHARLES WALCOTT, Jr.
OSRIC,	OWEN FAWCETT
ROSENCRANTZ, } Courtiers, {	J. DUELL
GUILDENSTERN, }	W. F. BURROUGHS
MARCELLUS, } Officers, {	MR. BURGESS
BERNARDO, }	MR. DILLON
FRANCISCO, a Soldier	NELSON DECKER
FIRST ACTOR	MR. CLINE
SECOND ACTOR	MR. EVANS
FIRST GRAVEDIGGER	E. A. EBERLE
SECOND GRAVEDIGGER	MR. FITZGERALD
PRIEST	MR. EVERDELL
GERTRUDE, Queen of Denmark, and Mother to Hamlet	MRS. J. W. WALLACK, Jr.
OPHELIA, Daughter of Polonius	MRS. FRANK S. CHANFRAU
ACTRESS	MRS. S. K. CHESTER

Lords, Ladies, Pages, Officers, Guards.

ORCHESTRAL SELECTIONS.

1. *QUVERTURE.*—"Hamlet." *Stoepel*
(Introducing the Danish National Hymn.)
2. *INTRODUZOINE AND POLONAISE,* - - - - - *Meyerbeer*
(Written for the Danish play, "Struensee.")
3. *GALOP.*—"Danish Hussars," - *National*
4. *GRAND MARCH.*—"Lohengrin," - *Wagner*
5. *FANTASIE,* - *Stoepel*
(On Ophelia's Songs and other Tunes of Shakespeare's Time.)

The Tragedy has been placed upon the Stage, under the immediate direction of Mr. BOOTH, by J. G. HANLEY, Stage Manager.

The Music all expressly composed, selected and arranged by ROBERT STOEPEL.

THE PRODUCTION AND MEMORABLE RUN OF "HAMLET."

Initial Performance, Saturday Evening, November 26, 1864.

25th Night	Saturday, December 24, 1864.
50th Night	Monday, January 23, 1865.
75th Night	Tuesday, February 21, 1865.
100th Night	Wednesday, March 22d, 1865.

Thursday, March 23, Shakespeare's Play of "Othello."

IAGO	Mr. EDWIN BOOTH
OTHELLO	CHARLES BARRON

fourth grand revival was to be *Romeo and Juliet*, but on March 23, just before it could open, the Winter Garden and everything in it was destroyed by fire.

Nothing daunted—rather, indeed, energized and elated at being set free from the cramped spaces and facilities of the Winter Garden—he plunged ahead to realize his dream of an ideal playhouse. He chose a site, engaged a partner to share in the financing, and went on the road to raise his own portion of the initial capital. He intended to open Booth's Theatre in the autumn of 1868, but the usual if unforeseeable problems of architects and artists delayed him until mid-season. At last it was ready—"the stateliest, the handsomest, and the best appointed structure of its class that can now be found on the American continent," declared William Winter in the *Tribune*. "It has been built to endure."[70]

But it did not endure. Booth was a poor businessman. He let the construction costs run up to more than double the original estimates. He poured money lavishly into productions without reckoning the returns. His "partner," Richard Robertson of Boston, who in fact had never put any of his own money into the venture, persuaded Booth in the autumn of 1871 to buy out his interest for over a quarter of a million dollars.[71] In June of 1873, being then a half million short of ownership, Booth turned over the management to his brother Junius. Then came the 1873 financial crash, and creditors great and small began clamoring for settlement. In January of 1874 Booth declared bankruptcy. A series of proprietors took over the theatre during the next decade, but in 1883 it was pulled down and replaced by a department store. Only a plaque high up on the building's Twenty-third Street wall reminded passersby that Booth's theatre once occupied the spot. The 1883 building has been pulled down and the plaque given to New York University.

Even during the few seasons in which Booth retained control of the building, he discovered that his grand managerial intentions were beyond his grasp. He had wanted to create a sort of dramatic museum or laboratory in which great plays could be put into definitive production; and, he had imagined, not only he but other leading actors, then and for years to come, supported by a first-rate resident company, would take turns at reviving and starring in those plays. But much time and money were needed to build great productions; and although more than sixty-five plays were staged there during his five seasons of management, no more than ten appear to have been "produced," the rest being mounted in scenery drawn from stock. He found, too, that leading actors were hard to come by, or more expensive than they were worth. Edwin Forrest refused to open the theatre in *Othello*.[72] Charles Fechter declined a bid to use Booth's *Hamlet* scenery and engaged at Niblo's instead.[73] Charlotte Cushman did come once for a six-week stand, but at a salary that ate up all the profits. Other old-timers, including James Hackett, John Owens, John Clarke, and James W. Wallack, simply did not draw. When Booth attempted to advance younger actors like Ned Adams and Lawrence Barrett by starring them in their own plays, the box-office returns were disastrous. "I cannot afford to *star* those who have proved unprofitable to me," he told Barrett, thus precipitating a quarrel that took many years to resolve.[74] Only Joe Jefferson, who played two long stands of *Rip Van Winkle*, and later the lovely Adelaide Neilson seem to have brought profit to the house. Furthermore it was not possible to maintain a strong supporting company. Actors who proved their worth soon departed for better incomes than Booth could offer them, and only the weak or the aging could be expected to stay on season after season.

Nonetheless there were unforgettable Shakespearean achievements. In *Romeo and Juliet* the scenery was triumphant. Its "picturesque Italian streets, luxurious gardens, gay and bright interiors, and the solemn, cypress-shaded precincts of the tomb" surpassed in realism, beauty, and variety anything ever seen in New York before.[75] According to the *World* critic,

Of the scenery nothing can be said in praise that is not justified. Scene painting in such hands as those of Messrs. Witham and Hilliard becomes a fine art. When the Shakespearean Revivals were had at the Winter Garden it seemed to us that archaeology and scenic art had done their utmost. Since then we have had the paste of Offenbach set in the finest style of Paris, and the scenery of "Genevieve" was the boast and wonder of New York. But now the diamond of poetry is set more exquisitely than was even the quartz of prurience. The scenery at Booth's is more effective by reason that it is more extensive. In the first scene we have not a house, nor a row, but a whole square of the Gothic architecture of Italy reproduced with a pains and a patience which would have brought plaudits if only a tithe of it had been exhibited. . . . The balcony scene is exquisite. The stage is

---

Illus. 96. (*opposite*) Souvenir program for the "Hundredth Night" of Booth's *Hamlet* at the Winter Garden Theatre.

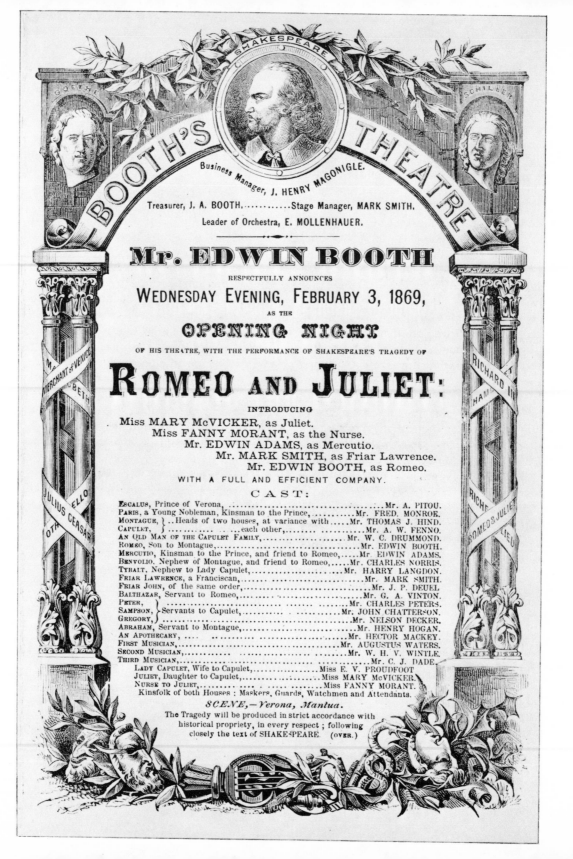

an Italian garden surrounded by brick and marble walls, . . . and Juliet's balcony, just seen at the right, is an exquisite and faithful bit of architecture. The facade of a Romanesque church, at least forty feet high, backs the square upon which Mercutio meets his death. The only bad scene is Juliet's bower, which is a monstrous melange of utterly impossible roses. But this is but a blemish upon a whole gallery of superb pictures.[76]

To William Winter, writing in the *Tribune*, the sweet fusion of poetry and scenic vista brought back the lost days of youth, "when the flowers smelled sweeter than they do now, and winds were balmier, and in the hush of the night there was a celestial mystery, and the stars seemed friends, and the affairs of human beings seemed infinitely remote and trivial, and one pair of eyes was worshipped, and one voice was all of music." Yet another critic, whose identity is lost to us, concluded that the ultimate resources of scenic art had here been absolutely exhausted: "It is doubtful whether human progress can much further go. Certainly within the next century it cannot be hoped that Shakespeare will be more thoroughly presented on the stage."[77]

Booth claimed in advance that he intended to "go even beyond Chas. Kean in my devotion to the sacred text of the late W.S." He would restore to the stage "the unadulterated plays of Shakspere: his 'Romeo and Juliet,' not so performed since the days of Betterton, I fancy."[78] He had forgotten that Charlotte Cushman had long since restored the proper Shakespearean ending, and perhaps he did not know that in 1846 Samuel Phelps had staged nearly the entire text at Sadler's Wells in London. His cuttings were considerably heavier than Phelps's.[79] He deleted all bawdry, of course; eliminated the narrative reprises by Benvolio in the middle of the play and by the Friar at the end; reduced passages bearing on the family feud in order to focus attention on the love story. He rearranged several scene endings to give Juliet the curtain speeches. He transposed passages to accommodate scene changing. He translated a number of lines in order to get rid of the "ringle, jingle, mingle of rhyme."[80] For all that, though, his version was closer to the original than any previously seen in the American theatre.

The scenery was probably the saving of that first pro-

duction at Booth's Theatre, for the acting ran into trouble. *Romeo and Juliet* is unendurable without a right Juliet, and Booth had seriously overestimated Mary McVicker's rightness in the role. The stepdaughter of J. H. McVicker, a Chicago manager, Miss McVicker had charmed Booth into an engagement to marry her, but her qualities could never win the sentimental affection of a theatre audience. She was an intelligent little body—brisk, sharp, and witty. William Winter thought she might have done well playing Irish girls in farces.[81] But as Juliet she was impossible. She was "no delicate geranium rising from a Sèvres vase," said the critic at the *Herald*. "She is a strong, practical, Western little woman, with but little artistic training, but a great deal of raw vigor and rude force; and, while she can never realize the graceful, buoyant, lovely Juliet of Shakespeare's creation, we have no doubt she would manage Romeo's business after marriage with considerable effect."[82] In the *World* she was described with killing coolness as a "young Chicago actress, whose stage appearance is at first not the most prepossessing, inasmuch as she has an immature face and an exceedingly fragile body, that seems ill-adapted to the exacting duties of her profession. With a face that is too small to be expressive, and too attenuated to be pleasing, and a voice deficient in quality and power, the first impression was not a favorable one of the young actress."[83] Booth as Romeo fared even worse in certain quarters. Expectably the *Herald* attacked him, carrying on its long-established anti-Booth campaign;[84] other attacks, according to the *World*, were inspired by disgruntled actors who had not been hired into Booth's company.[85] The *Herald* declared flatly that he "can't play Romeo," and said that in the Balcony Scene he clogged about the stage as if he were imitating a jig by the comic actress Lotta Crabtree. In the same scene, according to the *Daily Star*, "he writhes from head to foot like a jointed snake." Descending then from witty simile to childish name calling, the *Star* likened him to a sheep, a monkey, a parrot, "an idiot, a prancing, diddling, mincing baby girl."[86] Booth had in fact laid himself open to criticism, especially in the love scenes. In a letter to William Winter a few days later, he would admit to his "unseemly and crazy excitement of that evening"[87]—which more friendly critics noticed also but generously attributed to the extraordinary nervous pressures of an extraordinary opening night. He did manage to pull himself together soon thereafter. By February 27 the *Citizen* remarked that some of the hostile critics had

---

Illus. 97. (*opposite*) Program for the opening night of Booth's Theatre.

veered around and now praised what they had at first condemned.[88] On March 1, even the *Herald* half-apologized, acknowledging that Booth had "toned down his exuberance of passion for the fair Juliet," yet at once taking care to remind its readers of his earlier "agile but undignified impatience of feet, the at-times ludicrous by-play under the arch of the balcony which irresistibly suggested the active, bustling, glittering harlequin of pantomime."[89] None of this ridicule kept audiences away, however. *Romeo and Juliet* ran for ten weeks (fifty-eight performances) with undiminished popularity. In earlier days Booth's Romeo had fluttered maiden hearts throughout the country, but after 1869 he never played the part again.

He was uncomfortable in lover's roles. Perhaps it was his shyness, his sense of privacy, his unwillingness to hang his heart on his sleeve—perhaps indeed it was pride—that inhibited him from displaying love upon the stage. He enjoyed roughnecking through Petruchio, where there is no call whatever for sentiment. But Romeo embarrassed him; in Othello, too, as one usually friendly critic observed, he seemed "incapable of rising to the full expression of the amatory passion";[90] he would insist that Hamlet was not in love with Ophelia.[91] He even disliked Benedick: "This fellow is a lover," he once exclaimed to the young Otis Skinner, who as Claudio was waiting to make an entrance with him. "I loathe the whole pack of them. Always did. Even as a youngster I loved the villains." And Skinner marveled that "with such gentleness as his it was singular that his greatest effects should have been made in parts of sinister and diabolic character—Iago, Richard, Bertuccio, Macbeth, Pescara, Shylock."[92]

He would soon redeem himself in his diabolonian masterpiece. His second production at Booth's Theatre was *Othello* (April 12 to May 29, forty-two performances), and while it was obligatory that he lead off as the hero, after two weeks he exchanged roles with Ned Adams and thereafter shone in his favorite role of Iago. "We don't like his Othello," said the *Daily Star*, buttressing its prejudice with the expectable sarcasms. "But go and see his Iago if you have to be carried on a litter—it is the very best of all he has ever done, possibly of all he ever will do."[93]

This *Othello* production was scenically less spectacular than that of *Romeo and Juliet*, yet in its fifteen sets it was worthy of its place in the program. The art historian Henry Tuckerman observed how in the first act it delighted the audience to recognize romantic Venetian

Illus. 98. Edwin Booth as Othello.

scenes long since familiar to them through the writings of Byron and Ruskin or through the modern art of photography.[94] And from the *World* critic, of a Cyprus scene, "It is, indeed, a novelty to see a turreted building rising forty-five feet high, with bastions and towers standing out against a lighted void of atmosphere, with a great sweep of sky, we know not how far behind it, in which the white clouds seem from their very distance to hang suspended."[95] Again Booth was complimented, as he had been in *Romeo and Juliet*, for the by-play of the crowds of supernumeraries who filled up the more public scenes with realistic behavior—never in a "huddle," never staring

Illus. 99. Edwin Booth as Iago, by Thomas Hicks. Courtesy of the National Portrait Gallery, Smithsonian Institution, Washington, D.C.

at the audience, but genuinely concerned in the stage events, all having been told what to do and how to do it.[96]

Booth's acting of Othello was, of course, a marked improvement over his Romeo, though not even his friend William Winter could claim that it ranked with his finest conceptions. It was widely observed that he lacked the physical stature of an ideal Othello; and though partisans defended him on the foolish grounds that Arabs are a diminutive race and on the somewhat more sensible grounds that Garrick and Edmund Kean—both known to have been superb Othellos—were even smaller than Booth, yet size and temperament did count against him.[97] Apparently, too, he failed to recognize what John McCullough would come to know instinctively, that from the beginning of the play Othello is *not* doom-eager but almost ecstatic in his good fortune and well-being. According to the *Herald*, which, of course, put Booth down as "the worst Othello we have ever seen outside an amateur performance," he resembled a fiery Arab not at all but rather "a young Jesuit student, calm, cultivated, even subdued"; and his "lachrymal tone made the address to the Senate sound like the well-delivered appeal of an elderly schoolboy begging off a flogging."[98] As the critic for the *Evening Mail* more acutely perceived, through two acts of the play Booth seemed to confuse Othello with his own characterization of Hamlet: "Now comes Othello into the council chamber, and although greeted by the Duke quite heartily, no smile mars his solemnity, and walking slowly down the stage the well known *pose* is taken, one arm thrown across the breast, and the hand of the other gracefully supporting the resting chin (Hamlet in Othello) absorbing all the gloom into himself. . . . And why is this? 'Vanity of vanities, and all is vanity.' "[99]

Once he got into the third act, of course, the part caught up with him, so to speak, and once his suspicion, jealousy, and tiger rage were aroused, he was "swept along upon a veritable tempest of passion, and he carried his auditors with him as leaves are swept by the whirlwind."[100] When he moved into the fifth act, said the *World* critic, "the fierceness settles into an implacable firmness. He sees nothing but his great wrong, and he will kill her."[101] Yet there was a kind of barbaric nobility in the killing, which never sank from an expiation to a brutality. Here we must recall that, like Charles Fechter and certain other nineteenth-century Othellos, Booth altered the conventional placing of Desdemona's bed from a curtained alcove at upstage center to downstage left, with the head of the

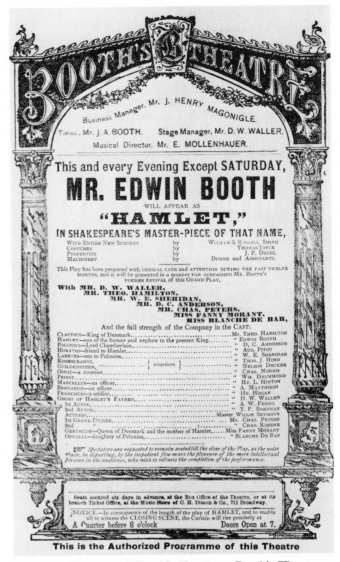

Illus. 100. Program of Booth's *Hamlet* at Booth's Theatre.

bed toward the audience. "It is of more importance that Othello's face should be seen than Desdemona's dead body," Booth explained to H. H. Furness, "and the killing is partly hidden at the same time."[102] We must recall, too, that he retained the old stage practice, at line 89 ("So, so"), of making Desdemona's death certain by a dagger thrust. Thus it was made to appear that she died of internal bleeding, after having time and strength enough to utter her final lines.[103] The critic at the *World* described the killing in the following terms:

The very blow of violence at the last becomes an agony of justice, and not a dastardly stab—he does not butcher her in his action, he slides the dagger under the bed clothes, with face averted; when it touches the victim he is shaken like a reed. His face is reflecting a greater anguish than comes of mortal hurt, and if in the slow bestowal of that cruel stab, as inch by inch the steel enters the body of Desdemona, we are horrified by the spectacle of suffering in the man, it must, at the same time, be conceded that this is a more artistic as it is a more terrible cruelty than the cool vengeance of another Othello who has been stabbing Desdemonas all over the country for the last twenty years, much as a lusty butcher performs the same feat on other innocents.[104]

Booth's own directive for the moment was "Hide your face in trembling hand while you stab and groan 'So, so'; the steel is piercing your own heart."[105]

When he turned to Iago on April 26 and gave Othello over to Ned Adams, everyone was pleased to note that the casting was now in better balance, and Winter could declare that New York was seeing "the best representation of a Shakespearean play that has been given here for years."[106] But little was written about Booth's Iago at the time, for his way with it had long since been set. As early as 1860, the *Post* had defined his Iago vividly—first in terms of what he was not:

He is no vulgar, melodramatic villain, full of scowlings and writhings, so transparent in his malice that Othello could not fail to see his motives; he does not go raving up and down, ranting his devilish designs at the top of his voice, in bellowing tones that would indeed have frighted the whole Isle of Cyprus; he is no slouched-hat and dark-lantern scoundrel, proclaiming to the world his intended villainy in a gruff stage whisper, and bearing his character writ upon his visage with all the malignant power that lurks in blackened eyebrows and a burnt-cork scowl.[107]

Shunning these clichés, which were presumably the stock-in-trade of most Iagos whom the *Post* critic had seen, Booth made a compelling bid for plausibility. "He is a frank, keen fellow, whom the simple-hearted grand Othello cannot choose but believe," wrote Lucia Calhoun in the *Galaxy*: "He has no stage winks and grimaces. . . . If Othello had suddenly turned upon him, at any moment of their interview, he would have seen only the grave, sympathetic, respectful, troubled face that was composed for

him to see." What impressed Miss Calhoun even more was the variety of clearly distinguished roles which Booth contained within this one role—his versatility: "To Othello he is the truthful, respectful adherent and friend, whose duty makes a painful disclosure obligatory upon him. To Desdemona he is the courteous servant, whom her beauty and her distress command. To Cassio he is the open and generous fellow-soldier, ready to take his part in disgrace. To Roderigo he is a dashing buck, whose villainy and whose pretensions the poor fool equally admires. To Emilia alone is he the inscrutable, black-browed schemer, whom she distrusts, but does not understand." And in the Senate Scene, Miss Calhoun said, where Iago has no lines, and in the final scene after declaring "never to speak word," he continued to hold attention by "the intensity of his being."[108]

In Booth's notes on Iago which he wrote out for H. H. Furness in 1885, he recommended a certain bluffness to underscore Iago's soldierly quality, admitting regretfully that his own characterization failed utterly in that particular. Otherwise his prescription chimes with the *Post* critic's earlier opinion. As he told Furness, "To portray Iago properly you must seem to be what all the characters think, and say, you are, not what the spectators know you to be; try to win even *them* by your sincerity. Don't *act* the villain, don't *look* it or *speak* it (by scowling and growling, I mean), but *think* it all the time. Be genial, sometimes jovial, always gentlemanly. Quick in motion as in thought; lithe and sinuous as a snake." To press home his point he made a suggestion which, in those days when every actor practiced and was strictly confined to a "line," must have been startling: "I think the 'light comedian' should play the villain's part, not the 'heavy man.' "[109]

Of all Booth's productions at his own theatre, that of *Hamlet* (January 5 to March 19, 1870, sixty-four performances) stirred the greatest excitement, drew the strongest box office, received the highest praise.[110] "In the production of *Hamlet* last night," the *Post* reported, "the most admired actor on the American stage achieved the greatest triumph he has yet known."[111] Over seventy substantial reviews of it were published, not only in New York papers but in Boston, Cincinnati, and as far away as Saint Paul, Minnesota. Even the *Herald*, amazingly, laid by its knives to rejoice in the event: "It was a genuine feast of reason, of beauty, of fashion, and of histrionic intelligence and splendor, both as regards actors, scenery, and audience. It was, in fact, just such a treat as 'pro-

Illus. 101. Edwin Booth as Hamlet.

latory message published in the *Leader*: "From the rising of the curtain until the going down thereof, you are my Hamlet."[113]

The opening was preceded by more than the usual amount of publicity, including several announcements of delay owing to the elaborateness of preparations. And for once Booth resorted to the "educational" device of issuing a brochure—to tell the public how this play could lift us out of "the narrow sphere of our daily lives into a loftier, grander region, whose atmosphere perforce shall purify and exalt our souls"; to present certain high-minded interpretations of the play and its hero, quoting Schlegel, Goethe, and Mrs. Jameson; to describe the sets, identify the entr'acte music, and list the half-dozen authorities that had been consulted for the costumes. The brochure emphasized that for the first time in the American theatre the play would be staged in the Norman architecture and Saxon dresses appropriate to tenth-century Denmark.[114] The costumes were not the usual bright-colored silks of Italian Renaissance or theatrical nondescript style, but heavy woolens, as befitted a cold northern country. The characters all wore blond wigs—all but one: Hamlet, whose father's beard was "a sable silvered," wore his own flowing black hair.

The scenery by Charles Witham and associates (eleven sets for fourteen scenes) delighted nearly everyone. On careful scrutiny of promptbooks and pictorial evidence one discovers that for the most part the sets followed the same ground plans and the same general style of decoration as the old Winter Garden sets for the "Hundred Nights *Hamlet*," but in size, solidity, consistency, and—with the rise-and-sink method of scene changing—fluidity of movement, they all seemed entirely new. "There were no makeshifts," said the *World* critic,

no expedients, no omissions, to suddenly recall the mind from the fanciful realm represented to the ungrateful theatric reality. In so perfect a combination of mechanical and artistic resources, the actors seemed for the time being to be impressed by the illusion about them. That new sense of reality which the witchery of paint had evoked in the spectators, seemed to lend a new freedom to the performers. They were in no danger of mistaking pasteboard boxes for battlements and carved oak panels for doors. The massive stone stairways they seemed to know would bear the tread of a regiment, and that distant blue above them got to be in their minds the very "brave o'erhanging firmament" itself, "fretted" —so far as anyone but the high ensconced deity of a stage carpenter could see—"with golden fire."[115]

fessionals' and critical old playgoers would almost risk the shortening of their span of life to enjoy."[112] George Fox and three or four other burlesque artists honored the production by getting up parodies of it. Shakespeare himself, watching from the "Dramatic Sphere, Spiritual World," sent Booth, through a medium, a long congratu-

Illus. 102. Charles Witham's watercolor of the Churchyard Scene for *Hamlet* at Booth's Theatre, 1870. Courtesy of the Harvard Theatre Collection.

Three sets were especially admired.[116] At the beginning, as a great bell was tolling midnight, the curtain rose on a view of the Castle of Elsinore. Behind low crenelated walls—the castle's outer defenses—the massive structure with its square keep and octagon watchtower rose toward stage left, bathed in the light of a full moon hanging low in the cloud-rifted sky. It was a deep set, the defense wall some thirty feet beyond the curtain line. Tall trees bordered the stage at either side. It was a scene of mystery, lighted only by a green glow from the footlights and white light of low intensity pouring down from the right. The principal set of the third act, called the Grand Hall of Audience, where Hamlet confronts Ophelia and later stages the Play Scene, was a marvelous construction. At either side of this hall a marble staircase rose some fifteen steps to a practical gallery which ran the width of the hall. The gallery was fronted by a carved stone railing surmounted by three curtained arched openings (vantage points for the King and Polonius to spy on Hamlet). Beneath the gallery and flanked by the staircases a broad, flat-arched opening provided the main entrance to the hall. Downstage of the staircases, arches gave to right and left into small side rooms, prettily lighted by stained-glass windows. Over all, as in a cathedral, hung a magnificent triple-vaulted ceiling, lifting one's vision and lending dignity and mystery to the scene. The Churchyard set in the fifth act was perhaps the most celebrated of them all. The scene was framed above and at the sides by leafage, and tombs and trees were scattered through the depth of the stage. A Gothic chapel toward stage left was half concealed behind a pyramidal yew tree. It was a night scene and moonlight fell in streaks through the branches. "Surely no 'God's acre' was ever more lovely than this!" exclaimed a correspondent to the *Evening*

Post. "The moonlight streams calmly over the little church, the green hillocks, the marble tombs, the graceful figure of Hamlet, and the sturdy and loquacious grave-digger who sings at his work, keeping time with his shovel as he throws up the earth and now and then a skull."[117] It was all so enchanting, so dreamlike and serene, that almost no one noticed the oddity that Ophelia's funeral was taking place at night.

The supporting company, if not brilliant throughout, behaved acceptably, but all eyes and ears were for Booth alone, and dozens of critics and thousands of playgoers were hypnotized into belief that in this role Booth could do no wrong. "His spare and almost attenuated frame, his thoughtful, and, indeed, habitually mournful expression; his hollow, low-pitched voice; his splendid dark eye; his jetty, disheveled locks, and a certain morbidness that is suggested by his whole look and bearing, carry conviction to the mass of beholders that in them they see as near an approach as possible to the Hamlet of Shakespeare."[118] Thus much wrote the *Times* critic, struggling to maintain his distance from "the mass of beholders." He could go on to assert that "there is a want of fire and *electricity* in the great test scenes," that "in passages of violent declamation, Mr. Booth appears to lack power," but resistance was useless: there was no stemming the current of Booth-worship. This "genteel and gentle" Hamlet, "pale and polite"—as Booth himself once jokingly described it[119]—became the only right one for an entire generation.

Hamlet, of course, was the role with which Booth was then, and is to this day, most often identified. From his first performance of it in San Francisco in 1853, when he was nineteen, until his last public appearance of all in 1891, he was always Hamlet. During those nearly four decades his Hamlet passed through many phases. From the first, it appears, his conception of the role differed from that of his father, or of the actors of the heroic school, by its quietness, gentleness, and grace. His early California critic, Ferdinand Ewer, attributed to it, in Hazlitt's phrase, "all the easy motion and the peaceful curves of a wave of the sea." Yet we gather that from time to time in the 1850s, while he settled his style, he was tempted even in Hamlet to make points, chew the carpet, and "act a bit" in order to stir up audiences. By 1860 when he arrived at the Winter Garden for the effective beginning of his New York career, Lucia Calhoun tells us that "certain spurts and dashes of power were

gone; certain striking but fantastic readings and bits of business had been abandoned. The actor had attained repose. His Hamlet was a lovely poem."[120]

As for the Hamlet of 1870, doubtless the most interesting interpretation of it is that of a twenty-one year old amateur, Charles Clarke, who has left us a 60,000-word manuscript description of Booth's performance. By 1870 the professional critics tended to take Booth's Hamlet for granted and to spend their comments on side issues, the physical staging or lesser points. But for Clarke, seeing it for the first time, it was an authentic tragedy which moved him deeply. It was the tragedy of "a man of first-class intellect and second-class will," a Hamlet who could face smaller challenges with clear courage and act on firm determination, but who, when confronted by the great challenge—to kill the King—was baffled. And when at last, on impulse and without reflection, he does the necessary deed, he is bewildered, appalled by his own action. In the deepest sense this Hamlet was for Clarke a tragedy and a morality, and the experience of it was exhilarating. He speaks of "all that Booth has done to drill my mind, and put an edge upon my sensibility; and instruct my emotions, and inform my imagination." He would like to reach up and cry "Oh Booth! Booth! as if his identity and power were somewhere just overhead and I was looking up toward them as to some source of mental health and light."[121]

As Booth grew older, his Hamlet matured in spirit and significance. When the young Hamlin Garland first saw it in 1884, he found in it "a sombre philosopher, a student of life and a man burdened with doubt." It was a Hamlet who seemed to know how his story would end and who approached his doom with dignified resolution. He had become what he admired in Horatio, the "man that is not passion's slave." He was "the good man enduring," "the passive suffering center"—settled in wisdom and purpose, much less a figure of pathos than a subject for tragic admiration.[122]

Booth's *Julius Caesar*, another of his major productions of Shakespeare at his own house, opened on Christmas night of 1871, and although scheduled for only eight weeks it lasted out the winter and ran for twelve (December 25 to March 16, eighty-five performances). That run was for the moment the longest that *Caesar* had ever known, though four years later when Jarrett and Palmer revived it at the same theatre, using pretty much the same scenery, they would keep it on for 103 performances.

In terms of theatre management the *Caesar* production was Booth's climactic achievement. Scenically, Charles Witham's Rome was finer in conception and finish than even his Verona or Elsinore had been. Histrionically, whereas *Hamlet* had been a personal triumph for Booth (*Hamlet* being in a sense a one-man show), in *Caesar* he brought together an entire team of leading actors—Lawrence Barrett, Frank Bangs, and D. W. Waller—capable of sharing the acting honors. Toward the end of the run, when Barrett had left to fill another commitment, Booth took the occasion to demonstrate his versatility: after ten weeks of playing Brutus, he put in a week as Cassius and another week as Antony.

Witham's scenery was "historical," of course, but frankly anachronistic. As befitted the grandeur of the play, and responding to popular expectations in stage decoration in the 1870s, it was not the rude brick Rome of the Republic but the marble Rome of Augustus—the Rome which in fact was rising again in state capitols, public libraries, and other official buildings all over America. The curtain rose on a "Grand Square in Rome," filled presently with a procession of well over a hundred lictors, guards, standard bearers, and citizens accompanying Caesar to the Lupercal games.[123] The facades of over a dozen splendid buildings flanked the square or rose above each other on the hills behind it, all distributed in such graceful composition and modeled with such care to proportion and perspective that reviewers claimed to have felt they had looked into a real view of a real city. The Senate Chamber Scene, as everyone recognized, was based upon Jean Léon Gérôme's recent but already famous painting *The Death of Caesar*—only Witham had vastly elaborated the architecture of it. Gérôme's painting, broad and low, cuts off just above the tops of his background columns: Witham, making use of the grand height of Booth's proscenium opening, introduced a lofty and coffered barrel-vaulted ceiling and, beyond it, the illusion of a long hall with a series of barrel vaults separating a series of domes. The Forum Scene, where Brutus and Antony deliver their glorious harangues—the rhetorical cornerstones of so much American political oratory in the nineteenth century—though less elaborate than the Grand Square of Act I, was likewise praised without stint. The mob of supernumeraries in this scene, according to *Appleton's Journal*, "are converted from the usual uncouth elements of a stage crowd into men and women who form a part of the picture, who are moved by the words addressed to them, who are swayed, excited, become turbulent—who . . . help to render the Brutus and Mark Antony the men they would seem."[124]

Booth presented Brutus as the philosophical man rather than the warrior, and that, said the *World* critic, was the Brutus that Shakespeare intended; but, he continued, since convention holds that nobility can be expressed only by huge actors, capable of the stock fury of the stage, we are sure to be told that Booth lacks the vigor and puissance for Brutus.[125] William Winter, too, anticipated this obvious attack and attempted to justify Booth's physical appearance by an appeal to history: "Brutus like Cassius, was lean and pale—and Mr. Booth's physical embodiment of the character is therefore entirely accurate."[126] Convention could not be forestalled, however, and the stale objection was registered far and wide. A more significant objection, which perhaps owed more to opening-night nervousness than to Booth's ultimate intentions, was a lack of repose, or, as the *Mail* put it, "too much of the feverish excitement which we admire in his Hamlet but which is unsuited to the present part."[127] The *Times*, in fact, suggested that not only in size but in tension he would be better suited to Cassius than to Brutus. And when he came to play Cassius toward the end of the run, he would hardly have been flattered to read in the *Herald* that "Cassius is a part in every way suited to Mr. Booth's genius. His conceptions are marked oftener by intensity than by breadth. Hence we find him most successful in the portrayal of what, for want of a better name, we may call the selfish passions." Just as his Iago had been acclaimed successful and his Othello not, so his Cassius was superior to his Brutus. "Envy, malignant hatred, avarice, or cunning, for instance, we should expect him to simulate more effectively than magnanimity or exalted patriotism." The *Herald* critic hastened to assure his readers that he was referring only to Booth's capacity as an artist, and not to his personal morals. Nonetheless it was a low blow.[128] But not so low as that struck by a scurrilous sheet called the *Season*, which wondered how Booth could be so morally callous as to stage the "assassination play": "How he then could have maintained his composure during that awful scene in which, in mockery, he played the part which John Wilkes Booth played with

Illus. 103. Charles Witham's watercolor of the "Grand Square in Rome" for *Julius Caesar* at Booth's Theatre. Courtesy of the Museum of the City of New York, Theatre and Music Collection.

Illus. 104. Edwin Booth as Richard III.

admiration and sympathy."[131] Of the half-dozen Shakespeare plays that Booth and Barrett took on the road when they played together in 1887–88 and 1888–89, they played *Julius Caesar* far oftener than any other, exhibiting those noblest Romans from coast to coast in every principal theatre town in America.

Booth mounted altogether eight major Shakespeare productions at his own theatre. Besides those already named there were *Macbeth* in March and April of 1870 (sixteen performances); *Much Ado about Nothing* in March of 1871 (fourteen performances); *The Winter's Tale*, which he did not act in but turned over to Barrett, a dedicated Leontes, in April and May of 1871 (forty-one performances); and *Richard III* in May of 1872 (sixteen performances).[132] This last was not Shakespeare's play, but Colley Cibber's, which he had once sneered at Charles Kean for perpetuating.[133] He would redeem himself on this point some years later (January 7, 1878) when he returned to Booth's Theatre under other management and performed Shakespeare's play in a version prepared by William Winter. Other remarkable contributions to the Shakespearean cause were his revival of *Richard II* at Daly's Theatre on November 8, 1875, and his performance of *King Lear* in a restored version at the same theatre a few days later. Winter placed Lear among Booth's finest characterizations and, indeed, "among the grandest achievements of the modern stage."[134]

The failure of Booth's Theatre was, in the long run, a good thing for Booth. He had wanted to revivify Shakespeare and the so-called legitimate drama with "Art," by which he meant principally *mise-en-scène*, especially of the "historically accurate" kind. It was enough that for a few seasons he participated in this grand nineteenth-century delusion that one got at the heart of Shakespeare's mystery by filling the stage with more and more realistic scenery. This notion was carried to such extravagant lengths in England by Henry Irving (and after Irving by Herbert Beerbohm Tree) that the plays were well-nigh displaced by the stage decoration. Then, as is well known, a revolt set in during the 1890s, led in its first phase by William Poel, whose goal was simply to banish scenery altogether and restore the plays to their original integrity on the plain, undecorated platform stage for which they had been written.

What is rarely noticed is that long before Poel got his campaign under way, certain critics in America had protested sharply against Booth's stage decoration, especially for *Hamlet*. As early as 1865, in a valedictory to the

such fearful earnestness, no one but Edwin Booth and his God can tell."[129]

It was Lawrence Barrett, of course, who was the supreme exponent of Cassius. He had played it at Niblo's in September of 1870, when he was said to have "rolled upon the stage like a red-hot bomb."[130] Here at Booth's, on the opening night he unequivocally "bore away the richest honors" for the well-aimed waspish sting of his performance. When he played Cassius again, opposite Davenport, in the 1875 Jarrett and Palmer revival, William Winter would declare that "he pervaded the play like the indomitable and remorseless figure of Fate, and he presented Cassius with such subtlety of thought, such power of intellectual passion, such vigorous and sonorous eloquence, and such force of identification and spontaneity as could not, and did not, fail to command the warmest

"Hundred Nights *Hamlet*," a critic who had knowledge-ably objected to historical error in the dresses and archi-tectural error in the scenery affirmed boldly that the entire scenic effort was an irrelevance and a nuisance: "The inherent depravity of stage decoration is such that when best it is worst, and among the agonies of the scene-painter one always sighs for a barn, or the golden days of Shakespeare himself, when actors moved in the sump-tuous costume of the time among scenes that merely sug-gested the situation, without dividing attention with the text."[135] Five years later the critic Richard Grant White, in an amusing essay called "The Clown's Real Pigling," demonstrated at length why it was that to present *Hamlet* in authentic historical settings was preposterous. The whole play is "one monstrous anachronism," he declared, and to warp and force the countless Elizabethan elements of the play, including above all the philosophizing person of Hamlet, into the furniture, dress, and architecture of tenth-century Denmark was simply absurd.[136] The critic Nym Crinkle, angered at the playgoers' desertion of the heroic school for what he took to be the sentimental school, denounced their "secret contempt for those demon-strative displays of grief and hate and love which once constituted the very *anima* of the tragic stage." All that the playgoers care for, he declared, is "the exact cut of the Danish soldier's breeches . . . and the style of furniture and decoration in Polonius's house."[137] In a review of the 1869 *Othello* a sneerer at the *Herald* hoped that "the day may not be far distant when some real actor will arise and scourge these carpenters and painters from the temple of Shakspearian genius."[138] Booth was shaken by these at-tacks. "What am I to do?" he responded. "If I read *Hamlet* as I read *Manfred*, it is simply a poem"; then only the intellectual few would respond to it. "I play it as it is writ-ten," he declared, "and put it on the stage according to every authority. There is not a costume, or decoration, or painting, that I have not some reason for introducing."[139]

A decade later in London when he was trying desper-ately amid shabby mountings at the Princess's to interest the public in his acting of Shakespeare, while across town at the Lyceum Henry Irving and his scene painters were drawing crowds to the thin gruel of Tennyson's *The Cup*, he came perforce to believe that excessive stage decora-tion was fool's fire. "The actor's art is judged by his cos-tume and the scenery," he complained in a letter to Wil-liam Winter. "If they are not 'esthetic' (God save the mark!) he makes no stir. . . . Chas. Kean, Fechter, & Irving have feasted the Londoners so richly they cannot

Illus. 105. Edwin Booth as Macbeth.

relish undecorated dishes. I was at the same ill work at home—but was fortunately checked, by fire first and afterwards by bankruptcy. I do not regret my losses now —since I've seen the evil results of 'grand revivals.' "[140] There were others in America—Lawrence Barrett, Au-gustin Daly, Richard Mansfield, E. H. Sothern, David Belasco—who would maintain the art of scenographic realism until the cinema would take it over and perfect it, but Booth contented himself with whatever scenic in-vestiture others would provide him, and wasted no more energy or authority upon the matter.

His genius lay in acting. Once he had shed the killing cares of management he was free to carry his acting—his brooding Brutus, his crimson Richelieu and mad Bertuc-cio, his cunning Iago, the agony of his Lear, the mystery of his Hamlet—across the Atlantic and to every corner of our own land.

Notes

I. *The Eighteenth Century*

1. The general histories of the eighteenth-century American theatre which are cited most frequently in the following pages are these: William Dunlap, *History of the American Theatre*, 2 vols. (London: Richard Bentley, 1833); John Bernard, *Retrospections of America, 1797–1811* (New York: Harper & Bros., 1887; reprint, Benjamin Blom, 1969); Joseph Norton Ireland, *Records of the New York Stage, from 1750 to 1860*, 2 vols. (New York: T. H. Morrell, 1866–67); George O. Seilhamer, *History of the American Theatre*, 3 vols. (Philadelphia: Globe Printing House, 1888–91; reprint, New York: Benjamin Blom, 1968); Arthur Hornblow, *A History of the Theatre in America*, 2 vols. (Philadelphia: J. B. Lippincott, 1919); George C. D. Odell, *Annals of the New York Stage*, 15 vols. (New York: Columbia University Press, 1927–49); Thomas Clark Pollock, *The Philadelphia Theatre in the Eighteenth Century* (Philadelphia: University of Pennsylvania Press, 1933); Hugh F. Rankin, *The Theater in Colonial America* (Chapel Hill: University of North Carolina Press, 1960).

2. Information about the earliest pre-Hallam stagings of Shakespeare appears in Dunlap, I, 31; Ireland, I, 1–12; Seilhamer, I, 1–18; Hornblow, I, 53–65; Odell, I, 41–45; Rankin, pp. 22–42.

3. Garrick to Grey Cooper, February 1, 1774. See David M. Little and George M. Kahrl, eds., *The Letters of David Garrick*, 3 vols. (Cambridge: Harvard University Press, 1963), III, 920.

4. Bernard, p. 8.

5. Bernard, p. 162.

6. The beginnings of the Hallam company have been variously reported. See Dunlap, I, 1–13; Ireland, I, 13–21; Seilhamer, I, 19–29; Hornblow, I, 66–75; Odell, I, 50–52; Rankin, pp. 43–50. See also Philip Highfill, Jr., "The British Background of the American Hallams," *Theatre Survey* XI (May 1970): 1–35.

7. Arthur H. Scouten, ed., *The London Stage, 1660–1800*, Part 3: *1729–1747*, 2 vols. (Carbondale: Southern Illinois University Press, 1961), II, 1117–1304.

8. George Winchester Stone, Jr., ed., *The London Stage, 1660–1800*, Part 4: *1747–1776*, 3 vols. (Carbondale: Southern Illinois University Press, 1962), I, 331–35.

9. Since the *Virginia Gazette* of August 28, 1752, announced the performance for "Friday next," the date has often been given as September 5. But as Hugh Rankin (p. 54) explains, when the Gregorian Calendar was adopted that year, the days between September 2 and 14 were omitted. For the Hallam company's first stand in Williamsburg, see Dunlap, I, 14–18; Seilhamer, I, 35–43; Hornblow, I, 79–87; Odell, I, 52–54; Rankin, pp. 50–59.

10. John Northbrooke, *A Treatise against Dicing, Dancing, Plays, and Interludes* (London, *ca.* 1577; reprint, London: The Shakespeare Society, 1843), pp. 59–68 of 1577 ed.

11. Eola Willis, *The Charleston Stage in the XVIII Century* (Columbia: The State Company, 1924), chap. 1.

12. Photographs of the Richmond Theatre are reproduced in Brooks McNamara, *The American Playhouse in the Eighteenth Century* (Cambridge: Harvard University Press, 1969), pp. 34–36.

13. Hornblow, I, 80; Rankin, p. 50.

14. Rankin, p. 54.

15. Charles Beecher Hogan, *Shakespeare in the Theatre, 1701–1800*, 2 vols. (Oxford: Clarendon Press, 1952–57), I, 309–19, II, 411–13.

16. Hornblow, I, 82–83; Rankin, p. 56.

17. Hornblow, I, 87; Rankin, p. 57.

18. For the American tours of the Hallam company, see Dunlap, I, 19–33; Ireland, I, 21–26; Seilhamer, I, 44–79; Hornblow, I, 88–96; Odell, I, 54–68; Pollock, pp. 7–12, 75–76; Rankin, pp. 60–73.

19. For Lewis Hallam, Jr., see Dunlap, I, 199–200, 287–95, etc.; Bernard, pp. 265–66; Ireland, I, 20; Hornblow, I, 98 ff.; Odell, I, 232, 340–41, 430–31, etc., II, 265; Rankin, pp. 75–76, 196–97.

20. Pollock, p. 21.

21. Odell, I, 90.

22. Quoted by Rankin, p. 83.

23. Pollock, pp. 77–84.

24. George O. Willard, *History of the Providence Stage, 1762–1891* (Providence: The Rhode Island News Company, 1891), p. 5.

25. Barnard Hewitt, *Theatre U.S.A., 1668–1957* (New York: McGraw-Hill, 1959), pp. 26–27.

26. Willard, pp. 12, 18; Rankin, pp. 99–100.

27. Odell, I, 85.

28. Rankin, p. 99.

29. For the theatregoing of George Washington, see Paul Leicester Ford, *Washington and the Theatre* (New York: The Dunlap Society, 1899).

30. For Margaret Cheer, see Seilhamer, I, 204–8; Hornblow, I, 121–22; Odell, I, 116, 141; Pollock, p. 19; Rankin, pp. 102, 128–29, 198–99.

31. Pollock, pp. 21–22, 85–106.

32. For John Henry and the Storer sisters, see Dunlap, I, 52 ff.; Ireland, I, 43–44, 46, 51; Seilhamer, I, 198–200; Hornblow, I, 124–27 ff.; Odell, I, 116 ff; Pollock, pp. 23–24 ff.; Rankin, pp. 120 ff., 197–98.

33. Seilhamer, I, 235–40; Rankin, pp. 140–52.

34. For Nancy Hallam, see Seilhamer, I, 278–81; Hornblow, I, 136–39; Odell, I, 171–73; Rankin, pp. 155–59.

35. Seilhamer, II, 51–53; Hornblow, I, 147; Rankin, p. 187.

36. Rankin, p. 191.

37. Hornblow, I, 158–61.

38. Pollock, pp. 41–48, 133–45.

39. For John Hodgkinson, see Dunlap, I, 183–92; Bernard, pp. 26–29, 257–58; Ireland, I, 95–96; Seilhamer, III, 28–42; Hornblow, I, 190–94; Odell, I, 313–14 ff., II, 10 ff., 246.

40. Odell, I, 370.

41. For James Fennell, see Dunlap, I, 231–33; Bernard, pp. 73–77, 292–93, 296–98; Ireland, I, 161; Seilhamer, III, 129–33; Hornblow, I, 207–8; Odell, II, 54, 352–53, etc.

42. For Charlotte Melmoth, see Dunlap, I, 201–3; Bernard, p. 266; Ireland, I, 105–6; Seilhamer, III, 78–81; Hornblow, I, 200; Odell, I, 332–33, 341, etc., II, 54, etc.

43. For Elizabeth Whitlock, see Dunlap, I, 238–39; Bernard, p. 264; Ireland, I, 151; Frances Ann Kemble, *Records of a Girlhood* (New York: Henry Holt, 1883), pp. 40–42, 105–6; Seilhamer, III, 134–35; Hornblow, I, 208–9; Odell, II, 150–61.

44. For Mrs. Ann Brunton Merry, later Mrs. Wignell, later Mrs. Warren, see Dunlap, I, 308, 334–41; Bernard, pp. 268–69; Ireland, I, 154–55; Hornblow, I, 213–14; Odell, I, 460, II, 120, 135, 238, 301.

45. For Thomas Abthorpe Cooper, see Joseph Norton Ireland, *A Memoir of the Professional Life of Thomas Abthorpe Cooper* (New York: The Dunlap Society, 1888). Also Dunlap, I, 341–52, II, *passim*; Bernard, pp. 164–68, 171–72,

267–68; Ireland, *Records*, I, 156–57; Noah Ludlow, *Dramatic Life as I Found It* (St. Louis: G. I. Jones & Co., 1880; reprint, Benjamin Blom, 1966), p. 234; Hornblow, I, 214–16; Odell, I, 452, II and III *passim*, IV, 75; Hewitt, pp. 72–78.

46. McNamara, pp. 104–18; William C. Young, *Documents of American Theatre History: Famous American Playhouses*, Vol. 1, *1716–1899* (Chicago: American Library Association, 1973), I, 35–39.

47. These figures, the estimate of a French visitor, are perhaps too small. Charles Durang said that when the theatre was enlarged in 1805 it held about 2,000, of which 960 were in the boxes; see Young, pp. 35–39.

48. Rankin, pp. 103, 161.

49. For Charles Ciceri, see Dunlap, I, 201–13; Hornblow, I, 201; Odell, I, 378–79, II, 6, 8, 14, 84, 85.

II. *The Wild Ones*

1. Price's connections with the Park are recorded in George C. D. Odell, *Annals of the New York Stage*, 15 vols. (New York: Columbia University Press, 1927–49), II–IV *passim*. For the fullest account of Price see Barnard Hewitt, " 'King Stephen' of the Park and Drury Lane," in *The Theatrical Manager in England and America*, ed. Joseph W. Donohue, Jr. (Princeton: Princeton University Press, 1971), pp. 87–141. See also Joseph Norton Ireland, *Records of the New York Stage, from 1750 to 1860*, 2 vols. (New York: T. H. Morrell, 1866–67), I, 251–52.

2. Principal accounts of Cooke's life and his American career are: William Dunlap, *The Life of George Frederick Cooke*, 2d ed., 2 vols. (London: Henry Colburn, 1815); *idem*, "Notes on the Life of George Frederick Cooke," in *Diary of William Dunlap*, 3 vols. (New York: New York Historical Society, 1930), II, 413–70; Ireland, I, 273–76; Arthur Hornblow, *A History of the Theatre in America*, 2 vols. (Philadelphia: J. B. Lippincott, 1919), I, 272–81; Odell, II, 348–90; William W. Clapp, *A Record of the Boston Stage* (Boston: James Munroe, 1853), pp. 118–28; William B. Wood, *Personal Recollections of the Stage* (Philadelphia: Henry Carey Baird, 1855), pp. 133, 156–70; Don B. Wilmeth, "Cooke among the Yankee Doodles," *Theatre Survey* XIV, no. 2 (November 1973): 1–32.

3. For James Boaden's generally hostile remarks about Cooke, see his *Memoirs of the Life of John Philip Kemble*, 2 vols. (London: Longman, Hurst, etc., 1825), II, 279–85.

4. In Lamb's 1802 review of Cooke's Richard III. See *The Works of Charles Lamb*, ed. Thomas Hutchinson (London: Oxford University Press, 1924), p. 48.

5. Cited in Bertram Joseph, *The Tragic Actor* (London: Routledge & Kegan Paul, 1959) p. 245.

6. Boaden, II, 523.

7. See Dunlap, *Cooke*, II, 350 ff. for this and following notes on Cooke's style.

8. Boaden, II, 279.

9. See Barnard Hewitt, *Theatre U.S.A., 1668 to 1957* (New York: McGraw-Hill, 1959), pp. 84–85.

10. Lamb, *Works*, pp. 45–48.

11. Boaden, II, 280.

12. Hewitt, " 'King Stephen' of the Park and Drury Lane," pp. 92–93.

13. Dunlap, *Cooke*, II, 152.

14. *Diary of William Dunlap*, II, 415.

15. Reviews from the *New York Columbian* are quoted in Odell, II, 356–59.

16. See Wilmeth, pp. 28–32, for tabulation of all Cooke's American performances.

17. For an account of Cooke's burial and subsequent events, see Don B. Wilmeth, "The Posthumous Career of George Frederick Cooke," *Theatre Notebook* XXIV, no. 2 (Winter 1969–70): 68–74.

18. Joseph N. Ireland, *Mrs. Duff* (Boston: James R. Osgood, 1882).

19. Among the many books about Kean, the most judicious account of his life and his American career is Harold N. Hillebrand's *Edmund Kean* (New York: Columbia University Press, 1933). See also Ireland, *Records*, I, 368–72, 462–63; Hornblow, I, 300–310. For his New York performances, see Odell, II, chap. 9, and III, chaps. 6 and 8; for Boston, Clapp, chaps. 12 and 15; for Philadelphia, Wood, chaps. 13 and 16, and Reese D. James, *Old Drury of Philadelphia* (Philadelphia: University of Pennsylvania Press, 1932). Recent appreciative essays may be found in Edward Wagenknecht, *Merely Players* (Norman: University of Oklahoma Press, 1966), pp. 30–54; and Richard Findlater, *The Player Kings* (New York: Stein & Day, 1971), pp. 72–93. See also Joseph, chap. 6; and Joseph W. Donohue, Jr., *Dramatic Character in the English Romantic Age*, (Princeton: Princeton University Press, 1970), *passim*.

20. Frances Ann Kemble, *Records of a Girlhood* (New York: Henry Holt, 1883), p. 119.

21. Kemble, pp. 429–30.

22. Hazlitt's opinions cited here are scattered through his early reviews of Kean, collected in *A View of the English Stage* (London: R. Stodart, 1818). See William Hazlitt, *Complete Works*, ed. P. P. Howe, 21 vols. (London: J. M. Dent & Sons, 1930–34), V.

23. John Keats, "On Edmund Kean as a Shakespearian Actor." See *The Poetical Works and Other Writings of John Keats*, ed. H. Buxton Forman, etc., 8 vols. (New York: Charles Scribner's Sons, 1938–39), V, 231.

24. *Leigh Hunt's Dramatic Criticism*, ed. Lawrence H. and Carolyn W. Houtchens (New York: Columbia University Press, 1949), p. 114.

25. Hazlitt, V, 182.

26. Hazlitt, V, 188.

27. Hazlitt, V, 207.

28. Hillebrand, pp. 201 ff.

29. Odell, II, 583–84.

30. Hillebrand, p. 204.

31. Odell, II, 588.

32. Hillebrand, p. 207.

33. Hillebrand, p. 206.

34. Clapp, pp. 185–93; Hillebrand, pp. 216–23.

35. Hillebrand, pp. 249–56.

36. For the details of this American visit, see Hillebrand, pp. 257–80; Odell, III, chaps. 6 and 8; Clapp, pp. 226–37; Wood, pp. 309–24.

37. Quoted in Hillebrand, p. 263.

38. The most detailed biographical account of the elder Booth is Book 1 of Stanley Kimmel, *The Mad Booths of Maryland* (Indianapolis: Bobbs-Merrill Co., 1940; rev. ed., New York: Dover, 1969), pp. 13–92. See also Ireland, *Records*, I, 389–94; Asia Booth Clarke, *Booth Memorials: Passages, Incidents, and Anecdotes in the Life of Junius Brutus Booth* (New York: Carleton, 1866); *idem*, *The Elder and the Younger Booth* (Boston: James R. Osgood, 1882); Thomas R. Gould, *The Tragedian: An Essay on the Histrionic Genius of Junius Brutus Booth* (New York: Hurd & Houghton, 1868); Hornblow, I, 320–27. For his New York appearances, see Odell, III–VI; for Boston, Clapp, pp. 195–202; for Providence, George O. Willard, *History of the Providence Stage, 1762–1891* (Providence: The Rhode Island News Company, 1891), pp. 85, 106–8, 132–36; for Philadelphia, Wood, pp. 271–74, 301, etc., and James; for New Orleans, John S. Kendall, *The Golden Age of the New Orleans Theatre* (Baton Rouge: Louisiana State University Press, 1952).

39. Gould, p. 31.

40. For Kean's Sir Giles, see Robert Hamilton Ball, *The Amazing Career of Sir Giles Overreach* (Princeton: Princeton University Press, 1939), pp. 59–97, etc. Ball describes Booth's Sir Giles at pp. 98–108 and 195–231.

41. Hazlitt, V, 354–55.

42. Hazlitt, V, 356.

43. Hazlitt, XVIII, 328.

44. Francis C. Wemyss, in *Theatrical Biography; or, The Life of an Actor and Manager* (Glasgow: R. Griffin, 1848), pp. 75–76, comments on the loss of reputation Booth suffered by this back-door entry into America.

45. Edwin Booth, "Some Words about My Father," in *Kean and Booth and Their Contemporaries*, ed. Brander Matthews and Laurence Hutton (Boston: L. Page, 1900), pp. 95–96.

46. The pigeon story was reported first in the Boston *Pearl and Literary Gazette* December 13, 1834, and then by the

Reverend James Freeman Clarke in "My Odd Adventure with Junius Brutus Booth," *Atlantic Monthly* VIII (September 1861): 296–301. Asia Booth Clarke reprinted it in *Booth Memorials*, pp. 114–25.

47. Richard Lockridge, *Darling of Misfortune: Edwin Booth, 1833–1893* (New York: Century Co., 1932), p. 24.

48. Charles H. Shattuck, *The Hamlet of Edwin Booth* (Urbana: University of Illinois Press, 1969), pp. 4–6.

49. James E. Murdoch, *The Stage; or, Recollections of Actors and Acting from an Experience of Fifty Years* (Philadelphia: J. M. Stoddart & Co., 1880), pp. 172–75.

50. Arthur Colby Sprague, *Shakespeare and the Actors* (Cambridge: Harvard University Press, 1945), p. 95.

51. Walt Whitman, *Complete Prose Works* (Philadelphia: David McKay, 1892), p. 427.

52. Murdoch, p. 180. See also Wood, p. 301.

53. Gould, pp. 30–32.

54. John Foster Kirk, "Shakespeare's Tragedies on the Stage," *Lippincott's Magazine of Popular Literature and Science* XXXIII (May and June 1884): 607–11.

55. Murdoch, p. 178.

56. Booth's statements about elocutionary effects are reported by Murdoch, pp. 275–76.

57. Gould, p. 86.

58. Gould, pp. 57–58.

59. Gould, p. 60.

60. Gould, pp. 126–27.

61. Gould, p. 106.

62. Gould, pp. 19–21.

63. Gould, p. 23. Murdoch, Noah M. Ludlow, and others express similarly enthusiastic appraisals.

64. Kirk, pp. 607–8.

65. See William C. Young, *Documents of American Theatre History: Famous American Playhouses*, Vol. 1, *1716–1899* (Chicago: American Library Association, 1973), pp. 59–160, for the principal documents describing the theatres built in this period.

III. *Three Natives—and Another Visitor*

1. Payne's New York appearances are chronicled in George C. D. Odell, *Annals of the New York Stage*, 15 vols. (New York: Columbia University Press, 1927–49), II. A brief account of his life as well as his Boston appearances is given in William W. Clapp, *A Record of the Boston Stage* (Boston: James Monroe, 1853), pp. 101–12. For his full biography, see Grace Overmyer, *America's First Hamlet* (New York: New York University Press, 1957). See also Joseph Norton Ireland, *Records of the New York Stage, from 1750 to 1860*, 2 vols. (New York: T. H. Morrell, 1866–67), I, 255–57.

2. Giles Playfair, *The Prodigy: A Study of the Strange Life of Master Betty* (London: Secker & Warburg, 1967). Among the more remarkable child Shakespeareans on the nineteenth-century American stage were Master Joseph Burke, the Irish Roscius, who arrived in New York in November of 1830, being then eleven years old, to play Shylock and Richard III; Jean Davenport (said to be the original of Dickens's "infant phenomenon," Ninetta Crummles), who was playing Shylock and Richard III in 1837 at the age of eleven; Kate Bateman, who in December of 1849 was playing Portia, Richmond, and Macbeth at the age of six; and her sister Ellen, who was the Shylock, the Richard III, and the Lady Macbeth at the age of four.

3. Clapp, p. 104.

4. Clapp, p. 103.

5. Overmyer, p. 382.

6. Francis Hodge, *Yankee Theatre: The Image of America on the Stage, 1825–1850* (Austin: University of Texas Press, 1964), p. 5.

7. For Hackett's New York performances, see Odell, III–VIII; for Boston, see Clapp, pp. 427–29. The fullest account of Hackett, attending mainly to his American Originals, is in Hodge, pp. 81–151. See also Ireland, I, 473–75; Arthur Hornblow, *A History of the Theatre in America*, 2 vols. (Philadelphia: J. B. Lippincott, 1919), II, 16–19. A fine essay on Hackett is in William Winter, *The Wallet of Time*, 2 vols. (New York: Moffat, Yard, & Co., 1913), I, 93–100. For Hackett's Falstaff see William Winter, *Shakespeare on the Stage, Third Series* (New York: Moffat, Yard, & Co., 1916), pp. 356–62, and Charles H. Shattuck, "Six Episodes in the Life of a Play," in *The Merry Wives of Windsor*, The Laurel Shakespeare, ed. Francis Fergusson (New York: Dell Publishing Co., 1966), pp. 27–30.

8. This sentiment of Charles J. Foster's appeared in "Sketch of James H. Hackett" in the *Spirit of the Times*, February 1862. It was reprinted by Hackett in *Notes and Comments upon Certain Plays and Actors of Shakespeare* (New York: Carleton, 1863), p. 333.

9. This Hackett-Kean promptbook has been published in facsimile: Alan S. Downer, ed., *King Richard III: Edmund Kean's Performance, As Recorded by James H. Hackett* (London: Society for Theatre Research, 1959).

10. Hackett, pp. 295–310.

11. Hackett, pp. 93–110.

12. Hackett, pp. 63–90, 191–253.

13. Hackett, pp. 13–59.

14. Hackett, pp. 268–95.

15. Hackett, pp. 117–87.

16. Part 6 of *Notes and Comments*, pp. 313–53, contains reviews of and Hackett's comments on Falstaff.

17. *New York Herald*, April 24, 1840.

18. Playbill of Booth's Theatre, December 24, 1869.

19. Hackett, pp. 352–53.

20. *Times* (London), November 2, 1839.

21. *Harper's New Monthly Magazine* XXXV (August 1867): 394–95.

22. His first London appearance was at Covent Garden Theatre on April 5, 1827. It is true, of course, that young Payne had a brief stage career in England in 1813. Thomas A. Cooper, who though English-born was generally regarded as American, failed in London in 1803 and again in December of 1827.

23. Maurice Morgann, *An Essay on the Dramatic Character of Sir John Falstaff* (London: T. Davies, 1777), p. 132. See Stuart Tave, *The Amiable Humorist* (Chicago: University of Chicago Press, 1960), pp. 127–34.

24. William Hazlitt, *Complete Works*, ed. P. P. Howe, 21 vols. (London: J. M. Dent and Sons, 1930–34), IV, 279.

25. Shattuck, pp. 24–27.

26. *Times* (London), November 2, 1839.

27. *Times* (London), February 7, 1845.

28. *Times* (London), June 27, 1851.

29. Hackett, pp. 322–23.

30. Clapp, p. 429.

31. Hackett, pp. 274, 281.

32. Allan Nevins, ed. *The Diary of Philip Hone, 1828–1851* (New York: Dodd, Mead, & Co., 1936), pp. 242, 367, etc. Hackett, p. 63, claimed that it was at Hone's table that he heard Adams's ideas on Hamlet; Hone (p. 384) told a quite different story.

33. Hackett, p. 75.

34. Charles H. Shattuck, *The Shakespeare Promptbooks* (Urbana: University of Illinois Press, 1965), pp. 306–8. Hackett did go to some trouble, however, to secure a copy of the promptbook of Macready's "restored" *King Lear*. See Shattuck, p. 214.

35. *Spirit of the Times*, June 2, 1855.

36. *Harper's New Monthly Magazine* XXXV (August 1867): 394–95.

37. *New York Herald*, December 14, 1869.

38. *Spirit of the Times*, December 18, 1869.

39. George Vandenhoff, *Leaves from an Actor's Notebook* (New York: D. Appleton & Co., 1860), pp. 200–201.

40. Frances Trollope, *Domestic Manners of the Americans*, ed. Donald Smalley (New York: Alfred A. Knopf, 1949), p. 340.

41. For Forrest's performances in New York see Odell, III–IX. The principal biographies of Forrest are: James Rees, *The Life of Edwin Forrest* (Philadelphia: T. B. Peterson & Brothers, 1874); William Rounseville Alger, *Life of Edwin Forrest*, 2 vols. (Philadelphia: J. B. Lippincott & Co., 1877); Montrose Moses, *The Fabulous Forrest* (Boston: Little, Brown & Co., 1929); and Richard Moody, *Edwin Forrest: First Star of the American Stage* (New York: Alfred A. Knopf, 1960). See also Ireland, I, 478–82. Valuable essays on Forrest are: Lawrence Barrett's "Edwin Forrest," in *Actors and Actresses of Great Britain and the United States*, ed. Brander Matthews and Laurence Hutton, 5 vols. (New York: Cassell & Co., 1886), IV, 33–67; Hornblow, II, 31–47; Edward Wagenknecht, *Merely Players* (Norman: University of Oklahoma Press, 1966), pp. 93–121. See also William Winter, *Shakespeare on the Stage* (New York: Moffatt, Yard, & Co., 1911).

42. William B. Wood, *Personal Recollections of the Stage* (Philadelphia: Henry Carey Baird, 1855), pp. 250–51.

43. Miss Placide seems to have held him off through 1825, when Forrest challenged Manager Caldwell to a duel to dispute her favors; she accepted him when he returned in 1828. See Moody, pp. 44–47, 92–93.

44. Quoted in Moody, pp. 63–64.

45. Alger, I, 158–63; Moody, pp. 76–78.

46. Alger, I, 251–52.

47. Alger, I, 177.

48. Moses, p. 335.

49. John Foster Kirk, "Shakespeare's Tragedies on the Stage," *Lippincott's Magazine of Popular Literature and Science* XXXIII (May and June 1884): 604.

50. George Beck's annotated promptbook of Forrest's *Hamlet* is in the Theatre Collection of the New York Public Library.

51. Moses, p. 195.

52. Alger, I, 324.

53. Odell, VII, 558, quoting the *New York Herald* of September 8, 1863.

54. Robert Hamilton Ball, *The Amazing Career of Sir Giles Overreach* (Princeton: Princeton University Press, 1939), pp. 232–37.

55. Moody, pp. 345–47. The statue is in the central hall of the Edwin Forrest Home in Philadelphia.

56. *Macready's Reminiscences*, ed. Sir Frederick Pollock (New York: Macmillan & Co., 1875), pp. 241–42.

57. The principal biographies of Macready are: William Archer, *William Charles Macready* (London: Kegan Paul, Trench, Trübner, & Co., 1890); J. C. Trewin, *Mr. Macready, A Nineteenth-Century Tragedian and His Theatre* (London: George C. Harrap & Co., 1955); and Alan S. Downer, *The Eminent Tragedian, William Charles Macready* (Cambridge: Harvard University Press, 1966). An excellent essay on Macready is in Wagenknecht, pp. 55–92. See also Ireland, I, 506–8, II, 407, 430, 545–46. For Macready's New York appearances, see Odell, III and IV.

58. Odell, III, 234, quoting the *New York Mirror* of October 7, 1826.

59. Frances Ann Kemble, *Records of Later Life* (New York: Henry Holt & Co., 1882), p. 637.

60. *Macready's Reminiscences*, p. 695.

61. George Henry Lewes, *On Actors and the Art of Acting* (London: Smith, Elder, & Co., 1875), pp. 38–39; *The Diaries of William Charles Macready*, ed. William Toynbee, 2 vols. (London: Chapman & Hall, 1912), II, June 9, 1839.

62. Lady Juliet Pollock, *Macready as I Knew Him* (London: Remington & Co., 1885), p. 11.

63. *Macready's Reminiscences*, pp. 86–87.

64. Odell, III, 234, quoting the *New York Mirror* of October 7, 1826.

65. Kirk, p. 612.

66. Odell, III, 234, quoting the *New York Mirror* of October 14, 1826.

67. Odell, III, 234, quoting the *New York Mirror* of October 21, 1826.

68. Quoted in Downer, p. 108.

69. Downer, p. 72.

70. Charles H. Shattuck, ed., *William Charles Macready's "King John"* (Urbana: University of Illinois Press, 1962), pp. 27–28.

71. *Literary Gazette*, January 15, 1831.

72. Kirk, p. 613.

73. Downer, p. 75, cites this anecdote from the *Theatrical Journal* III (1842): 189. For Macready's own version of the event, see his *Reminiscences*, p. 166.

74. Lady Pollock, p. 121.

75. *Macready's Reminiscences*, pp. 708–9.

76. Lady Pollock, p. 118.

77. Alger, I, 172.

78. Moody, p. 88.

79. His openings in London were *The Gladiator*, October 17, 1836; *Othello*, October 24; *King Lear*, November 4; *Damon and Pythias*, November 10; *Macbeth*, November 30; *Virginius*, February 7, 1837; *Brutus*, February 13; *Pizarro*, February 20; *Richard III*, February 27.

80. Generous sections of favorable reviews are quoted by Alger, I, 299–320.

81. *Spectator*, December 17, 1836.

82. *Diaries*, I, October 14, 1836.

83. Archer, chap. 4.

84. Alger, I, 317.

85. *Diaries*, I, November 10, 1836.

86. Forster's reviews appeared in the *Examiner* on October 23, 1836 (*The Gladiator*), October 30 (*Othello*), November 6 (*King Lear*), November 13 (*Damon and Pythias*), February 12, 1837 (*Macbeth*), and March 5 (*Richard III*).

87. *Diaries*, II, September 20, 1843.

88. *Diaries*, II, October 3, 1843.

89. Downer, p. 258; Moody, pp. 206–11.

90. *Diaries*, II, September 7, 9, and 15, 1844.

91. Quoted by Alger, I, 398.

92. Forrest's openings were February 17 (*Othello*), February 21 (*Macbeth*), March 6 (*King Lear*), March 14 (*Damon and Pythias*), March 26 (*Metamora*).

93. Alger, I, 391–92.

94. Archer, p. 171.

95. *Spectator*, February 22, 1845.

96. Joseph Leach, *Bright Particular Star: The Life and Times of Charlotte Cushman* (New Haven: Yale University Press, 1970), p. 150.

97. *Spectator*, March 29, 1845.

98. Alger, I, 421.

99. Macready's provincial tour is traceable in his *Diaries*, II, February 19 to May 7, 1845. See supplemental entries in *Macready's Reminiscences*, pp. 564–68.

100. Macready asserted Forster's absence from the *Examiner* in a handbill of November 22, 1848. See Downer, p. 294. Evidence that Forster was housebound may be noted in Macready's diary entries for January 28, February 3 and 15, and March 22, 1845.

101. Alger, I, 392–93.

102. *Diaries*, II, March 2, 1846, and following.

103. John Coleman, *Players and Playwrights I Have Known*, 2 vols. (London: Chatto & Windus, 1888) I, 33.

104. Moody, p. 236.

105. Alger, I, 420–21.

106. Moody, p. 252; Downer, p. 291.

107. *Diaries*, II, November 20, 1848.

108. Downer, pp. 293–94.

109. *Diaries*, II, December 2, 1848.

110. Sol Smith, *Theatrical Management in the West and South for Thirty Years* (New York: Harper & Brothers, 1868), p. 217.

111. *New Orleans Picayune*, March 21, 1849, reprinted in *Spirit of the Times*, April 7.

112. *Diaries*, II, April 2, 1849.

113. The events that followed are covered in great detail in Richard Moody, *The Astor Place Riot* (Bloomington: Indiana University Press, 1958).

114. *Diaries*, II, April 12, 1849.

115. In Shakespeare's play Macduff does not enter earlier than Macbeth, but in the early nineteenth-century stage version Macduff takes Ross's lines in I.2.

116. *Diaries*, II, May 7, 1849; Downer, pp. 297–99; Moody, pp. 101–14.

117. For the climactic night of riot, see *Diaries*, II, May 10, 1849, and following, with supplemental entries in *Macready's Reminiscences*, pp. 615–24; Downer, pp. 299–310; Moody, pp. 114–221.

118. Adam Badeau, *The Vagabond* (New York: Rudd & Carleton, 1859), pp. 120–27, 286–92.

119. Archimedes' "place to stand."

120. *Harper's Magazine* XXVIII (December 1863): 132–33.

121. Major studies of Miss Cushman are: Emma Stebbins, *Charlotte Cushman: Her Letters and Memories of Her Life* (Boston: Houghton, Osgood, & Co., 1878); Clara Erskine Clement, *Charlotte Cushman* (Boston: James R. Osgood & Co., 1882); and Leach. See also Ireland, II, 159–64; Hornblow, II, 124–30. Shorter essays may be found in Gamaliel Bradford, *Biography and the Human Heart* (Boston: Houghton Mifflin Co., 1932), pp. 95–124; William Winter, *Other Days; Being Chronicles and Memories of the Stage* (New York: Moffat, Yard, & Co., 1908), pp. 152–77; *idem*, *Wallet of Time*, I, 159–76.

122. James E. Murdoch, *The Stage; or, Recollections of Actors and Acting from an Experience of Fifty Years* (Philadelphia: J. M. Stoddart & Co., 1880), p. 237.

123. Leach, p. 41.

124. Stebbins, p. 23.

125. Her New York performances are recorded in Odell, IV–VII and IX.

126. For this date, often given as May 8 (e.g., Leach, p. 69), see Odell, IV, 149.

127. Clement, p. 25.

128. *Diaries*, II, October 23, 1843.

129. *Diaries*, II, November 10 and 13, 1843.

130. Vandenhoff, p. 195.

131. *Diaries*, II, December 4, 1843.

132. Leach, pp. 120–21.

133. Quoted in Leach, p. 123.

134. *Diaries*, II, November 12, 1843.

135. Leach, p. 113.

136. *Macready's Reminiscences*, p. 96.

137. John Coleman, *Fifty Years of an Actor's Life*, 2 vols. (London: Hutchinson & Co., 1904), I, 306.

138. Leach, *passim*, is the only biographer who discusses all of Miss Cushman's female attachments. See p. 210 for Elizabeth Barrett Browning on the subject of "female marriage."

139. *Diaries*, II, December 4–23, 1843.

140. Leach, p. 122.

141. Leach, pp. 128–30.

142. *Times* (London), February 14, 1845.

143. *Spectator* and *Examiner*, both February 15, 1845.

144. Quoted in Stebbins, p. 52.

145. *Spirit of the Times*, May 31, 1845.

146. *Examiner*, October 9, 1847.

147. Vandenhoff, p. 196.

148. *Observer* (London), March 2, 1845.

149. Manager Webster was sympathetic to her restoration of the text. He had himself restored *Taming of the Shrew* in March 1844.

150. Leach, pp. 169–70.

151. *Spectator*, January 3, 1846.

152. *Times* (London), December 30, 1845.

153. *Athenaeum*, January 3, 1846.

154. Westland Marston, *Our Recent Actors*, 2 vols. (Boston: Roberts Brothers, 1888), II, 75–76.

155. Coleman, *Fifty Years*, II, 363.

156. Noah Ludlow, *Dramatic Life as I Found It* (St. Louis: G. I. Jones & Co., 1880; reprint, New York: Benjamin Blom, 1966), p. 316.

157. Quoted in Stebbins, p. 63.

158. Marston, II, 76.

159. *Times* (London), October 14, 1847.

160. An intensely social person, she numbered among her friends such distinguished American writers as Longfellow, Hawthorne, Lowell, Bryant, and Lanier; in England she knew the Brownings, the Carlyles, the Trollopes, Lord Houghton, the Duke of Devonshire, and many others; among the artists she neighbored with and patronized in Rome were William Page, John Gibson, Hiram Powers, Randolph Rogers, and W. W. Story.

161. Winter, *Shakespeare on the Stage*, p. 554.

162. Richard Lockridge, *Darling of Misfortune: Edwin Booth, 1833–1893* (New York: Century Co., 1932), p. 95.

163. Winter, *Shakespeare on the Stage*, p. 502.

164. Murdoch, p. 240.

165. Winter, *Shakespeare on the Stage*, p. 502.

166. Marston, II, 79–80.

IV. *Fresh Fashions from Abroad*

1. Frances Trollope, *Domestic Manners of the Americans*, ed. Donald Smalley (New York: Alfred A. Knopf, 1949), p. 340.

2. Trollope, p. 134.

3. Allan Nevins, ed., *The Diary of Philip Hone, 1828–1851* (New York: Dodd, Mead, & Co., 1936), p. 74.

4. For Kemble's biography, see Jane Williamson, *Charles Kemble, Man of the Theatre* (Lincoln: University of Nebraska Press, 1970). See also Joseph Norton Ireland, *Records of the New York Stage, from 1750 to 1860*, 2 vols. (New York: T. H. Morrell, 1866–67), II, 38–40. For the Kembles' New York appearances, see George C. D. Odell, *Annals of the New York Stage*, 15 vols. (New York: Columbia University Press, 1927–49), III.

5. Westland Marston, *Our Recent Actors*, 2 vols. (Boston: Roberts Brothers, 1888), I, 133; William Bodham

Donne, *Essays on the Drama* (London: John W. Parker & Son, 1858), p. 183.

6. *Macready's Reminiscences*, ed. Sir Frederick Pollock (New York: Macmillan & Co., 1875), p. 59.

7. William Robson, *The Old Play-Goer* (London: Longman, Brown, Green, & Longmans 1854), p. 44.

8. Frances Anne Butler, *Journal*, 2 vols. (London: John Murray, 1835), I, 112.

9. Donne, p. 175.

10. Quoted in Odell, III, 604.

11. Butler, I, 179–86.

12. Quoted in Odell, III, 606.

13. Marston, I, 128.

14. Butler, I, 138–40.

15. Quoted in Barnard Hewitt, *Theatre U.S.A., 1668–1957* (New York: McGraw-Hill, 1959), p. 111.

16. There are several modern biographies of Fanny Kemble: Dorothy Bobbé, *Fanny Kemble* (New York: Minton, Balch, & Co., 1931); Leota S. Driver, *Fanny Kemble* (Chapel Hill: University of North Carolina Press, 1933); Margaret Armstrong, *Fanny Kemble, A Passionate Victorian* (New York: Macmillan Co., 1938); Constance Wright, *Fanny Kemble and the Lovely Land* (New York: Dodd, Mead, & Co., 1972). See also Ireland, II, 40–43; Arthur Hornblow, *A History of the Theatre in America*, 2 vols. (Philadelphia: J. B. Lippincott, 1919), II, 114–17.

17. Quoted in Bobbé, p. 71.

18. Quoted in Hewitt, p. 113.

19. Quoted in Bobbé, p. 68.

20. Frances Anne Kemble, *Records of a Girlhood* (New York: Henry Holt, 1883), p. 569.

21. Butler, I, 150.

22. *New York Mirror*, September 29, 1832. Quoted in Hewitt, pp. 111–14.

23. Kemble, pp. 552–53.

24. Butler, II, 82.

25. Butler, II, 26.

26. Butler, II, 177–78.

27. Francis C. Wemyss, *Theatrical Biography; or, The Life of an Actor and Manager* (Glasgow: R. Griffin, 1848), p. 182.

28. George Henry Lewes, *On Actors and the Art of Acting* (London: Smith, Elder & Co., 1875), pp. 12–22.

29. Marston, I, 192.

30. Lewes, p. 21.

31. Quoted in William G. B. Carson, *Letters of Mr. and Mrs. Charles Kean Relating to Their American Tours* (St. Louis: Washington University, 1945), p. 31.

32. For Charles Kean's first New York appearances, see Odell, III. For Ellen Tree's, see Odell, IV. For their joint appearances as Mr. and Mrs. Kean, see Odell, IV, V, and VII.

33. Hone, p. 52.

34. James Henry Hackett, *Notes and Comments upon Certain Plays and Actors of Shakespeare* (New York: Carleton, 1863), p. 181.

35. John William Cole, *The Life and Theatrical Times of Charles Kean, F.S.A.*, 2 vols. (London: Richard Bentley, 1859), I, 333.

36. Cole, I, 334.

37. *Spirit of the Times*, September 6, 1845.

38. Kemble, p. 200.

39. Quoted in Odell, IV, 121.

40. For their New York appearances, see Odell, V. See also Ireland, I, 635–38, II, 182–85, 314, 447 ff.

41. Hone, p. 753.

42. *Spirit of the Times*, January 17, 1846.

43. Hone, p. 752.

44. Odell, V, 174–77.

45. Kean's *Richard III* promptbooks are in the Folger Shakespeare Library. His scene and costume designs are in the Folger and in the Enthoven Collection, Victoria and Albert Museum.

46. Charles H. Shattuck, "Macready Prompt-Books," *Theatre Notebook* XVI (Autumn 1961): 7–10; *idem*, "A Victorian Stage Manager: George Cressall Ellis," *Theatre Notebook* XXII (Spring 1968): 102–12.

47. Odell, V, 252–55; Charles H. Shattuck, *William Charles Macready's "King John"* (Urbana: University of Illinois Press, 1962).

48. William L. Keese, *William E. Burton, Actor, Author, and Manager: A Sketch of His Career* (New York: G. P. Putnam's Sons, 1885); *idem*, *William E. Burton: A Sketch of His Career Other Than That of Actor* (New York: The Dunlap Society, 1891). See also Ireland, II, 511 ff.; Hornblow, II, 121–23. For Burton's New York appearances, see Odell, IV–VII.

49. Keese [1885], p. 122.

50. Keese [1891], pp. 28–36.

51. Keese [1885], pp. 177–206.

52. Quoted in Keese [1885], p. 125.

53. James E. Murdoch, *The Stage; or, Recollections of Actors and Acting from an Experience of Fifty Years* (Philadelphia: J. M. Stoddart & Co., 1880), pp. 224–25.

54. Keese [1885], pp. 136–37.

55. Keese [1885], pp. 124–25.

56. Odell, VI.

57. *New York Albion*, September 27, 1851.

58. Joseph Jefferson, *The Autobiography* (New York: Century Co., 1889), pp. 107–8.

59. *New York Albion*, April 3, 1852, quoted in Odell, VI, 129.

60. *Spirit of the Times*, April 10, 1852.

61. Odell, VI, 210; *Spirit of the Times*, March 19, 1853.

62. Odell, VI, 290–93.

63. W. May Phelps and John Forbes-Robertson, *The Life and Life-Work of Samuel Phelps* (London: Sampson Low, Marston, Searle, & Rivington, 1886), pp. 128–38.

64. *Spirit of the Times*, February 11, 1854; *New York Herald*, February 4, 1854; *New York Tribune*, February 4, 1854.

65. Odell, VI, 282–83; *Spirit of the Times*, February 11, 18, 25, March 4, 11, 1854; *New York Herald*, February 8, 1854; *New York Tribune*, February 7, 1854.

66. Several promptbooks of the *Dream*, by John Moore, John Wright, and George Becks, are preserved in the Folger Shakespeare Library and the Theatre Collection of the New York Public Library. It is not easy to distinguish which of their details reflect Burton's production and which reflect the Broadway production or later productions by Augustin Daly.

67. Odell, VI, 293–94; *Spirit of the Times*, April 15, 1854; *New York Herald*, April 12, 1854; *New York Tribune*, April 12, 1854.

68. This promptbook of Moore's is in the Folger Shakespeare Library, as are his promptbook and his stage manager's workbook for Burton's production.

69. Keese [1885], p. 175.

70. He would revive it for a few performances at the Metropolitan on April 6, 1857.

71. Odell, VI, 437; *Spirit of the Times*, February 16, 23, 1856, and April 11, 1857; *New York Herald*, February 14, 1856; *New York Tribune*, February 14, 1856.

72. John Martin (1789–1854), English artist and engraver. His *Illustrations to Milton's Paradise Lost* was published in folio by Septimus Prowett in London, 1825, and his work was used in several editions of *Paradise Lost* during the nineteenth century.

V. *Masters of the Craft*

1. In 1901, Edwin Francis Edgett of the *Boston Transcript* "edited" *Edward Loomis Davenport, A Biography* for the Dunlap Society publications (new ser., 14). This work, the only book-length study of Davenport, was based on a manuscript of unknown authorship found among the papers of Davenport's daughter Fanny. See also Joseph Norton Ireland, *Records of the New York Stage, from 1750 to 1860*, 2 vols. (New York: T. H. Morrell, 1866–67), II, 403; Arthur Hornblow, *A History of the Theatre in America*, 2 vols. (Philadelphia: J. B. Lippincott, 1919), II, 134–36. For Davenport's New York appearances, see George C. D. Odell, *Annals of the New York Stage*, 15 vols. (New York: Columbia University Press, 1927–49), IV–X.

2. Edgett, p. 118.

3. Edgett, p. 110.

4. Eric W. Barnes, *The Lady of Fashion: The Life and the Theatre of Anna Cora Mowatt* (New York: Charles Scribner's Sons, 1954), p. 217 ff.

5. Edgett, p. 24.

6. Edgett, p. 29.

7. Edgett, p. 38.

8. For Macready's opinions which follow, see *The Diaries of William Charles Macready*, ed. William Toynbee, 2 vols. (London: Chapman & Hall, 1912), II, entries of November 16 and 20, 1850; January 14, 22, and 27, 1851.

9. Edgett, p. 39.

10. Edgett, p. 42.

11. Edgett, pp. 43–44.

12. Laurence Hutton, *Plays and Players* (New York: Hurd & Houghton, 1875), p. 156.

13. William Winter, *Life and Art of Edwin Booth*, new ed. (Boston: Joseph Knight Co., 1893; rev., 1894), p. 149.

14. Edgett, p. 30.

15. This promptbook is *King Lear*, no. 4, in the promptbook collection of the Folger Shakespeare Library.

16. Clara Morris, *Life on the Stage* (New York: McClure, Phillips, & Co., 1901), p. 187.

17. William Winter, *Shakespeare on the Stage, Second Series* (New York: Moffat, Yard, & Co., 1915), p. 604.

18. Edgett, p. 49.

19. Henry Dickinson Stone, *Personal Recollections of the Drama; or, Theatrical Reminiscences* (Albany: Charles van Benthuysen & Sons, 1873), p. 122.

20. William Winter, *Shakespeare on the Stage* [First Series] (New York: Moffat, Yard, & Co., 1911), p. 168.

21. Winter, *Shakespeare on the Stage* [First Series], pp. 336–37.

22. Morris, p. 185.

23. Adam Badeau, *The Vagabond* (New York: Rudd & Carleton, 1859), p. 74.

24. Robert Hamilton Ball, *The Amazing Career of Sir Giles Overreach* (Princeton: Princeton University Press, 1939), pp. 280–307.

25. Winter, *Life and Art of Edwin Booth*, p. 149.

26. Morris, p. 186.

27. Edgett, p. 114; Winter, *Shakespeare on the Stage, Second Series*, pp. 603–6.

28. For a thorough account of the 1875 *Caesar*, see Richard Lee Benson, "Jarrett and Palmer's 1875 Production of *Julius Caesar*: A Reconstruction" (Ph.D. diss., University of Illinois, 1968).

29. Mason's record of the Davenport and Barrett stage

business is at the Boston Athenaeum. Other records by George Becks and by Leon John Vincent are in the Theatre Collection of the New York Public Library, and one by James Taylor is at Harvard.

30. Edgett, p. 114.

31. *New York Tribune*, December 28, 1875.

32. The only book-length study of McCullough is Susie C. Clark, *John McCullough as Man, Actor, and Spirit* (Boston: Murray & Emery, 1905). It contains reliable information and a good deal of review material, but the last third of its 356 pages is devoted to his life and opinions beyond the grave. William Winter was responsible for a slender volume, *In Memory of John McCullough* (New York: DeVinne Press, 1889), and for essays on McCullough's life and work in *Other Days; Being Chronicles and Memories of the Stage* (New York: Moffat, Yard, & Co., 1908), *The Wallet of Time*, 2 vols. (New York: Moffat, Yard, & Co., 1913), I, *Shakespeare on the Stage* [First Series], *Shakespeare on the Stage, Second Series*, and *Shakespeare on the Stage, Third Series* (New York: Moffat, Yard, & Co., 1916). See also Hornblow, II, 225–28; Garff B. Wilson, *A History of American Acting* (Bloomington: Indiana University Press, 1966), pp. 30–37. For McCullough's New York appearances, see Odell, VII–XII.

33. This term for the postwar generation is, of course, Lewis Mumford's: *The Brown Decades: A Study of the Arts in America, 1865–1895*, 2d ed. (New York: Dover Publications, 1955).

34. Winter, *Wallet of Time*, I, 263.

35. Winter, *Other Days*, p. 214.

36. *Daily Alta California*, May 28, 1876, quoted in Clark, p. 49.

37. *Spirit of the Times*, May 9, 1874.

38. *New York Tribune*, May 5, 1874.

39. *New York Herald*, May 5, 1874.

40. These quotations from Wheeler (May 1878) appear in Percy MacKaye's *Epoch: The Life of Steele MacKaye, Genius of the Theatre*, 2 vols. (New York: Boni & Liveright, 1927), I, 270–71.

41. *Spirit of the Times*, April 7, 1877.

42. See *San Francisco Theatre Research*, W.P.A. Project 10677 (San Francisco, 1938–), VI, 121.

43. *Boston Globe*, February 1878, quoted in Clark, p. 81.

44. Winter, *Shakespeare on the Stage* [First Series], p. 169.

45. *Ibid.*, pp. 476–77.

46. For Winter's opinions, see the *New York Tribune*, May 19, 1874, and *Shakespeare on the Stage* [First Series], pp. 352–54.

47. *St. Louis Republican*, March 19, 1874, quoted in Clark, p. 70.

48. *New York Times*, May 19, 1874; December 8, 1882.

49. For Winter's opinions, see the *New York Tribune*, April 12, 1877, quoted in Clark, pp. 93–96; and *Shakespeare on the Stage* [First Series], pp. 105–7.

50. *New York Herald*, April 12, 1877; December 4, 1880.

51. *New York Times*, December 4, 1880.

52. *New York Dramatic Mirror*, December 3, 1881.

53. For Winter's opinions, see the *New York Tribune*, April 25, 1877, quoted in Clark, pp. 96–100; and *Shakespeare on the Stage, Second Series*, pp. 452–62.

54. His promptbook of *King Lear*, which is in the Harvard Theatre Collection, is a curious object. It was originally marked for Charles Kean by his prompter T. W. Edmonds on proofsheets of a Kean edition. The American actor Harry Edwards erased the original markings and re-marked it for McCullough.

55. For Winter's opinions, see the *New York Tribune*, April 14, 1877; *Wallet of Time*, I, 275–77; and *Shakespeare on the Stage* [First Series], pp. 282–86.

56. *New York Times*, April 14, 1877.

57. *Spirit of the Times*, April 28, 1877.

58. Edward Tuckerman Mason, *The Othello of Tommaso Salvini* (New York: G. P. Putnam's Sons, 1890), pp. 67 ff.

59. *New York Herald*, April 14, 1877.

60. *Times* (London), May 16, 1881.

61. *Theatre*, June 1, 1881.

62. *Athenaeum*, May 21, 1881.

63. The principal biographical studies of Booth are: Asia Booth Clarke, *The Elder and the Younger Booth* (Boston: J. R. Osgood, 1882); Winter, *Life and Art of Edwin Booth*; Edwina Booth Grossmann, *Edwin Booth: Recollections by His Daughter and Letters to Her and His Friends* (New York: Century Co., 1894); Charles Townsend Copeland, *Edwin Booth* (Boston: Small, Maynard & Company, 1901); Richard Lockridge, *Darling of Misfortune: Edwin Booth, 1833–1893* (New York: Century Co., 1932); Stanley Kimmel, *The Mad Booths of Maryland* (Indianapolis: Bobbs-Merrill Co., 1940; rev. ed., New York: Dover, 1969); Eleanor Ruggles, *Prince of Players, Edwin Booth* (New York: W. W. Norton & Co., 1953). See also Katherine Goodale, *Behind the Scenes with Edwin Booth* (Boston: Houghton Mifflin Co., 1931); Edward Wagenknecht, "Edwin Booth," in *Merely Players* (Norman: University of Oklahoma Press, 1966); Charles H. Shattuck, *The Hamlet of Edwin Booth* (Urbana: University of Illinois Press, 1969); Daniel J. Watermeier, *Between Actor and Critic, Selected Letters of Edwin Booth and William Winter* (Princeton: Princeton University Press, 1971); Charles H. Shattuck, "The Theatrical Management of Edwin Booth," in *The Theatrical Manager in England and America*, ed. Joseph W.

Donohue (Princeton University Press, 1971). For Booth's New York appearances, see Odell, VI–XIV.

64. *Boston Evening Traveller*, February 3, 1869.

65. See Illustration 93. The portion of the building nearest the viewer was not properly a part of the theatre, but an office building fronting on Sixth Avenue. It measured 79 by 34 feet and was five stories tall. Booth designed it as studios for his various artist friends, but it was in fact taken up by shops, a secretarial school, and other commercial enterprises. The top floor was Booth's residence.

Published statements of the dimensions of the theatre are wildly contradictory. I extract the following, some of them being approximations. From west to east (the stage being at the east end) it was 155 feet long, and from north to south it was 79 feet wide through the auditorium section and about 99 feet through the stage section. The extra 20 feet offstage left provided a paint room at stage level and tiers of dressing rooms above. The building was 70 feet tall to the cornice line and about 120 feet tall to the top of the towers. The lobby at the west end, containing stairs to the balconies, measured about 18 by 76 feet. The auditorium was about 76 feet wide and about 70 feet from back wall to curtain line. According to the *Boston Evening Traveller*, the main floor seated 576 persons and the three balconies 1,195—a total of 1,771, not counting standees and occupants of the six proscenium boxes. The stage house measured 55 feet from curtain line to back wall, about 76 feet across, about 96 feet from stage floor to roof, and 32 feet from floor to bottom of cellarage. We can only guess at the width and height of the proscenium opening: from 45 to 50 feet across and perhaps 60 feet tall.

66. *New York World*, February 4, 1869.

67. For an account of Booth's early ventures in management, see Shattuck, "Theatrical Management of Edwin Booth," pp. 143–65.

68. Booth to Emma Cary, August 26, 1864, in Grossmann, p. 164.

69. Letter from Booth to Adam Badeau, October 14, 1864, Folger Shakespeare Library.

70. *New York Tribune*, February 4, 1869.

71. For the Robertson story, see Shattuck, "Theatrical Management of Edwin Booth," pp. 165–75.

72. Barton Hill, "Personal Recollections of Edwin Booth," *New York Dramatic Mirror*, December 26, 1896.

73. Fechter's letter excusing himself from the invitation is in Booth's book of souvenir letters at The Players.

74. Quoted in Ruggles, p. 240. Much of the correspondence leading to this quarrel is preserved at The Players.

75. The phrases are William Winter's, in the *New York Tribune*, February 4, 1869.

76. *New York World*, February 4, 1869.

77. Unidentified clipping at p. 29 of Booth's 1869 scrapbook, The Players.

78. Booth to Emma Cary, September 27, 1868, in Grossmann, p. 176.

79. According to Shirley S. Allen, in *Samuel Phelps and Sadler's Wells Theatre* (Middletown: Wesleyan University Press, 1971), p. 217, Phelps cut 490 lines. Gerald Honaker, in "Edwin Booth, Producer" (Ph.D. diss., Indiana University, 1969), pp. 139–44, shows Booth's cuts to number 770.

80. Letter from Booth to H. L. Hinton, undated, Folger Shakespeare Library.

81. Winter, *Life and Art of Edwin Booth*, p. 94.

82. *New York Herald*, February 8, 1869.

83. *New York World*, February 4, 1869.

84. The *New York Herald*, under James Gordon Bennett, savagely denounced Booth's return to the stage in 1866, nine months after the assassination of President Lincoln. On Booth's opening night the audience awarded Bennett "three groans." It then became fixed policy at the *Herald* to attack Booth's work.

85. *New York World*, February 23, 1869.

86. *New York Daily Star*, February 5, 1869.

87. Watermeier, p. 20.

88. *New York Citizen*, February 27, 1869.

89. *New York Herald*, March 1, 1869.

90. *New York World*, April 16, 1869.

91. Shattuck, *Hamlet of Edwin Booth*, p. xxi.

92. Otis Skinner, *Footlights and Spotlights* (Indianapolis: Bobbs-Merrill Co., 1924), p. 172.

93. *New York Daily Star*, April 13, 1869.

94. *New York Evening Post*, May 17, 1869.

95. *New York World*, April 16, 1869.

96. *New York Commercial Advertiser*, April 19, 1869; *New York World*, April 16, 1869.

97. The "ethnic" defense appears in the *New York Commercial Advertiser*, April 19, 1869; the *New York Citizen*, April 14, 1869; Winter, *Life and Art of Edwin Booth*, p. 295; and elsewhere.

98. *New York Herald*, April 25, 1869.

99. *New York Evening Mail*, April 24, 1869.

100. Winter, *Shakespeare on the Stage* [First Series], p. 268.

101. *New York World*, April 16, 1869.

102. Horace Howard Furness, *A New Variorum Edition of Shakespeare: Othello* (New York: J. B. Lippincott & Co., 1886), p. 292.

103. Arthur Colby Sprague, *Shakespeare and the Actors* (Cambridge: Harvard University Press, 1945), pp. 214–16; Furness, pp. 302–7.

104. *New York World*, April 16, 1869.

105. Furness, p. 303.

106. *New York Tribune*, April 28, 1869.

107. *New York Evening Post*, December 19, 1860. For a comprehensive account, see Arthur Colby Sprague, "Edwin Booth as Iago," in *Shakespearian Players and Performances* (Cambridge: Harvard University Press, 1953), pp. 121–35.

108. *Galaxy*, January 1869, p. 83.

109. Furness, pp. 214 and 146.

110. For a comprehensive account of Booth's *Hamlet*, see Shattuck, *Hamlet of Edwin Booth*, pp. 67–98.

111. *New York Post*, January 6, 1870.

112. *New York Herald*, January 6, 1870.

113. *New York Leader*, January 8, 1870.

114. The brochure, called *Booth's Theatre: Hamlet*, was compiled by Arthur Matthison, a young English actor, singer, and man of letters, who was a member of Booth's company.

115. *New York World*, January 6, 1870.

116. Watercolors of the 1870 sets are in Booth's souvenir promptbook, now in the Harvard Theatre Collection. Sketches of the Winter Garden sets were printed in the Booth-Hinton acting edition of the play, published in 1866. All these are reproduced in Shattuck, *Hamlet of Edwin Booth*.

117. *New York Evening Post*, February 28, 1870.

118. *New York Times*, January 7, 1870.

119. Letter from Booth to Adam Badeau, October 14, 1864, Folger Shakespeare Library.

120. *Galaxy*, January 1869, p. 78.

121. The Clarke manuscript is in the Folger Shakespeare Library.

122. The opinions of Ewer, Clarke, and Garland are given more fully in Shattuck, *Hamlet of Edwin Booth*. Garland's unpublished lecture on Booth's Hamlet is in the Garland Archive at the Library of the University of Southern California.

123. Witham's watercolors of this scene and the Senate Chamber are preserved at the Museum of the City of New York.

124. "Table Talk," *Appleton's Journal*, January 20, 1872.

125. *New York World*, December 28, 1871.

126. *New York Tribune*, December 26, 1871.

127. *New York Mail*, December 27, 1871.

128. *New York Herald*, March 5, 1872.

129. *Season* (New York), December 30, 1871.

130. *New York World*, September 6, 1870.

131. *New York Tribune*, March 31, 1876.

132. Other Shakespeare plays performed at Booth's apparently without especial production included *Henry IV* and *The Merry Wives of Windsor* by James Henry Hackett;

Henry VIII by Charlotte Cushman; and *As You Like It* by Carlotta Leclercq and Adelaide Neilson.

133. Booth to Emma Cary, September 27, 1868, in Grossmann, p. 176.

134. Winter, *Shakespeare on the Stage, Second Series*, p. 450.

135. *New York Evening Post*, March 22, 1865.

136. *Galaxy*, March 1870, pp. 397–406.

137. *New York World*, January 9, 1870.

138. *New York Herald*, April 25, 1860.

139. *New York Globe*, March 11, 1870.

140. Booth to William Winter, January 22, 1881, in Watermeier, p. 180.

Index

24/5